Liberal Journalism and American Education, 1914–1941

Liberal Journalism and American Education, 1914–1941

James M. Wallace

RUTGERS UNIVERSITY PRESS
New Brunswick and London

Library of Congress Cataloging-in-Publication Data

Wallace, James M.
    Liberal journalism and American education, 1914–1941 / James M.
Wallace.
        p.   cm.
    Includes bibliographical references and index.
    ISBN 0-8135-1662-5 (cloth)   ISBN 0-8135-1663-3 (pbk.)
    1. Education—United States—History—20th century. 2. Journalism
and education—United States—History—20th century. 3. Politics
and education—United States—History—20th century.
    4. Progressivism in education—United States—History—20th century.
    5. Liberalism—United States—History—20th century. I. Title.
    LA209.W28   1991
    370'.973—dc20   90-45946
                                                                          CIP

British Cataloging-in-Publication information available

*To the memory of my parents, who taught me
to appreciate both education and history*

Contents

Part III   ACTIVE LIBERALISM REVIVES, 1930–1941

Foreword

In this illuminating book James Wallace shows that liberalism
—an ideology battered by radicals in the 1960s and 1970s and
coyly dismissed by conservatives in the 1980s as "the L-word"—
was and is alive and well in social thought about education. By
examining liberal journalism in *The New Republic* and *The Nation*, he locates progressivism in education as part of the larger
political, social, and intellectual currents of the years from 1914
to 1941 and beyond. Education remained a constant concern of
the writers in these journals throughout major shifts in the political economy.

These left-liberal intellectuals probed the connections between education, reformist goals, and societal change. They
wrote vivid descriptions of progressive classrooms, violations of
academic freedom, student activism, the impact of the Great
Depression on schools, New Deal programs for youth, and
many other events. But they went beyond reportage to interpretation and policy advocacy. They regarded educational discourse as an arena for debating what kind of future Americans
should strive for.

In the process these writers left a record of social criticism un-
paralleled in educational journalism during those years. Unlike
the mass media that typically treated schooling in superficial

descriptive terms or indulged in simplistic criticism, and unlike professional journals that spoke to the initiated in pedagogese, authors in *The New Republic* and *The Nation* addressed basic issues in language that instructed and motivated the intellectuals and activists who were the chief audience of the journals. One of the pleasures of Wallace's book is the spirited and pointed prose he quotes.

The writers in these journals did not believe that education was above politics or that politics could be understood without examining educational imperatives. Reflecting their vantage point, Wallace sketches a complex picture of how politics and educational ideology and practice intertwined. Thus he conjoins subjects that are often treated separately in the history of education. Although shifting their tone and message in discussing different national political leaders and programs as they changed from Progressive to conservative to New Dealer, writers in these journals consistently argued the centrality of education in democratic theory and practice. They exposed the power politics of schooling and urged coalitions to challenge entrenched privilege. They believed that penetrating and coherent criticism was essential to effective educational reform. Education was not a casual part of their agenda, influenced chiefly by a fickle "issue-attention cycle," but an intrinsic component of the liberal project.

In his vivid re-creation and analysis of this liberal educational journalism, Wallace illuminates the past and challenges the present era when much educational reform is shallow in diagnosis, inequitable in impact, and conservative in philosophy.

David Tyack
STANFORD UNIVERSITY
July 1990

Preface

Writing this book has been a pleasant, interesting, and satisfying experience, and the most pleasurable part of the entire process will be to thank the many people who inspired my interest in history and education and who assisted me as I wrote and revised the text. I have not been able to incorporate all the advice I have received, so some of those who assisted me may not be able to find their suggestions reflected in the pages that follow. Nonetheless, the many dialogues I have had with a variety of people have helped in shaping the book, and I appreciate their contributions.

I can most easily acknowledge my gratitude by thanking people in rough chronological order. I am grateful to my high school history teacher, Barbara Lewando Zulauf, and to my college history professor, Tom Bassett, for introducing me to political, social, and intellectual history, and for helping me see that history could be both interesting and important. And I wish that Dr. Milton Kraft, my first education professor, were still alive so that he could see in this book some of the impact of his teaching about progressive education and John Dewey.

I am grateful to my former wife, Norma Autenrieth, for support and encouragement at all times, and particularly when I was writing the first version of this study. I thank Theodore

Sizer and Stanley Bolster for their careful reading of various drafts, for helpful critiques, and for unfailing assistance.

I am grateful for informative interviews I conducted with Bruce Bliven, Freda Kirchwey, Alvin Johnson, Elizabeth Dana, and Agnes de Lima. Correspondence and an interview with Agnes de Lima's daughter, Sigrid de Lima Greene, were helpful. She also loaned me materials concerning her mother, which, at her request, I deposited in the Vassar College Library. Barbara Hollenbeck provided information on the Civilian Conservation Corps and gave me access to tapes of interviews with men who had served in the Corps.

I appreciate financial assistance I received from Harvard University, as well as a research grant from the United States Office of Education. David Purpel and Ralph Mosher encouraged me and adjusted my work schedule with the Harvard teacher education program so that I could complete the original research. I am also grateful to Peter Carbone, George Thomas, and other colleagues on the board of *The Harvard Educational Review* for many stimulating discussions of our mutual research interests.

The study was originally inspired by Lawrence Cremin's *Transformation of the School,* and I am grateful to Dr. Cremin for responding to my inquiries and for well-timed words of encouragement. His recent untimely death is a loss to his many friends and admirers in the fields of education and history. David Tyack, Michael B. Katz, and Susan Sokol-Blosser gave me useful suggestions for revision of an early version of this study.

Dr. Tyack deserves a special note of gratitude. He has taken an interest in my work, and I in his, ever since we shared an office at Reed College in 1966–1967. Over the years since then he has suggested useful materials, answered my many questions, read chapters and entire drafts, given me helpful advice, and finally written a generous foreword. I am delighted to note how much I value his friendship and scholarly wisdom.

My colleagues at Lewis and Clark College have been consistently supportive, and the College has given me research grants at several critical points. Suzy Downey and Maureen Nesbitt skillfully typed several chapters.

I have had interesting and useful correspondence with Patricia Aljberg Graham, Larry Cuban, David Tyack, Joyce Antler,

Lawrence Cremin, Theodore Sizer, Jo Ann Boydston, and with staff members of *The Nation* and *The New Republic*.

I acknowledge the invaluable assistance of librarians at the Widener, Houghton, and Education libraries of Harvard University; the Butler and Teachers College libraries at Columbia University; the libraries of Reed College, Vassar College, Portland State University, the Northwest Regional Educational Laboratory, and Multnomah County. I am particularly grateful to librarians at Lewis and Clark College for conducting computer searches, ordering books, and in other ways assisting my research. Louise Gerity, Elaine Heras, Elizabeth Walter, and Randy Collver have been particularly helpful.

I have benefited from opportunities to present drafts of chapters at meetings of the American Educational Research Association, the History of Education Society, the Pacific Northwest Labor Studies Association, and the American Educational Studies Association. I wish to thank program coordinators, reviewers, respondents, and other colleagues in those organizations for their interest and encouragement. I particularly appreciate specific suggestions I received from Wayne Urban, Charles Howlett, and Rita Saslaw.

I received helpful critiques from editors and anonymous reviewers for *The Journal of the Midwest History of Education Society*, *Labor Studies Journal*, *The Educational Forum*, *Educational Foundations*, and *Insights*. I thank the editors for permission to use material (some substantially changed) previously published in their journals.

One of the many pleasures of this research has been exploring new and used bookstores from Maine to Hawaii and searching for books on progressive politics, journalism, and education. I am grateful to the proprietors and clerks for helping me rescue from dusty oblivion some of the classic works in these fields.

I want to thank Marlie Wasserman, associate director and editor-in-chief of the Rutgers University Press, for her patience and encouragement while I have been revising and editing this book. Her colleagues at Rutgers, Kenneth Arnold, Marilyn Campbell, Stephen Maikowski, and Dina Bednarczyk have been consistently helpful. I appreciate Willa Speiser's careful copyediting and tactful guidance during the final stages of the revision process.

I appreciate the efforts of several people who helped search for an appropriate photograph for the cover: Sharon Cohen, Joyce Antler, David Evans, and my good friend Charles Stones. I am particularly grateful to David Ment, archivist, and Kate Rousmaniere, manuscripts curator, at the Milbank Memorial Library, Teachers College, Columbia University, for their interested assistance. Ms. Rousmaniere's search of the Bank Street Archives, now housed at Teachers College, turned up the excellent photograph used on the cover.

The members of my men's group have been gratifyingly supportive as I have worked on this book. Finally, I want to give special thanks to my wife, Mary Guenther, and to my children and her children for heartening interest and encouragement.

I conclude with the usual disclaimer, but one which is true and wholehearted: I appreciate all the help I have received from colleagues, friends, and relatives, and cheerfully exonerate them from blame for errors and misinterpretations which may remain. I am continuing my study of related topics, so would welcome correspondence from anyone who has criticisms or suggestions concerning the book or the issues with which it deals.

James M. Wallace
LEWIS AND CLARK COLLEGE
October, 1990

Liberal Journalism and American Education, 1914–1941

1

Introduction: Liberal Journalism and American Education

In the fall of 1914 Randolph Bourne—soon to be known as one of America's leading young intellectuals—visited the high school in Bloomfield, New Jersey, from which he had graduated eleven years before. A brilliant, intense young man, he sat in the back of a classroom and attentively watched the teacher and students. He was not favorably impressed by what he saw. In his report on the visit, published in the first issue of *The New Republic*, Bourne noted that many students were justifiably bored by class activities that had little relevance to any of their present and future needs. But through years of conditioning the pupils had developed "that good-humored tolerance which has to take the place of enthusiastic interest in our American school." They joined loyally with their teacher in "slowly putting the hour out of its agony."[1]

The class was clearly unrelated to anything in business, industry, or the professions, and Bourne tried to think if it might have any parallels in adult life.

> I smiled, indeed, when it occurred to me that the only possible thing I could think of was a State Legislature. Was not the teacher a sort of Speaker putting through the business of the session, enforcing a sublimated parliamentary

order, forcing his members to address only the chair and avoid any but a formal recognition of their colleagues? How amused, I thought, would Socrates have been to come upon these thousands of little training-schools for incipient legislators! He might have recognized what admirably experienced and docile Congressmen such a discipline as this would make, if there were the least chance of any of these pupils ever reaching the House, but he might have wondered what earthly connection it had with the atmosphere and business of workshop and factory and office and store and home into which all these children would so obviously be going.

Schooling, then, was disconnected from real life, but Bourne was bothered also by the psychological assumptions on which the class seemed to be based. The students were expected to think without talking, as though these were completely separate activities. The atmosphere was constraining, unstimulating, inert. Learning was not seen as a process in which students would actively use their minds to solve problems.[2]

Bourne was sensitive not only to the internal dynamics of the lesson but also to the external influences on the school: "Now I know all about the logic of the classroom, the economies of time, money, and management that have to be met. . . . Hand-educated children have had to go the way of hand-made buttons." But in an early critique of the "cult of efficiency" in education, Bourne declared that there was a fundamental difference between the masses of machinery brought together in a factory and the masses of children in school.[3] "The difference is that, unlike cotton looms, massed children make a social group and that the mind and personality can only be developed by the freely interstimulating play of minds in a group."

Bourne concluded his depressing observations with what might be labeled criticism by definition: "Call this thing that goes on in the modern schoolroom schooling, if you like. Only don't call it education."

Thus at the very beginning of *The New Republic*'s history, Bourne identified some of the educational issues with which liberal journalists would be concerned during the next three decades: the aims and functions of schools; the psychology underlying the learning process; the role of the teacher; the place of efficiency in schools; and the reciprocal impact of school and society upon one another. The fact that the article reflected the views of the editors had been noted in a letter from editor Herbert Croly to Bourne: "The article which you sent in this morning has already been read and has been cordially and even enthusiastically accepted. We are all delighted with it."[4]

With this article Randolph Bourne began *The New Republic*'s tradition of perceptive educational commentary. This tradition was a natural expression of the convictions of the journal's founders. Dorothy and Willard Straight, wealthy progressives who provided the funds for founding *The New Republic*, were profoundly interested in education. In fact, they had originally conferred with Croly, who became its first editor, not about founding a journal, but about starting "some kind of school, perhaps a university to be located in Washington and to be devoted to education for the public service."[5] The Straights and Croly decided instead to start a weekly journal of opinion, but the motivation for the venture was equally educational. David Seideman's history of the early *New Republic* notes that the journal's planners expected it to "take the lead in a national renewal in education, literature, and government."[6] The editors often paired education and journalism as means of progress and reform. On the journal's first anniversary in 1915, the editors listed among their most important duties the need to "advocate better schools and press."[7] And in 1939, near the end of the period covered by this study, the editors applauded a statement on behalf of democracy and free inquiry that had been issued by a group of journalists and educators. They quoted extensively from the document, which concluded: "Our role is to fulfill our true function as educators and journalists in a democratic society by keeping free channels of knowledge so that the people can examine the facts with the critical intelligence necessary for intelligent appraisal and choice."[8]

Croly, even before the journal's first issue, had indicated his interest in having good coverage of education. He wrote to Bourne in June 1914 that Charles Beard had recommended him, saying: "I have liked very much what I have seen of your work and I feel sure that you could become a valuable contributor to a periodical such as we hope to start."[9] Three months later he made his expectations more specific: "You will be exceedingly useful to the paper in case your writing can include a more or less systematic dealing with educational and religious topics. I agree absolutely with the slight indication in your letter of the point of view you would like to take both in education and religion."[10]

The New Republic's fellow journal, *The Nation*, which had been published since 1865, had long since established a pattern of insightful analysis of educational developments, and this too was an expression of the beliefs of the founder. E. L. Godkin's original prospectus for *The Nation* had stated as one of the journal's main purposes "the fixing of public attention upon the political importance of public education and the dangers which a system like ours runs from the neglect of it in any portion of our territory."[11]

Both journals have always seen their roles as educative ones. Partly for this reason, and because they have been addressed to educated audiences, both have had a consistent interest in educational matters.[12] They have functioned both as advocates of progressive innovation and as critics of particular educational developments. They have critiqued educational bureaucracy, elitism, and narrow interest-group pressures. They have helped define and redefine the role of education in a democratic society. They have contributed to the debate over what kind of a social future the schools were trying to build. And some of their editors and writers have gone beyond their journalistic functions and participated actively in educational projects, particularly those related to progressive education.[13]

The New Republic and *The Nation* are periodicals of small circulation, addressed primarily to liberal intellectuals. The journals and their editors have played significant roles in American liberal thought and culture and have analyzed educational matters as part of larger political and social developments. Writers like Bourne, Walter Lippmann, Oswald Garrison Villard, Agnes de Lima, Alvin Johnson, and John Dewey gave the two journals reputations as outlets for some of the best American educational commentary and criticism in this century.[14] John Dewey and Alvin Johnson (longtime director of the progressive New School for Social Research) served on the editorial boards of both journals. And Dewey wrote 179 articles, many of them on education, for *The New Republic*—more than for any other journal.[15]

Scholars who have written about America's educational past, including Lawrence Cremin, Patricia Graham, Sol Cohen, Chester Bowers, Walter Feinberg, and Clarence Karier, have drawn on *The Nation* and *The New Republic* as exemplars and transmitters of liberal thought on educational developments.[16] With these and other studies as background, an integrated analysis of the relationships between liberal journalism and American education during the period 1914–1941 may help illuminate issues of social, intellectual, educational, and journalistic history. And, at the very least, it may remind educators of their need for the kind of incisive, thoughtful criticism the liberal journals provide, and encourage journalists to continue to supply such criticism.

This study encompasses the years from the beginnings of World War I to America's entry into World War II. Brief as it is in the sweep of history, this span of time includes three periods that can illustrate significant changes in politics, in liberal journalism, and in the response of the journals to educational developments.

In 1914 World War I started in Europe and the progressive movement peaked in America. *The New Republic* began publication in that year, and *The Nation* changed editors, from classicist Paul Elmer More to his fellow professor, Harold Fuller.[17] During the first part of the 1914–1921 period, the differing educational coverage of the two journals reflected the divergent Wilsonian and Rooseveltian political commitments of the two weeklies. *The Nation*, representing an older, individualistic approach to reform, was somewhat suspicious of new educational trends. *The New Republic*, as the leading journalistic proponent of a newer collective liberalism, gave sustained attention and support to various progressive experiments.[18] But when *Nation* owner Oswald Villard took over the editorship in 1918, he adopted "new liberal" political policies much like those of *The New Republic*, and the educational commentary of his journal shifted accordingly. This transition to a new liberalism in education was evident in three issues with which the journals were particularly concerned during this period: the efficiency movement, academic freedom, and the role of the schools in social reform.

The years from 1921 to 1930 include the Republican administrations of Harding, Coolidge, and Hoover, through the onset of the Great Depression. During this period of liberal political failure, the journals, seeking deeper and more long-range solutions to America's problems, gave extensive attention to cultural and educational developments. They concentrated their educational commentary during the 1920s on the worker education movement, on child-centered progressive schools, and on the defense of education against super-patriots, religious sectarians, and business interests. In 1930 Herbert Croly, the great founding editor of *The New Republic*, died, marking the end of an era for that journal.

With the beginning of the Depression, the content and emphasis of the journals' political commentary changed drastically, and the educational coverage shifted in response. During the 1920s the liberal journals had promoted education as an alternative to political action or as a long-range way of rebuilding progressive politics. But during the 1930s, when liberals were again experiencing some political success, the journals modified the emphasis of their educational commentary and sought to infuse progressive educational perspectives into some of the political programs of the decade.

The 1930–1941 period was marked politically by the Depression, Franklin Roosevelt's New Deal, the growth of a threatening fascism in Europe, and the drift toward American participation in World War II. In the field of education, the journals focused their attention on the impact of the Depression on schools and colleges, educators' responses to the Depression (including the politics of teacher unions), the "revolt on the campus," and New Deal youth programs.[19] Several of these issues were inextricably intertwined with the journals' participation in, and final break with, the popular front with the Communists.[20]

■

The Nation and *The New Republic* have received considerable attention in reinterpretations of American progressivism and liberalism.[21] An analysis of the place of education in the ideas and actions of the liberal journalists may help in the effort to develop a balanced assessment of their roles and of the larger political movements in which they were so actively involved. Peter Filene reminded historians in 1970 that progressivism was an "overgrown and treacherous field of historical controversy" and even tried to demonstrate that the progressive movement "never existed."[22] But Filene's position has not slowed the debate, which began long before 1970 and continues today in full force. Was progressivism, as William O'Neill has written, "more an age of modernization than of reform"? Was it primarily a "quest for social justice" or, as Robert Wiebe has claimed, essentially a "search for order"?[23] Or was it even the "triumph of conservatism," as Gabriel Kolko has proposed?[24] And, whatever the essential nature of progressivism, to what degree did its policies and practices survive the 1920s and reappear in modified form in the 1930s?[25]

Although this study can provide only partial responses to such large historiographical questions, the educational thought of liberal journalists like Croly and Villard and of others who wrote for their journals was an integral part of their broader social philosophies, and should be considered as historians reinterpret their work and influence within this broader context. The following chapters will indicate that the liberal journals helped both to define and to keep alive political and educational progressivism during this unsettled period of American history.

Responding to the deep social conflicts of the 1960s and to the broad revisionist interpretations of thinkers like Wiebe and Kolko, educational scholars have sought new perspectives on progressive education. Historians such as Walter Feinberg, Harvey Kantor, Michael B. Katz, and Paul Violas have criticized progressive education (and schooling in general) as an instrument of a fundamentally conservative social order. More traditional historians like Diane Ravitch have written rebuttals to such attacks on the "democratic-liberal tradition."[26] But during the 1980s, steps toward a creative integration of progressive and revisionist interpretations have been taken by David Tyack, Robert Lowe, Elisabeth Hansot, William Reese, Ira Katznelon, Margaret Weir, and other scholars.[27]

A good recent example of a partial rapprochement between divergent scholarly camps—or at least a growing shared appreciation between them—is a dialogue between Katz, leader of the revisionist educational historians, and Lawrence Cremin, acknowledged dean of liberal educational scholars, over Cremin's latest book, *The Metropolitan Experience*. While Katz thinks Cremin's "urban liberalism" is an inadequate response to world and national crises, and that his consensus-oriented approach fails to see that America is "an arena filled by the conflict between irreconcilable groups," Katz appreciates Cremin's massive contributions to educational history and his critiques of cultural traditionalists like Allan Bloom and E. D. Hirsch. Katz

writes: "As he attacks conservative educational critics and the
mind-numbing impact of commercial television, Cremin, for
me, is on the side of the angels. His vision of education is generous, humane, and democratic. I think of him as one of the
last great educational liberals, more sympathetic to John Dewey
than to anyone writing about education today."

For his part, Cremin says "I very much appreciate the care
with which Michael Katz has read *The Metropolitan Experience*
and the questions he has asked of it. He and I have surely disagreed over the years, but with a mutual respect that I have
found gratifying." He goes on to say: "I have 'joined' neither
the historians of the left nor the historians of the right, though
I have learned from both."[28]

At the end of his essay, Cremin writes of educational historiography:

> Some work will surely continue to focus on the schools and
> colleges, but other work will deal more broadly with a wide
> range of educative situations and institutions. There will
> be a diversity of questions, approaches, paradigms, and
> problematics. . . . But the benefits to scholars, practi-
> tioners, policy makers and the public will be legion, not
> least in the illumination of educational problems that have
> long been seen as intractable because they have been
> viewed too narrowly and in isolation from the relation-
> ships and contexts that give them meaning.[29]

This study was originally inspired by Cremin's *Transformation
of the School*, and it has been shaped by insights derived from
historians ranging from conservative to radical. It is offered as
a modest contribution to history which deals, as Cremin says,
"with a wide range of educative situations and institutions."[30]
The liberal journals surely warrant recognition and analysis
among those institutions. An interpretation of the ideas and activities of the liberal journalists, who had an intense awareness
of the weight of the past and were consciously trying to shape
history, may contribute to an emerging synthesis in educational
historiography.

The role that the liberal journalists assigned to themselves
was to look below the level of daily events and to report on significant developments and ideological transitions in society,
particularly in the political economy. Beyond that, they inter-

preted the meaning of those events and transitions and proposed policy solutions to the problems they analyzed. The journalists showed the relevance of education to broader changes in society and provided a forum in which leading liberal thinkers could show how education connected with those changes and how it could promote liberal goals.[31]

■

These ideas may be summarized in four central messages that will receive varying emphasis in the chapters that follow. The first is that—underneath superficially shifting responses to specific political and educational issues—the journals maintained the consistent position that education was an essential element in their democratic theory and in their programs of reform. The journals' commitment to reformist education varied less than their support for particular political programs. While the journals changed their allegiances to political parties and leaders, and while they emphasized different roles for persuasion and power in social change, they never lost their commitment to education as a central, but not exclusive, means of promoting what Croly called "the promise of American life."[32] In so doing they expressed a liberal version of the characteristic American belief noted by Lawrence Cremin: that "certain long-term reforms in society were better achieved through education than through politics, indeed that education was a form of politics insofar as it altered traditional relationships among individuals and groups."[33]

The second message—a corollary of the first—is that the educational commentary in the weeklies provided one of the ways in which the liberal journalists set forth their vision of a better world. Indeed, the journals' analysis of education became "a means of debating what sort of future the society should strive for."[34] Interpreting this message requires, as Cremin has written, a determination to give "as much attention to the intellectual history of education as to the social history . . . believing that whenever people set out to educate, they usually have in mind, explicitly or otherwise, some conception of the kind of individual and the kind of society they would like to see result from that education."[35]

The third message is that in promoting their vision of reform the liberal journalists continuously sought to build coalitions with other progressives and liberals, particularly those involved in a variety of educational enterprises. And in so doing, the journals depended less on the vain hope that elite groups could be persuaded to accept necessary reforms in society and education and more on the power of organized progressives working together to force needed social changes. Although these coalitions never succeeded in gaining broad political power, they did maintain pressure from the left on the movers and shakers of American society.

The final message is that the liberal journalists, whatever their current political positions, consistently functioned as what Michael Walzer calls "connected critics" of educational developments.[36] Even while serving as active participants in some progressive educational enterprises, the journalists provided sound, thoughtful, intellectual criticism of the varied educational institutions and processes that characterize American society. They can thus remind contemporary liberals and educators that such connected criticism is essential as we continue to struggle to improve and reform education and the society in which it operates.

In each of the next three sections, dealing respectively with the periods 1914–1921, 1921–1930, and 1930–1941, an introductory chapter will review major developments in politics, liberal journalism, and education. Subsequent chapters will then show how these broad changes were reflected in the educational reporting, analysis, and policy positions of the liberal journals.

PART I

From Persuasion to Power, 1914–1921

2

Liberalism, Old and New

Nearly three decades ago, in one of the most-quoted statements in American educational historiography, Lawrence Cremin asserted that progressive education was "the educational phase of American Progressivism writ large."[1] While Cremin's general insight has come to be accepted as a truism, it has also stimulated a minor scholarly industry of concurrence, elaboration, and reinterpretation.[2]

Since Cremin's influential book appeared, historians have asked challenging and fundamental questions about the broad progressive movement: Was progressivism basically an economic or a political movement? What were the varying influences of capitalism and democracy on the events of the period? Was the working class a victim of progressivism or a participant in it?[3] All of these questions about political progressivism "writ large" have had their counterparts in the historiography of educational progressivism "writ small."[4] And all of them influence the way historians and their readers interpret current educational issues. Do educators and educational scholars have a genuinely reformist tradition to look to for guidance, or must they engage in their work with regrets about the errors, limited vision—and even the antisocial motivations—of their political and educational predecessors?[5]

Further exploration of the progressive movement, and of some of the journalistic sources on which Cremin drew, shows that a qualification of Cremin's famous statement is in order.[6] Progressive education was the educational strand of only *part* of the progressive movement: that element which has come to be called "the new liberalism." There was, during the heyday of progressivism, a "crossroads of liberalism," in which the most advanced social liberals were vigorous advocates of progressive education, and particularly of its reformist branch, while more traditional laissez-faire liberals, although actively involved in the broad progressive movement, nevertheless did not accept progressivism in education as part of their program.

Charles Forcey has written the most comprehensive and persuasive account of the "new liberalism" that coalesced around Theodore Roosevelt during the pre–World War I period and of its divergence from the "old liberalism" of Woodrow Wilson's supporters.[7] Although his book was published nearly thirty years ago, in the same year as Cremin's *Transformation of the School*, it continues to influence studies of progressivism and still stands as one of the key interpretations of the development of the philosophy of modern American liberalism.[8]

Forcey traced the intellectual paths that led Herbert Croly, Walter Lippmann, and Walter Weyl to participate in the formulation of a new Hamiltonian liberalism that called for an activist national government, accepted industrial concentrations, favored labor unions, promoted economic planning, and sought reform in and through major social institutions, including education.[9] And he showed how their ideas, somewhat mangled in the political process, were partly reflected in Theodore Roosevelt's Progressive party platform in 1912. Two years after Woodrow Wilson's victory over Roosevelt in 1912, Croly, Weyl, and Lippmann went on to found *The New Republic*, which for many years was the most influential journalistic exponent of the new liberalism. In that same key election of 1912, the leading existing liberal journal, *The Nation*, supported Wilson, who was propounding a modified version of the classical American version of Jeffersonian liberalism. These journals were exemplars of two divergent emphases in American political progressivism, and their different political philosophies were reflected in contrasting responses to educational developments and particularly to progressive education.

The critical election of 1912 provided the clearest confrontation between the differing positions of *The Nation*'s editors and *The New Republic*'s founders. In that year, both groups of liberals agreed on the extremes of the ticket: neither could support Socialist Eugene Debs or Republican President William Howard Taft. *The Nation*, edited by classicist Paul Elmer More, backed Wilson, who seemed to be the most consistent supporter of Jeffersonian liberalism. The group that was to found *The New Republic*, including Croly, Weyl, Lippmann, and Willard Straight (who with his wife would become the journal's financial angel), supported Roosevelt and his Progressive party.[10]

This distinction between the old and new liberalisms can, of course, be drawn too starkly: Jeffersonian individualism versus Hamiltonian centralism; Wilson's New Freedom versus Roosevelt's New Nationalism; the nineteenth century versus the twentieth; and, in journalism, *The Nation* versus the emerging *New Republic*. But however they may overcontrast the situation, these labels do serve to identify two divergent trends within the liberal movement.

Political designations evolved along with changing events and philosophies. *The New Republic*, during the 1914–1916 period, called itself progressive. But when the editors began to shift to support of President Wilson, they took his "liberal" tag unto themselves, and dropped "progressive" as too reminiscent of their atrophied allegiance to Roosevelt.[11] Roosevelt, incidentally, did not respond gracefully to criticism by the *New Republic* group, referring to the editors as "nice, well-meaning geese— early Victorian geese."[12] And he displayed his bigotry by stating that the journal "was run by three anemic gentiles and three international Jews."[13]

The Nation, meanwhile, under the editorship of Harold Fuller, who succeeded More in 1914, continued to support Wilson and the New Freedom policies he was pragmatically modifying and in some respects abandoning. The realities of power forced Wilson, as Arthur Schlesinger, Jr., has written, to "nationalize the New Freedom." He found it necessary, as Croly had proposed, to use Hamiltonian means for his Jeffersonian ends.[14]

In early 1918, Fuller resigned as editor of *The Nation*, and Oswald Garrison Villard took over. Villard abandoned the laissez-faire policies of his predecessors and soon made the journal into a vigorous advocate of the new liberalism. His point of view permeated editorials, articles, and even the choice of book reviewers. In his memoirs, Villard recalled that period: "I was captain and supercargo, purser and recruiting officer, and I had the complete satisfaction of molding my historic journal according to my exact wishes and beliefs."[15]

It is evident then, as Forcey pointed out, that a shift of political opinion among many intellectuals did take place at the "crossroads of liberalism" in the progressive era. Some exponents of Jeffersonian liberalism now found it necessary to support the use of the positive state to achieve their objectives.[16] In journalism, *The Nation* took an analogous turn to the left, staking out a position much like that of *The New Republic*.[17] And, when *The Nation* shifted to the new liberalism, it began to selectively support the reformist strand of the new education as well.

The editors of *The New Republic* were pragmatic liberals who wanted to see education—along with other institutions—used as agents of social reconstruction.[18] The pre-1918 *Nation* also saw itself as a reformist journal (this was perhaps its chief distinction from the confessed conservatives of the period), but saw reform largely in terms of restoration. It feared that progressive education would cause a loss of traditional standards and weaken the ability of education to preserve the finer things in life. Consistent with this position, *The Nation* gave more attention to higher education during this period than did *The New Republic*, devoting considerable space to defending the colleges as bastions for the maintenance of cultural values and tending to ignore the lower schools or to contemplate their new activities with misgivings.

The contrast between the two journals before 1918 was evident in their responses to two of John Dewey's books: *Schools of Tomorrow* (written with his daughter Evelyn), published in 1915, and *Democracy and Education*, which appeared in 1916.[19] *The New Republic*'s review of *Schools of Tomorrow* (probably written by Randolph Bourne) applauded Dewey's use of ideas from Rousseau. It declared that the Deweys had updated Rousseau's "old vision . . . of having each child unfold his or her powers and tastes, gripping and adjusting the world to him and himself to the world." The book gave the reviewer the hope that such a vision might now be realized, not only in private schools, but—through such approaches as the Gary Plan—in schools serving the broader public as well.[20]

The Nation's review was—characteristically—more lengthy, scholarly, and critical than *The New Republic*'s. While the reviewer did not completely reject the purposes of the new education described in the book, he noted that schooling that emphasized practicality could easily "descend to the dead level of materialism." He also expressed the fear that too rapid educational change might "endanger the cultural training which our high schools are giving." And he questioned the attempt in the Gary schools, as described by the Deweys, to convince students of the utility of all subject matter: "All education should be practical in the sense that it should fit into some useful scheme of the universe; but the use of some portions of it need not necessarily be felt by students until long after they have left school."[21]

The following year *Democracy and Education*, Dewey's educational magnum opus, appeared, and the two journals gave it treatment comparable to that of the earlier book. Walter Lippmann's brief review in *The New Republic* was adulatory and even included an unorthodox note of praise for Dewey's "tightly packed and organized" style. Lippmann was impressed by Dewey's sense of the social role of the school and by his grasp of the historical changes which had affected that role. He shared Dewey's antipathy to the traditional school "inherited from a society in which there was a sharp division of social classes, in which culture was the property of leisure and drudgery the fate of ordinary men, in which commands came from on high, that is, from God through the rich, in which obedience was a greater virtue than self-direction . . . and science had not yet come to break down exclusiveness and offer endless hope to mankind." Lippmann welcomed *Democracy and Education* as a force in the creation of a new school for a new society: "It is a great book because it expresses more deeply and more comprehensively than any other that could be named the best hope of liberal men."[22]

The *Nation*'s review of *Democracy and Education* was not unfriendly, but it lacked Lippmann's enthusiastic, uncritical tone. The reviewer, Princeton philosophy professor Warner Fite, questioned Dewey's dialectical pattern of thought: "Perhaps it is wrong to expect a pragmatic philosopher to 'stand' anywhere. His business rather is to move." Fite noted Dewey's effort to integrate the various dualisms with which he was grappling—individual and society, culture and utility, discipline and interest—but felt that Dewey tended to emphasize the second item in each pair. This, to Fite, was an outgrowth of "the 'social' obsession which underlies all of Professor Dewey's thinking."

And, in a statement given wide circulation by Cremin, he wrote, "In spite of Mr. Dewey's fine defense of individualism, his moral ideal is really that of 'the good mixer.'"[23]

The contrast between the two reviews is clear: Lippmann accepted Dewey's social and economic program in full; it appealed to him as a reformer eager to cast off the dead hand of the past and to build a more just and creative future. It also reinforced Lippmann's faith that science—as he had declared two years earlier in *Drift and Mastery*—might be the "modern communion" that would bind men together in their struggle for better lives.[24]

Fite, on the other hand, instead of welcoming Dewey as an ally, saw him partly as a potential threat. Dewey's philosophy questioned the emphasis of most existing education on individualism, culture, and external discipline. It proposed to infuse schools with a greater emphasis on social goals and activities, and stressed student interest rather than the disciplinary value of subject matter. In short, while Lippmann saw Dewey as the prophet of more relevant education and a better social order, Fite feared him as the leader of an assault on established values. It is no exaggeration to say that Lippmann evaluated Dewey with the eyes of the future, and Fite with the eyes of the past.

■

The January 1918 issue of *The Nation* carried the announcement that Harold Fuller had resigned as editor and that Oswald Garrison Villard, grandson of the great abolitionist William Lloyd Garrison, would now assume responsibility for the journal.[25] The shift from Fuller to Villard represented a clear movement from the old to the new liberalism, although it was immediately instigated by the fact that Fuller had been outspokenly pro-Allied, while Villard insisted on maintaining a pacifist position concerning the European conflict. *The Nation's* leftward move helped attract many new readers and was apparently welcome to some of the old subscribers as well. A "reader's-eye-view" of the change was given in a letter that the journal carried in early 1919:

> Nowadays on opening one's *Nation* each week one is conscious of an expectation which did not exist a few months ago. . . .

No longer do we read academic discussions on such dessicated subjects as the split infinitive in Shakespeare. A
growing interest in and toleration of so-called radicalism
has become obvious to the most casual reader, until we
find open sympathy for, if not espousal of, advanced Socialism, Anarchism, and even Bolshevism—and the end is
not yet.

That which is happening to the *Nation* is evidently that
which is transforming many of us as individuals. We are
becoming aware that we are to live in a world of new conditions, one in which the old order not only changeth, but
may well disappear altogether.[26]

The new editorial policy encompassed education along with
other domestic concerns. Writers and reviewers placed less emphasis on traditional cultural values and mental discipline and
more on the social and reformist role of education. They became increasingly vigorous in their attack on business domination of schools and colleges and spoke out for strong teachers'
organizations. In short, they moved closer to the "new liberal"
positions already held by Dewey and his allies on *The New Republic*.

A more favorable attitude toward Deweyan pragmatism was
one of the noticeable changes in Villard's *Nation*. Where reviews of Dewey's earlier books had been somewhat suspicious
and critical, the response to his *Reconstruction in Philosophy*,
which appeared in 1920, was entirely positive. The fact that
Boyd Bode, a pragmatist whose ideas, according to Cremin,
"closely resembled the spirit and temper of Dewey's" was asked
to review the book was itself evidence of the change in *The Nation*.[27]

Bode described the book as "the most comprehensive and
enlightening pragmatic document that has yet appeared." He
agreed with Dewey's claim that philosophy had historically
been a conservative force and that science could help liberate
philosophy as it had other fields. The social implications of the
book were clear from Bode's commentary. He saw pragmatism
as a "tool or an instrument for the reorganization of experience, not an explication of a preexistent reality," and concluded
with the statement that "the book is a masterpiece. It formu-
lates and applies, with splendid insight, an outlook upon life
that represents one of the potent social forces of the present

time. It is in itself a reconstruction in philosophy, and it is a powerful plea to philosophy to forsake its sterile practices and become in a significant sense a guide of life."[28]

Articles and reviews of this sort indicated that Villard's *Nation*, as an emerging voice of the new liberalism, was sympathetic with the pragmatic philosophy that underlay the new education. It was equally supportive of educational ventures that grew out of that democratic, experimental point of view. In early 1918 preliminary plans for the New School for Social Research were released (an undertaking in which *New Republic* editors were actively involved). A *Nation* editorial, written by H. R. Mussey, praised the founders for their vision of an educational institution, based on freedom and creativity, which minimized administration and liberated students from rigid curricular boundaries. Mussey hoped that such an institution might be independent of the "legal control of boards composed largely of business men, or of governors politically chosen." Such institutions "have difficulty providing the surroundings in which the frank discussion of existing social conditions with a view to their radical reconstruction, if necessary, can be easily and effectively carried on."[29]

As plans for the New School were gradually formulated, *The Nation* continued to applaud the proposal. An article by James Harvey Robinson, one of the founders of the school, described the new venture as a response to the problems of social reconstruction created or exposed by the war. Robinson hoped that the institution might help bridge the yawning gulf between theory and practice in the social sciences. In a Deweyan reconciliation of dualisms, he declared that "all intelligent practice is based on theory, and all theories that are calculated to aid in reform are nothing but broad and critical ways of viewing practice."

Robinson identified the political, educational, and journalistic commitments of the school, saying that the regular students "should show promise of becoming high-class editorial writers, original teachers, public administrators or [show] their capacity for taking responsible positions where it is essential to deal with the problems of labor." The school should produce a better type of political leader, as well as "a new kind of teacher, who if he gets an opportunity may bring the instruction in the schools and colleges into closer connection with our needs; a new type of secretary of city clubs who can organize and direct public opinion; a new type of editorial writer, who can make our newspapers and magazines a source of public enlightenment beyond what they are now."[30]

Given the interest in the enterprise, the editors asked several leading educators to comment on the plans that were being developed for the New School. Alexander Meiklejohn, president of Amherst College, noted that some traditional subject matter and values were being ignored in the planning, but approved of the proposal, noting that the school "appeals to men who wish to know how society should be changed rather than to those who wish to know that it should be." And Francis Hand wrote: "It is to be hoped that the freedom of the new school from any suspicion of capitalistic bias will win the confidence of labor."[31]

■

It is clear then, that—amidst its varied constituencies—the progressive movement had its right and left wings, represented in journalism by the pre-1918 *Nation* and the *New Republic*; that there were significant differences in the political and educational policies of the two journals during that period; and that under a "new liberal" editor after 1918, *The Nation* began to adopt positions on politics and education similar to those already taken by its fellow journal. This shift to the new liberalism in philosophy and in support for educational experiments will be traced in the journals' reactions to three educational controversies of the 1914–1921 period: efficiency, academic freedom, and reformist education.

3

Education and Efficiency

The Nation and *The New Republic* were, during the prewar period, consistently hostile to the domination of the schools by business ideologies and values. They expressed this hostility in a number of ways, including their opposition to narrow vocational education, but their positions can be explored most meaningfully in their attitudes toward the application of business efficiency to education.[1]

The relationships of these two journals to American business and its generally conservative outlook were complex, ambiguous, and changing. At the beginning of this period, in spite of their differences, both were organs of middle-class reform; neither sought an alliance with the working class against the rest of society. The editors of *The New Republic*, whose magazine was subsidized by the inherited, business-derived wealth of Dorothy and Willard Straight, had in their books expressed an inordinate faith that enlightened businessmen might "civilize the whole class conflict."[2] No doubt at this stage the examples of public-spirited persons like the Straights influenced their thinking about the role of business in American life.[3]

Yet in spite of their hope that businessmen eventually might become agents of social transformation, *The New Republic* editors were suspicious of the existing influence of business. They

lost no opportunity to denounce the conservative role of businessmen in the affairs of the nation, including the schools. As
Charles Forcey has pointed out, Croly, Lippmann, and Walter
Weyl as editors were soon putting their faith in industrial democracy rather than in business as the preferred instrument of
social change.[4]

Thus, almost from the beginning of its history, *The New Republic* opposed business conservatism from the left. The *Nation*'s early opposition to business, however, might be said to
come neither from the left nor the right, but from above. Richard Hofstadter identifies E. L. Godkin, founder of *The Nation*,
as the "pre-eminent journalist and philosopher" of the laissez-
faire liberals who felt that their status and influence were under
attack during the Gilded Age of the late nineteenth century.[5]
And Hofstadter's "status revolution" interpretation can continue to apply to editors More and Fuller. Under their leadership *The Nation* looked down on the new business leadership
and its shoddy values. Until Villard took over in 1918, the journal, as Henry May has shown, was a representative of the "genteel tradition"; as such it resisted the encroachment of philistine
"progress" in many areas of life, including education.[6]

Both journals were thus suspicious of the "pecuniary interests," although on somewhat different grounds. Their attitudes
toward business were expressed in articles and editorials on a
variety of subjects and were clearly evident in discussions of efficiency and education.

In the case of *The New Republic* there was a complicating factor. Croly, Weyl, and Lippmann came to their journalistic endeavors with considerable admiration for the efficiency
movement. Like many other progressives, they were interested
in the application of what they saw as scientific efficiency practices to government, conservation, labor relations, and education.[7] *The New Republic* was thus in a position to support
efficiency as a means, but to reject many of the conservative
ends to which businessmen tried to apply it. The pre-Villard
Nation also saw that efficiency could not stand alone as a social
goal, but it was almost automatically suspicious of efficiency in
itself. The whole efficiency movement represented elements of
a new industrial society that its editors could not quite accept.
Both journals, although approaching the problem from different directions, reached similar conclusions regarding efficiency
practices in education.

The New Republic's position on efficiency in education was the corollary of its position on efficiency in industry. That was made clear in a 1916 editorial that reported on a meeting of the Taylor Society—a leading promoter of the efficiency movement—and concluded that "our greatest need in America today is a working agreement between democracy and science." The issue influenced political discussions, with Republican presidential candidate Charles E. Hughes accusing the Wilson administration of gross inefficiency. Lippmann, however, had earlier stated *The New Republic*'s preference for Wilson and declared that "efficiency will never be a popular cause in America until it is tied securely to radical liberalism."[8]

Randolph Bourne, in *The New Republic*'s first issue, had criticized somewhat obliquely the penetration of efficiency practices into the schools. He had struck a theme that he would continually express in his educational writings. In 1916 he put the matter into perspective, separating efficient means from human goals:

A school system whose object was little more than to abolish illiteracy and prepare the more fortunate for college was bound to fall an easy prey to the mechanical organizer. . . . The machinery was developed before the moving ideals were worked out. . . . It is so easy to forget that this tightening of the machinery is only in order that the product may be finer and richer. . . . To institutionalize a social function is always the line of least resistance.[9]

But it is in Bourne's articles on the Gary Plan that one sees most clearly the new liberal attitude toward efficiency and education. In 1915 Bourne wrote a series of five *New Republic* articles about Superintendent William Wirt's educational innovations in Gary, Indiana. Bourne visited the Gary schools in March 1915 and was impressed by what he saw as their democratic spirit, by the enthusiasm with which students carried on their studies, and by the numerous connections being made between the life of the school and that of the outside community.[10]

The Gary schools had been cited as an example of the application of scientific management to education, but Bourne saw them in a different light.[11] He reported Wirt's belief that the public was unlikely to increase its investment in education and that thus the only hope for improvement was the more intensive use of resources. But Bourne declared that this change had been undertaken "with none of the spirit of the 'efficiency expert' or mechanical administrator." He could not agree with some critics that the Gary schools were the educational counterparts of the new steel industry that was burgeoning in Gary. On the contrary: "That these schools [challenge] in their democratic organization and opportunity, their versatility and joy of initiative, most of the ideas and principles upon which enterprises like those of Judge Gary's have been founded, is one of those ironical accidents which will happen."[12]

Bourne returned to this theme in his second article, declaring that "Mr. Wirt has been accused of 'business efficiency,' but this is scarcely the term for so artistically elegant a scheme of economy. . . . Such economy is creative; it enriches, not impoverishes."[13] In fact, one of the major themes of Bourne's article and subsequent book was that the Gary schools had succeeded in freeing teachers and students from lock-step mechanical educational procedures.

As Bourne observed later, these articles constituted a "mere impressionistic survey" of Wirt's innovations.[14] He seems to have spent most of his time visiting classes, giving little attention to exploring the administrative intricacies of the system. Had he done so he might have seen more clearly—and warned against—the incipient tendencies toward conservative, business-oriented, economy-emphasizing efficiency that were to become the target of later liberal critics.

Bourne's good friend Agnes de Lima felt that he wrote rather uncritically about the Gary schools.[15] And F. S. Hoyt, who handled the publishing details of *The Gary Schools*, warned Bourne against being "too eulogistic of Mr. Wirt." Bourne made a valiant effort to temper his fervor for the experiment.[16] Just after completing the manuscript he wrote to a friend, Elizabeth Sergeant: "The Gary work is a fearful thing. I tried to be official and descriptive and to quench all unqualified enthusiasm with the result that I am duller than the most cautious schoolman."[17]

Bourne may well have been deluded in his belief that the Gary schools were free of negative efficiency practices, but the important point is that in his articles and book he expressed unremitting hostility to mechanical efficiency approaches to educational and human concerns. Part of his favorable response to the Gary schools was based precisely on his belief that they were free of such life-destroying influences.

Bourne's mentor, John Dewey, put the issue in a broader context and reminded readers of the influence of social class in a 1916 article in *The New Republic*:

> It is for education to bring the light of science and the power of work to the aid of every soul that it may discover its quality. For in a spiritually democratic society every individual would realize distinction. Culture would then be for the first time in human history an individual achievement and not a class possession. . . .
>
> Our public education is the potential means for effecting the transfiguration of the mechanics of modern life into sentiment and imagination.[18]

And in a 1918 review of Helen Marot's *Creative Industry*, Dewey added his authority to the convictions expressed by Lippmann and Bourne that scientific efficiency must be accompanied by democracy in education, industry, and society. He noted that "even the movement for 'scientific management' got no further in its psychology than the importance of standardizing methods of production; it never perceived the importance of enlisting the cooperation of the workers in discovering and fixing these standards for themselves."[19]

■

While *New Republic* writers and editors were attacking efficiency that was not based on democracy, the pre-Villard *Nation* was assailing it as part of new educational trends that it saw as leading to an excess of democracy. In 1916 an editorial commented on the National Education Association convention at which teachers were being offered a number of sessions responding to the current mania for efficiency. The editors noted that efficiency was becoming the "watchword of public education," but that if schools became too standardized and mechanized, "such efficiency was no better than a steamroller."

The editors noted the general, but only partly laudable, effort to democratize opportunity by making people equally efficient in earning a living and in carrying on the other activities of life. But the editors seemed to fear that the schools might become *too* efficient in this area; that the very success of the school tended to "relieve parents of all sense of responsibility in the instruction of their children. The more the schools undertake, the more the parents shirk. The result is bound to be a levelling of minds and manners."

What the editors were objecting to, of course, was the assumption by the school of a wider variety of social functions. And it was in these terms that they saw the efficiency movement; it was part of a whole trend—which they rejected—away from traditional cultural education and toward practical, vocational, materialistic training.

The Nation also feared the effects of the efficiency movement on instructors. In the same editorial they questioned the adoption of mechanical methods and procedures that would inhibit the "character and originality of the individual teacher."[20] And two years earlier they had given Columbia's president, Nicholas Murray Butler, a rare note of praise for opposing "the foolish and wrong-headed proposal of applying to the teaching body of a university the mechanical tests of the efficiency engineer."

But if efficiency practices were deadening for teachers, they were even more so for students, who were, after all, the chief concern of the educational process. Thus the editors had also condemned Butler for his proposal that physical examinations be required of Columbia's entrants. They saw such a plan as the expression of a misdirected "itch for perfection." In regard to his professors Butler had written, "A University is precluded from being efficient in the mechanical or business sense by its essential character and essential policies." *The Nation*, referring to Butler's statement, added: "Most true—and applicable just as truly to the spirit in which the university should regard its body of students as to that in which it should view questions of faculty organization."[21]

■

While the pre-1918 *Nation* had suspected educational efficiency partly because of its apparent connection with vocational training, the growth of the school's functions, and "extreme democracy," under Villard the journal took a position more like that of *The New Republic*.[22] (In 1911 Villard had been one of the founders of the Efficiency Society of New York.)[23] The similarities of the journals' stands on the related issues of efficiency, the influence of business on education, and the social role of education were evident in 1919 reviews of Thorstein Veblen's *The Higher Learning in America*. The *New Republic* review, written by British political scientist Harold Laski, quoted Veblen's charge that "the University apes the great business organization. It lays emphasis upon its quantitative output—the number of its students, the writing in bulk of its professors."

Like Veblen, Laski deplored the conservative effect of the business domination that created this atmosphere: "In every subject that nearly touches the business world, heterodoxy is at a discount." And Laski shared Veblen's conviction that university control by trustees had to be abolished if the institutions were to be free to pursue their truly creative functions. But although Laski saw *The Higher Learning in America* as "the profoundest analysis that has been made of the weaknesses of the American university system," he could not accept Veblen's nonreformist conclusions. Laski insisted that the university could not "decry utilitarian pursuits; for the simple and satisfactory reason that its main business is the service of man. Veblen's own hypothesis is open to the danger which follows every worshipper of research for its own sake; he takes his laboratory and calls it life."[24]

The Nation's reviewer, Joseph Jastrow, was also generally positive about *The Higher Learning in America*. He was clearly taken by Veblen's pungent, ironic style, and quoted liberally from the book. Jastrow agreed with Veblen that "business success is by common consent, and quite uncritically, taken to be conclusive evidence in matters that have no relation to education." He summarized Veblen's observations on efficiency in education: "Every item of the mechanism of teaching must be standardized and made to tell a statistical tale, which alone falls within the comprehension of the laity." He deplored with Veblen the practice of making educational decisions primarily on budgetary grounds.

Veblen had criticized the colleges for treating their faculties as employees, and Jastrow agreed with him that the professors were partly to blame for permitting this business-oriented practice to develop. "Unquestionably, the commercializing [of higher education] . . . has been hastened and aggravated by the false spirit of concession, even the warm adoption of the programme, which the academy should have resisted wisely and vigorously and well."

Jastrow's only criticism of the book was precisely that made by Laski in *The New Republic*: Veblen assumed that "the scholar desires to be or should be nothing more than a scholar." Where Veblen sought to conceal his moralism and humanitarianism behind a screen of pure, disinterested scholarship, Jastrow explicitly advocated a sense of social concern and an assumption by university personnel of responsibility for human betterment.[25]

These reviews point up Veblen's ambiguous relationship to the representatives of "the new liberalism." The journals, in their usual eclectic fashion, accepted much of Veblen's argument while rejecting his elitist conclusions. They welcomed him as an ally in the denunciation of the pecuniary domination of science and technology, but while Veblen sought to substitute direction by technicians for that domination, the liberal journals followed Dewey in demanding greater democratic control.[26]

Certainly thinkers like Dewey had more in common intellectually with scientists than with businessmen; but such liberals opposed granting inordinate power to any group. Thus they opposed Veblen's putatively amoral and socially disinterested role for higher education.[27] They rejected his position that research should take place in a social and moral vacuum; instead, they insisted that research and education must be dedicated to human welfare—which could not be promoted by either the old commercial-industrial elite or by a new scientific-technical elite.

Members of *The New Republic* group had had an early and short-lived faith in a business elite; the pre-1918 *Nation* had put excessive confidence in a scholarly cultural elite. But Villard's *Nation* joined *The New Republic* in insisting that democratic control had to be strengthened to prevent the accretion of unrestrained power by any group, however wise, efficient, or benevolent.

The journals' positions on efficiency and education may be seen most clearly within this broad context. Both *The Nation* and *The New Republic* recognized the need for rational economy measures in schools and colleges but deplored the use of the efficiency fad as a means of lowering justified expenditures. But Fuller's *Nation* associated efficiency with practical, hyper-democratic trends in the schools and condemned the entire package; *The New Republic*, on the other handed, resisted efficiency measures that were closely tied to business-oriented conservatism. And under Villard, *The Nation* came to share the new liberal position of its sister journal—that science and efficiency were only creative to the extent that they were accompanied by an extension of democracy.

The efficiency movement provides one example of a transition that was evident in other issues, including academic freedom. As *The Nation* moved leftward under Villard, it came to rely less on the vain hope that educators and others could persuade powerful groups in society to change their ways. Instead, it advocated the use of power, exercised collectively by teachers and other workers, as an instrument of institutional and social change. *The Nation* thus became not just an advocate of progressivism in education, but—like *The New Republic*—a supporter of the reformist wing of that movement.

4

Scholars and Their Bosses

Throughout their histories *The Nation* and *The New Republic* have defended academic freedom at all levels of education.[1] Given their commitment to free inquiry and their wide readership among teachers and professors, this is not surprising. But a change in the means proposed for dealing with academic-freedom issues illustrates further the contrasts between the old and new liberalism. Under "old liberal" editors More and Fuller, *The Nation* failed to advocate structural changes that would have helped teachers defend their rights, but under "new liberal" Villard, *The Nation* joined *The New Republic* in forcefully promoting organizations and unions as instruments of self-defense for teachers. In short, the new liberalism added power to persuasion in support of academic freedom and democratic governance.

The magazines often considered together the issues of academic freedom and governance. Since violations of academic freedom were usually committed by trustees or by administrators acting as their agents, the journals frequently used the same editorials and articles to defend individual instructors and

NOTE: This chapter takes its title from the title of a *Nation* editorial on academic freedom (TN 112 [9 February 1921]: 199–200).

to attack the existing pattern of school and university management.

The liberal editors and writers did not have a long tradition of academic freedom on which to build their cases. At this time teachers in elementary and secondary schools were, in most parts of the country, still very much at the mercy of local school boards.[2] In higher education, it was only in a few of the larger and more sophisticated universities that professors had, since the 1890s, begun to demand freedom to speak and write as their studies and their consciences dictated.[3] And as Ellen Schrecker has shown, even in those institutions, at least through World War I, professors consistently lost in their confrontations with administrators and trustees.[4] Thus the journals were supporting a nascent, not an established, movement when they backed teachers and professors in their quest for academic freedom and democratic governance.

The contrast between the journals on these issues during the pre-Villard period was evident in their responses to the formation of the American Association of University Professors (AAUP) in 1915. *The Nation* carried a rather bland report by Morris Jastrow, one of the participants. Jastrow noted the group's decision to exclude college presidents from membership, but handled this largely as a technical issue. Similar treatment was accorded discussions of tenure and academic ranking, but singularly lacking was any attention to the professorial dissatisfaction that lay behind the formation of the AAUP.[5]

The New Republic, however, was more familiar with the various pressures that had led to the new organization. Two years earlier Herbert Croly had been the only nonprofessor to serve on an academic-freedom committee formed by several learned societies. John Dewey and Alvin Johnson, both *New Republic* contributors and later editorial board members, were among the founders of the AAUP, and Dewey was its first president.[6] It is understandable, then, that the journal saw the new organization in broader perspective. The editors ignored technicalities and commented on the central issue:

> Several of the speakers seemed to be morbidly afraid that the association might be popularly misconceived as a labor union. Almost they did protest too much. A union of professors must differ essentially from a union of wage-earn-

ers, but the new association is seeking none the less an object analogous to that of an ordinary union. It is seeking increasing independence for its members by means of organization and community of spirit.[7]

During the pre-Villard period, *The Nation* gave little attention to the vulnerability of teachers or to their need for collective action. Consistent with their moralistic, individualistic worldview, the editors seemed to hope that offending boards and trustees could be persuaded to deal more justly with their faculties and to take their social responsibilities more seriously. Not atypical, though more vigorously expressed than usual, was *The Nation*'s comment on the 1915 dismissal of Scott Nearing by the trustees of the University of Pennsylvania. The editors declared that the idea that the university was "not altogether a private institution . . . will have to be pried out of these gentlemen's heads."[8]

But while *The Nation* looked primarily to persuasion as the means of progress, *The New Republic* unequivocally supported collective action by educators as well as their membership on governing boards. In early 1915 the journal carried an article that proposed that teachers gain representation on school committees. The author, F. I Davenport, acknowledged the major difficulty in such a program: that teachers had been too effectively "drilled in reverence for properly constituted authority" and were thus unwilling to assume this responsibility.[9] *The New Republic* assumed the task of undermining this sense of reverence and of promoting collective action by educators. In a Veblenesque editorial in July 1915 the editors called for greater public and faculty participation on university governing boards. They admitted that the existing pattern of governance might have been tolerable when boards of trustees were top-heavy with ministers. "But with the passing of control from the ghostly to the moneyed element, the gulf between trustee and professor has become extreme." The editors hoped that a peaceful sharing of power might take place but had suggestions for faculty action in the likely event that this did not occur:

Trustees who really envisage the modern university as a public service . . . will gladly share their power. If they do not, they will demonstrate how radically their own conception of a university differs from the general one, and it will be the duty of professors to assert their rights by all of those forms of collective organization whereby controlled classes from the beginning of time have made their ideas effective.[10]

The New Republic soon gave a hearing to one of the professors who tried to "assert their rights." When Charles Beard and James Harvey Robinson resigned from Columbia University to protest the firing of two antiwar professors, the journal gave Beard a forum for a detailed description of various trustee actions aimed at silencing dissent. The education committee of the Board had in 1916 "grilled" Beard on his beliefs and had instructed him to warn his colleagues "against teachings 'likely to inculcate disrespect for American institutions.'" The following year the trustees passed resolutions establishing a committee to determine if "certain doctrines" were being taught in the university. In response, the Faculty of Political Science unanimously adopted the following statement:

> Whereas the resolution of the trustees by its very terms implies a general doctrinal inquisition, insults the members of the Faculty by questioning their loyalty to their country, violates every principle of academic freedom, and betrays a profound misconception of the true function of the university in the advancement of learning, *Be it Resolved* that we will not individually or collectively lend any countenance to such an inquiry.[11]

But such ringing statements had little effect on the conservative and militaristic trustees of established institutions. While continuing to protest violations of academic freedom in existing universities, Croly and other *New Republic* editors joined with Dorothy Straight to help create an institution with true faculty governance and a clear commitment to academic freedom. In 1919 they helped establish the New School for Social Research, with Beard, Robinson, and Henry Dana (one of the fired Columbia professors) among its first faculty members. A critical element in this new venture in social research and adult education was "faculty control of institutional policy."[12] Planning meetings for the school were held in *The New Republic* offices, and both journals devoted considerable space to encouraging the new academic experiment.[13] The New School may be seen, in fact, as an early example of the kind of educational effort that would claim the attention of the liberal journalists during the coming decade. Unable to have much impact on larger political events, both journals would look elsewhere for signs of hope, partly by exploring promising experiments in progressive education and adult education.

■

After what Villard called "the revolution in 'The Nation' of 1918," that journal joined *The New Republic* in recommending vigorous collective action by teachers.[14] Two weeks after the 11 November armistice, *The Nation* responded to the numerous attacks on academic freedom and to attempts to use the schools as instruments of reactionary propaganda by declaring that "the sooner all the teachers organize to protect themselves and rid the schools of politics, the better." An article by Joseph Swain two months earlier had concluded similarly: "If the nation cannot be made to see its duty, then the teachers, by concerted action and collective bargaining, must compel the nation to wake up."[15]

During the "Red Scare" of 1919–1920, schools and colleges became prime targets for conservative attacks. Robert Murray has written: "Because of its professed desire to foster open-mindedness, the educational system was second only to labor in the amount of criticism which it received and the suspicion which it aroused."[16] In 1920, the year of the infamous Palmer raids and other assaults on freedom, *The Nation*'s editors registered a firm protest against the action of Pennsylvania's superintendent of schools, who had denied teachers the right to join unions. The journal, having lost faith in the power of persuasion to change the actions of officials, gave the responsibility to the aggrieved educators: "It will be the fault of the teachers themselves if they go on accepting this 'new freedom' and allow the disciplinary necessities of an army to determine their rights and duties. We have only one counsel for the teachers of this country: that is to unite to secure the right of free teaching and a proper remuneration for their work."[17] (The journal's shift from its previous support of Wilson was suggested here by its sarcastic use of his phrase "new freedom.")

Partly because of changed conditions, but also because of its new editorship, *The Nation* had moved a substantial distance from the positions it had taken earlier. A 1919 editorial contended that the AAUP had "failed lamentably" to defend academic freedom during the war and praised those professors who were organizing locals of the American Federation of Teachers. The editors took the occasion to indulge in a rare bit of introspection: "Of course, such a step has been greeted in some quarters as a sign that Bolshevist principles are invading our institutions of learning, and it is no doubt true that the *Nation* itself would have been pained and shocked, a dozen years ago, by the news."[18] Now, however, *The Nation* was greeting the unionizing of professors with enthusiasm, rather than with pain and shock. On this, as on other issues, Villard's journal had come around to the more aggressive and power-oriented position already vigorously expressed by *The New Republic*.[19]

There are several explanations for the attention given by the liberal journals to academic freedom and school and college governance during this period. A basic reason, of course, is that the journals were written by and read by intellectuals. The editors and writers were college graduates with an intense interest in educational issues, and the journals' readers also constituted a highly educated group, many of whom were faculty members of schools and colleges.[20] To such persons, questions of academic freedom and governance were not subjects of esoteric interest—they were of immediate personal and professional concern.

Furthermore, the personnel of both journals wanted intellectuals to play larger roles in American society—which they could do only in an atmosphere of free inquiry. The pre-1918 *Nation* hoped that college graduates might help arrest what it saw as a mass drift toward narrow practicality in life. And even when it changed its social goals somewhat under Villard, *The Nation* clung to its hope that university-trained experts might play major roles in reform.

The New Republic, although more committed to popular democracy than the early *Nation*, also hoped that college faculties and graduates might exert an influence out of proportion to their numbers. A 1915 editorial in that journal contended that issues of academic freedom and governance were "as vital as any in American life, because the universities are coming more and more to focus the thought of the nation. We depend upon them as upon no other institution to inspire and discipline the democracy."[21] The individual interest of faculty members converged with the social interest; questions of academic freedom and governance were of national as well as personal concern.

The preceding explanations, however, might have held true even if the journals had been representatives of intellectual conservatism. Liberals were not the only supporters of academic freedom. But during much of this period it was liberals who were under attack, in politics and journalism as well as in schools and colleges.[22] There was thus a community of interest among academic and journalistic liberals. During the war, for example, *The Outlook* attacked *The New Republic* as one of America's "public enemies" and included it along with the Hearst press, German-language papers, and the International Workers of the World among the "sappers and miners" of America.[23]

Such attacks occurred even though *The New Republic* supported America's participation in the war. The journal had merely exercised its right to be critical of the conduct of the war and of the motives of the allies. But *The Nation* fiercely opposed American involvement and went through a well-publicized clash with government censorship.[24] Such events, intensified during the Red Scare, impelled liberals to unite in support of their rights. Thus the journals' vigorous fight for academic freedom may also be seen partly as an effort at self-defense. Attacks on liberals in any field had to be repelled if liberalism itself was to be safe.

There is a somewhat broader explanation for *The Nation*'s and *The New Republic*'s defenses of academic freedom. Concern for individual freedom was central to the social philosophies of both the old and the new liberalism. But, as has been noted, the old liberalism placed more emphasis on individualistic means for the defense of this freedom; the new liberalism recognized that in an increasingly corporate, bureaucratic society, collective means were required for individualistic ends. A corollary of this belief was evident in *The Nation*'s shift in emphasis from persuasion to power. During its "old liberal" stage *The Nation* had an extravagant faith in the rationality of humankind and in the ability of intellectuals to convince those in power to act more justly and humanely. But Villard, chastened by America's experience in World War I and disillusioned by what he saw as Wilson's false leadership, no longer believed that those who controlled America's institutions would willingly acquiesce in a diminution of their powers. Villard was, of course, a pacifist, and never proposed violence or class conflict as a solution to social problems. But he did join the editors of *The New Republic* in vigorously supporting efforts by suppressed groups—whether educators or laborers—to nonviolently and collectively demand and promote their rights.

Thus, by 1921 *The Nation* and *The New Republic* had staked out policies on academic freedom and governance to which they would adhere throughout their later histories.[25] And although their positions on these matters did not afterward undergo any essential change, the situations to which they applied them varied greatly. During the 1920s, with liberalism on the defensive, unions of teachers and professors made little headway. But then, in the 1930s, the journals supported an American Federation of Teachers that was militant and partly successful—and was wracked by serious factional disputes. The responses of *The Nation* and *The New Republic* to these developments will illuminate further the complex relationships between the journals and educational movements and organizations.

5

Education and Reform

In *The Transformation of the School* Lawrence Cremin described three main branches of progressive education: the scientific, the child-centered, and the reformist.[1] All three elements were present in progressive education during the 1914–1921 period, but the liberal journals were primarily interested in promoting the reformist forces in the movement. The term *reformist,* of course, covers a wide range of philosophies, including both the mild, genteel brand of progress through persuasion advocated by the pre-Villard *Nation* and the more vigorous, power-oriented approach which it joined *The New Republic* in supporting after 1918.

Cremin also pointed out "the inextricable relationships between social reform, reform *through* education, and reform *of* education."[2] An exploration of these relationships—which were of particular concern to the liberal journals—will further explain some of the connections among progressive politics, journalism, and education.

Political labels for this period are slippery, but perhaps the most appropriate term for the educational position of Fuller's *Nation* is "pre-progressive." *The Nation* rarely indulged in unrestrained polemics against the new education, but assessed it calmly and moderately, often damning it with faint praise. The editors recognized a certain worth in progressive education, but consistently expressed the hope that traditional cultural values would not be lost in the new era. And while Fuller's *Nation* rejected much of the emerging educational philosophy, it maintained an essential faith in schools as agents of moderate reform. It did not join in the truly conservative response described by Rush Welter, in which some of the more hidebound thinkers "substituted representation for education" in their democratic theory.[3]

The Nation under editor Fuller saw itself as a reformist journal, but insisted that progress would come through the efforts of benevolent middle-class people like its editors and readers. Writers for the magazine took almost as much pleasure in hurling verbiage at the grubby radicals as at the bloated plutocrats. The journal criticized "social-justice shouters" and worried about educational threats to benign individualism.[4] In his review of Bourne's *The Gary Schools*, for example, Fuller wrote:

> The Gary system has been thrust to the fore at a critical period in the history of this country, and the very nicety with which it appears to respond to present tendencies should make one the more suspicious of it as a cure-all. At a time when the excesses of the 'uplift' movement have resulted in a general letting down of the sense of responsibility on the part of the victims of economic pressure, Mr. Wirt proposes a plan in which discipline is almost entirely relaxed.[5]

Besides misinterpreting Wirt's program, Fuller was expressing the concern that continually plagues individualistic reformers. While acknowledging the problems of "the victims of economic pressure," he could not accept the new educational responses to them. His hope seemed to be that the old disciplinary education might still be adequate. In short, although he had a mild commitment to education as a means of reform, he could not support the changes within education itself that might make reform possible.

Similar views were expressed by other *Nation* writers. In 1915 Warner Fite criticized the idea that state universities were more important in a democracy than private colleges. Fite saw the state institutions as too utilitarian, while private colleges were essential precisely because of their distance from mundane concerns: "It is mere socialistic nonsense to suppose that an institution which lies outside of the political system performs no 'social function.'"[6]

The old liberalism was reflected also in an editorial in the same issue which objected to the emphasis of educators on "social values" and criticized the educational trend toward "extreme democracy." The editors concluded that "at present the schools are . . . in much the same position as the clergyman who, when he might be interpreting Holy Writ, is telling his congregation how they should vote."[7]

There was one area, however, in which Fuller's Nation was outspoken on reform of and through education. The journal—true to the values of its founder, E. L. Godkin—consistently called for better educational opportunities for blacks.[8] In a statement by Villard, it applauded the work of the General Education Board in raising the standards for black education. And it rejected the widely held view that black education should be simple training for menial vocations. The journal applauded the efforts of those blacks who, against great odds, acquired a higher education, and insisted that the way should be kept clear for all who had the ambition and ability to follow them.[9]

But even this position, advanced though it was for the time, was not an expression of the "new liberalism." The Nation's position was that blacks should have educational opportunity equal to that available for whites. This fell far short of a proposal that education should help to create a new social order. The Nation wanted blacks to be able to work their way into white society; it was not yet ready to say that education for either race might assist in the radical reconstruction of that society.

Thus Fuller's Nation held generally to the view that the schools should tend to their primary function of producing worthy individuals who would work within a basically sound economy and polity to elevate its moral tone. There were, admittedly, serious problems in society, but these were caused primarily by weaknesses of individual character and training. What was needed was neither a new education nor a new society, but a means of making the old work more effectively.

The New Republic, on the other hand, was dissatisfied not only with the character of individuals but with the economic, political, and educational system that produced them. The editors were more acceptant than Fuller of the irreversible technological revolution that had taken place, and more critical of the

antiquated and inadequate social structures that were struggling to deal with the results of that revolution. They shared
Veblen's view that institutions, always left over from the past,
had to be restructured to meet current needs.[10] Given the inevitable conservative tendency of social institutions, it became the
responsibility of liberals to seek environmental as well as individual change.

Thus one finds in *The New Republic* during this period, more
than in *The Nation*, encouragement for economic planning, se-
lective enthusiasm for some aspects of socialism, and greater
support for organized labor. The capitalist system was not a
given; it was not an expression of natural law, and humans
could mold it and modify it as they saw fit. As with the economy, so with education; recognizing that schools had a built-in
inertia, people should attempt all the more vigorously to adjust
the structure, content, and methods of education so as to promote fundamental social change.

Randolph Bourne promoted a reformist role for schools
both through his positive reports on educational experiments
and in his interpretation of Dewey's educational ideas. Part of
Bourne's enthusiasm for the Gary schools was based on his belief that they provided new institutional patterns, new techniques, and new approaches to content that would help to
develop both more creative individuals and a more just social
order. Bourne's views were, as he declared, "the product of an
enthusiasm for the educational philosophy of John Dewey."
And if his articles were sometimes little more than translations
of Dewey's views, what, he asked, "is a good philosophy for except to paraphrase?"[11]

In a 1915 article, Bourne told his readers that Dewey's ideas
were profoundly radical and that Dewey was "in the paradoxical situation of a revolutionist with an innate contempt for propaganda." Bourne admired Dewey for bringing order out of
social and intellectual chaos. Dewey's philosophy embodied
"some of the wisest words ever set to paper," and demonstrated
"the unity of all democratic strivings, the social movement, the
new educational ideas, the freer ethics, the popular revolt in
politics . . . and the applicability to all of them of scientific
methods."[12]

But *New Republic* readers did not receive Dewey's ideas only
in translation. Dewey spoke for himself in over fifty-two articles, notes, letters, and reviews written for *The New Republic*

during this period. In these writings, Dewey missed few opportunities to promote his hope for reform of and through education. He was particularly outspoken in his opposition to attempts to separate vocational and liberal education and, in his first *New Republic* article, denounced such schemes as part of an effort to make education a prop to an unjust economic system: "Every ground of public opinion protests against any use of the public school system which takes for granted the perpetuity of the existing industrial regime, whose inevitable effect is to perpetuate it, with all its antagonisms of employer and employed, producer and consumer."[13]

Four months later Dewey again protested proposals to divide the schools into academic and vocational branches. Calls for separate vocational programs arose out of the selfish ambitions of "commercial bodies and employers of labor [to] procure a state-supported system of schools in their own special behalf." Such suggestions were based on the conservative desire to maintain a stratified society. If successful, such splits would promote further divisions along religious or national-origin lines, and the schools would lose their roles as unifiers of culture.[14] Here, as in many of his *New Republic* articles, Dewey expressed one of his central educational ideas: that the schools should not passively reflect social trends but should, rather, resist and counteract the rigidities and injustices of society.

While Bourne and Dewey were calling for reforms that would enable education to promote desired social changes, Walter Lippmann, as Rush Welter has noted, was calling for a more educative politics.[15] Lippmann tried above all to be a realist and to assess accurately humankind's limited rationality. Yet he combined his interests in charismatic leadership and the use of myths to guide social groups with a consistent call for political activity that would help enlighten the electorate.

Lippmann recognized that the liberal Jeffersonian ideal of government was no longer viable—that in politics there were inevitably "insiders and outsiders," leaders and followers. But he blamed the failure of many of the progressives' administrative reforms on the fact that leaders had failed to instruct the public on the issues: "The power which has educated the insiders has left the outsiders uninformed. So they listen to the largest hope and follow the most magnetic personality."[16]

Throughout his life Lippmann carried on a dialogue with himself and others concerning human rationality. As Cremin

wrote, the more Lippmann "contemplated the new metropolitan world that was coming into being, the more he abandoned the hopeful socialism with which he began in favor of a
pessimistic elitism that held out little hope for a society gov-
erned by average men and women."[17] But during his association with *The New Republic* Lippmann emphasized the need
for an electorate as broadly and as realistically educated as possible. He fully understood human egocentricity, the role of
the unconscious in motivation, and the public's susceptibility
to propaganda, and yet—because he retained a basic faith in
the democratic process—he persisted in the belief that humans could be educated well enough to enable a free society to
function.[18]

■

Under Villard's leadership *The Nation* took positions on education and reform similar to those of *The New Republic*. After
1918 *The Nation* ceased to give space to peevish traditionalists
who bemoaned the increasing "socialization of education." Instead there was a growing enthusiasm for such reformist ventures as the New School for Social Research and the Boston
Trade Union College.[19] There was encouragement for "the effort to relate the universities more closely to community needs
and of spontaneous movements among the workers themselves
for a full educational opportunity." Such innovations encouraged the hope that Americans might "eventually emulate the
French in recognizing 'the moral obligation to be intelligent.'"[20]

An editorial note in early 1921 indicated how elements of
The Nation's new educational outlook could converge. The editors praised a recent convention of the American Federation of
Teachers that had adopted a liberal policy on Americanization
programs in schools. The assembled teachers had taken a stand
in favor of cultural pluralism; they had rejected the view that
Americanization meant discarding immigrant traits and adopting the Anglo-Saxon characteristics of the "true" American. In
their brief statement the editors demonstrated their rejection
of a narrow chauvinism and their belief that schools should
function as critics of society: "Whatever demagogues may do,
teachers have a more self-respecting task than to praise the
country for qualities which it does not possess; it is their obliga-

tion to point out the national shortcomings as well as the national virtues."[21]

Nation editors and contributors had come to accept the "new liberal" position that the schools *should* go beyond cultural transmission and participate in social criticism and transformation. But there was less unanimity on the degree to which education *could* play a role in social change. At one extreme, Harold Laski, paraphrasing H. G. Wells, declared extravagantly that in England "we are running a race between education and revolution. If labor gives to institutions like the Workingmen's Educational Association the support and funds they deserve, some way out of the present chaos may be found."[22]

But a more cautious M. H. Hedges—in an early statement of educational "reproduction theory"—raised doubts about the reforming power of the schools: "Education is not . . . an extrasocial process by which society is constantly freshened and transformed. Rather it lies within society and tends to reproduce in miniature the society which has borne it." Hedges was referring to existing educational institutions, which, he claimed, promoted either the Puritan ideal of Jonathan Edwards ("celestial propaganda") or the utilitarian ethic of Benjamin Franklin. He hoped that these outworn views of education might give way to a pioneering spirit more suited to the modern age. If colleges could begin to "supply students with a sense of a 'total universe of good' that is not fictitious, and to awaken in them the will to act on behalf of that universe," there might be grounds for optimism. But Hedges could not sustain so sanguine a view and concluded dimly that "the chances for the colleges to answer the needs of this generation . . . are small."[23]

Hedges is a convenient exemplar of the educational views of many postwar liberals. The experience of war abroad and reaction at home had deepened the liberal conviction that society was in need of drastic reformation; the hope that education might be an agent of cultural renewal would not die; and yet there was a sense of pessimism and a fear that what education should do, it actually could not do. It was partly this feeling of futility that strengthened the flight of so many liberals during the 1920s from politics to aesthetics and of many educators from reformist to child-centered schools.[24]

■

In 1918 the Commission on the Reorganization of Secondary
Education issued its influential report, the "Cardinal Principles
of Secondary Education." Early the next year the editors of *The
New Republic* published their reaction to the report in a clear
and forceful expression of their position on education and reform. Characteristically, the editors ascribed to the document a
more radically reformist cast than the authors probably intended. The editors noted that America had always relied on
education as "the chief bulwark of democracy," but that the
school had functioned in a largely self-correcting social economy. Society was no longer self-improving, however, and both
conservatives and radicals were demanding that the government assume a greater role in moral and political education in
order to keep the social machinery running. This implied "both
a radical break with the past and a long step toward collectivism
in education."

Conservatives and radicals disagreed on the ideals and
methods of education, however. Conservatives glorified discipline, obedience, and an unexamined loyalty to authority. They
believed in an "intellectual police power" to keep the people on
the "charted paths of virtue and truth." Radicals, on the other
hand, emphasized the reform of institutions, not the demand
for loyalty: "Social education must . . . start from the idea not
only of the decrepitude of the old education but from the gross
deficiencies of the affiliated social economy." In this context the
editors cited the Cardinal Principles as an appropriate ideal for
America's schools, but recorded the sad fact that "our existing
educational system fails flagrantly to realize that ideal." In
order for the Commission's goals to be achieved, the state
should "guarantee to all its citizens through the schools the economic independence which its social economy has failed to
guarantee."[25]

Rush Welter has pointed out that in conservative hands such
doctrine can make education a substitute for reform rather
than an adjunct to it:

> What sophisticated business practice has accomplished, in-
> deed, is to associate the competitive democratic values of
> Jacksonian and post-Jacksonian liberalism with the mod-
> ern business system by improving educational oppor-

tunities for personal success within it and leading to it. In effect, progressive businessmen have transferred economic individualism from business to the schools and thus reconciled their innovations with traditional American values.[26]

Realistically recognizing that an open educational system might help preserve a closed economy, conservatives thus sometimes joined liberals in support of public schools.

But the editors of *The New Republic* saw a deeper role for education. They recognized that power was unequally distributed, and that power was the key to progress for suppressed groups. Thus the state should "through its schools deliberately confer so far as possible the substance and opportunity of power on all its citizens." By so doing, the government would itself "serve as the chief agency of radical but remedial social change." The editors—after their vigorous presentation of these essentially Deweyan doctrines—closed appropriately by letting Dewey speak for himself. The goal of the new education should be, in his words, "to produce in schools a projection in type of the society which we should like to realize, and by forming minds in accord with it, gradually to modify the larger and more recalcitrant features of adult society."[27]

The school, then, was not to mirror existing society, nor was it merely to take the strain off an unjust system and thus help it survive. It was, within the limits of its own freedom of action, to mold itself in the image of democratic ideals; it would then be able to help develop individuals with enough power to help move society in desired directions.

■

"When the cheering stopped" and the ailing President Wilson was replaced by Warren Harding in 1921, political liberalism—at least as represented by *The Nation* and *The New Republic*—had taken on its modern form.[28] The doctrine of a strong activist government, forcefully put forth by Croly and his *New Republic* colleagues, had also been adopted by Villard's *Nation*. And its educational corollary, reformist progressive education, was being promulgated in both journals by the editors as well as by influential liberals like John Dewey, Charles Beard, and James Harvey Robinson.

This was no starry-eyed belief that education could be the chief agent of social reform, but it did mean that the school might be the growing edge of culture.[29] Education—partly through strong, organized collective action by educators themselves—could expand its own power and then help empower individuals and groups to participate constructively and energetically in social and political transformation.

In spite of the war and the "twilight of idols" like Roosevelt and Wilson, the liberal journals promoted the belief that reform and progress were possible and that the school could transcend its social context enough to enable it to play a significant role in social reconstruction.[30] If the optimistic enthusiasm of Randolph Bourne's early educational articles was no longer possible, the core of the faith still lived. The emotional edge of progressive belief had been blunted by the disillusioning experiences of the war years, but the editors of *The New Republic* and *The Nation* still held to the conviction that humankind was potentially educable and rational; that institutions retained some malleability and plasticity; and that there was continuing important work to be done by an educative journalism and a reformist education.

But in all their hopes for reform, it is clear that the liberal journalists, particularly those associated with *The New Republic*, overestimated their influence. As James Weinstein wrote in 1968: "To the extent that various independent liberals deceived themselves . . . it was in confusing their own pragmatic or problem-oriented liberalism with that of the corporate liberalism of the highly ideological business and political leaders. If they allowed themselves to be used, it was because they had the conceit to consider their intelligence and social values equal to the influence of the industrial and financial institutions that were the heart and muscle of American power."[31]

So in spite of an excess of optimism about their own power, by 1921, in *The Nation*'s fifty-sixth year and *The New Republic*'s seventh, the liberal journals had established themselves as thoughtful critics of American politics, society, culture, and education. During the decade to follow they would never lack for opportunities to exercise their critical capacities. But even during the discouraging days of the 1920s they would find in the world of education forces and movements that would call forth their powers as advocates as well as critics.

PART II

Lean Years for Liberals, 1921–1930

6

The Eclipse of Progressivism

Ring out the old; ring in something a little older." With these cheerless words the editors of *The New Republic*, in March 1921, greeted the inauguration of Warren G. Harding as President of the United States.[1] Their disdain for Harding was indicated again two weeks later by the biblical title they gave to an editorial on his inaugural speech: "Ephraim feedeth on wind." The editors exposed Harding's emptiness and confusion with apt quotations from his speech, asking finally: "Why not acknowledge now . . . that to expect much from the author of this Inaugural is to be as unwisely optimistic about President Harding as President Harding is about the whole world?"[2]

The Nation was equally disheartened at the prospect of four years—or more—of reaction. Its editors began their commentary on the Harding era with the observation: "Forward, march—straight to the rear! This is the inaugural command of our new Commander-in-Chief, President Harding. We are not even to be allowed to stand still, but are to advance backwards just as rapidly as possible—to normalcy by way of stability."[3]

This chapter takes its title from that given by Croly to a major editorial statement in *TNR* 24 (27 October 1920): 210–216. *The Nation* used the same appropriate eclipse metaphor in 1920. Quoted in Alan P. Grimes, *The Political Liberalism of the New York "Nation": 1865–1932* (Chapel Hill: University of North Carolina Press, 1953), 96.

However, 1921 was not the beginning of disillusionment for the liberal weeklies, but merely another milestone on the declining road from the heady progressive days of 1914. *The New Republic* had had the ambiguous fortune to begin publication in 1914 at the peak of the progressive movement and during the outbreak of World War I. Since that time it had observed with horror the exposure of its original hero, Theodore Roosevelt, as a chauvinistic "pseudo-progressive." It had found a new idol in Woodrow Wilson and followed (and perhaps helped push) him into a war that accomplished few of the goals for which liberals supported it.[4] Henry Fairlie, referring recently to *The New Republic*'s role in Wilson's choice to take America into the war, has written: "Of all the voices that prepared American public opinion (and to some extent, Wilson's own mind) to accept the inevitability of that decision, the most consistent, intellectually forceful, and zealous was that of this then infant magazine."[5]

The Nation had been equally discouraged by the events of the preceding years but could afford to be a bit more self-righteous than *The New Republic*, having been identified with fewer discredited causes. In 1912 it had supported the victorious Wilson for President against Roosevelt and Taft, and it had firmly opposed America's participation in the war. But with these major differences behind them, the two journals were now allied as observers of and participants in the liberal political failure that characterized the postwar years. They had supported Wilson's professed hopes for "peace without victory," and had then found it necessary to oppose the Versailles Treaty when it dashed such prospects. And in opposing the Treaty the liberal journalists had been chagrined to find themselves in a strange misalliance with some of America's most virulent conservatives.[6]

The Nation and *The New Republic* resisted with little success the wave of reactionary hysteria that swept over the nation during the Red Scare of 1919–1920. They had refused the Hobson's choice of Harding or Cox that had been offered by the two major parties in 1920. Villard had quoted in *The Nation* the statement that the choice was between "Debs or Dubs," and had cast his vote for the Socialist candidate, Debs.[7] It is a measure of Herbert Croly's estrangement from majoritarian politics that he "endorsed the Farmer-Labor Party candidate and plunged *The New Republic* into left-wing opposition—a stance from which it would not waver for the next forty years."[8]

The liberal journals thus went into the decade of the "Republican ascendancy" in a mood much less optimistic than that which they had felt in 1914. They were chastened not only by national failure, but by their own, and by that of the progressive movement generally. What John Hicks has described as "the abject conservatism of the Harding-Coolidge era" was upon them.[9]

■

The 1920s continue to be reinterpreted by historians, literary critics, social psychologists, and others, and while there are many issues of the decade on which consensus is not possible, there are some broad areas of agreement. Most historians characterize the era as one of general but unsound prosperity (with farmers, miners, and textile workers among the many groups left behind), and as one of undistinguished and unrealistic governmental leadership—at its worst, under Harding, corrupt and cynical—at its best, under Hoover, shortsighted and inflexible.[10]

In the social, literary, and intellectual realms, historians have seen the era as one of flight from responsibility. Many intellectuals abandoned in disgust their fruitless efforts to reform society or to elevate its taste. Some dramatically expressed their alienation from American values by choosing to live and work in Paris and other European cities. An even larger number remained physically in the United States but became "internal expatriates" who deliberately cut themselves off from the interests and standards of most Americans. Many in this group were among those who, as Norman Thomas said, had "no illusions but one. And that is that they can live like Babbitt and think like Mencken."[11]

Historians will continue to squabble over their interpretations of the 1920s, but most would agree that the decade was characterized by a decided swing away from the progressive enthusiasms of the preceding period. Page Smith has recently written that in the 1920s the American spirit of reform was "perhaps at its lowest ebb."[12] A question that is critical for educational developments during the 1920s is the one posed by Arthur Link in his classic article, "What Happened to the Progressive Movement in the 1920s?"[13] It is clear that conservatism was in the ascendancy nationally, but how powerful and effective was the liberal remnant? Link maintained that it had considerable influence, especially in Congress; that it was able to forestall some conservative legislation, such as the attempted sale of Muscle Shoals to private interests; that it was able to enact certain key progressive measures such as the 1928 Flood Control Act; and that finally—and ironically—some of the legislation passed by the conservatives themselves was in the progressive tradition.[14]

A reader of the liberal journals during the 1920s certainly had no doubts concerning the survival and vigor of an articulate and outspoken progressivism. But it is clear that *The Nation* and *The New Republic* played a different role during this decade. Where they had once hovered close to the centers of power (as in *The New Republic*'s relationships with Roosevelt and Wilson and Villard's with Colonel House), they now found themselves in the position of supporting, but still criticizing, political losers. Where they had once found grounds for cautious optimism concerning the future, they now inclined toward a caustic pessimism. Where politics had once seemed the major arena in which to promote progress and reform, now Croly, at least, gave increased attention to religion, economics, and education.[15] John Judis writes: "He rejected both the quest for a new Lincoln . . . and for enlightened business leadership. . . . Croly also called for 'the participation of the workers in the management of industry as an essential part of a democratic industrial policy and of democratic education for citizenship.'"[16]

Walter Weyl, in 1919, wrote a denunciation of "Tired Radicals." This label was picked up and used by Norman Thomas, William Leuchtenberg, and others to describe the liberal journalists and their allies, but the appellation is not entirely accurate. Indeed it has been said of the untiring Villard, who edited *The Nation* from 1918 to 1932, that he "made more acres of public men acutely miserable, per unit of circulation, than any other editor alive."[17]

A fair assessment of the liberal journalists during the 1920s would describe them not as "tired radicals," but as more realistic liberals. Croly's last case of hero worship occurred in early 1920, with Herbert Hoover as the object of his political affection.[18] But this was a short-lived infatuation, and Croly became increasingly wary of giving his loyalty to any politician. He came to believe that the ostensible progressive successes of the earlier era had been constructed on sand, and now proposed to go beneath the level of short-term results and build more solidly and more deeply. In a 1922 editorial appropriately titled "Sick of Politics," he wrote that "the chief function of the wise liberal during the next generation is to investigate the ability of individuals and groups to bring about an improved quality of human relations by other than political means." Croly's other means were, as Arthur Schlesinger, Jr., has indicated, "education, psychology, and finally perhaps religion."[19]

So, although the liberal journals were not politically irrelevant in the 1920s, they were chastened and changed, and their influence was consequently of a different nature. Instead of defining and encouraging a progressivism that was in power, they had to help build a liberalism capable of and worthy of assuming power. And it may be that such journals perform a more constructive function in periods of conservatism than during eras of progress and reform. As Arthur Schlesinger, Jr., has indicated, the intellectuals represented by such journals play a useful role in coordinating unrest. The assessment by Bruce Bliven (Croly's successor as editor) is particularly applicable to the 1920s: "A paper like the *New Republic* is badly needed, if only to be the eggheads' Committee of Correspondence."[20]

■

The liberal journals thus still had an important, if altered, mission to perform during the 1920s, but their degree of success in accomplishing it is difficult to evaluate. One of the earliest histories of the 1914–1929 period concluded that journalism of opinion probably had less influence during the 1920s than during the previous 'age of the muckrakers.'" Though this was true of some periodicals, *The Nation* and *The New Republic* at least were reaching a wider readership in the postwar decade. The combined circulation of the two journals rose from approximately 25,000 in 1916 to over 65,000 in 1921. And at no time during the 1920s did their total circulation ever slip below the 1927 figure of 55,000.[21]

While it is difficult to assess the influence of the journals on the liberal movement, it is somewhat easier to appraise the impact of the chief editors on their respective journals. During this decade the weeklies continued to be in considerable measure the personal journalistic expressions of Villard and Croly, two men who were similar in influence but very different in intellect and temperament.

Croly was a brilliant, original thinker—a scholar in journalism—but he wrote slowly, painfully, and ponderously. Villard was more professional as a journalist and had a more readable style than Croly's. But Villard's ideas were more derivative, and he made no contributions to political thought comparable to Croly's *Promise of American Life*.[22] Croly's thought was subtle, hypothetical, and pragmatic, while Villard's (although he considered himself a pragmatist) was more moralistic and dogmatic. John Hicks's comparison is apt: "Less emotional than Villard, and considerably more philosophic in his approach to public problems, Croly was equally dedicated to the idea of reform."[23]

Croly's associates described him as shy and withdrawn, while Villard was a commanding figure who did a great deal of polemical public speaking and gloried in the moral combat of his numerous causes. And Villard was a thoroughgoing pacifist (Humes has ironically noted his "violent hatred of war"), while Croly supported World War I and continued to insist that war could be justified under certain circumstances. But in spite of their contrasting personalities, Croly and Villard both served effectively during this period as editors of the two most influential liberal journals in America.[24]

The Nation had undergone its greatest recent transformation in 1918 when Villard assumed its editorship. The journal became controversial enough to inspire this bit of doggerel, which Sinclair Lewis wrote for its sixtieth anniversary:

> *The Nation* is a yellow scold.
> I like it.
> It's subsidized by German gold.
> I like it.
> It makes you hot, it makes you sore,
> It's either silly or a bore;
> It's all the things I most abhor—
> I like it.[25]

Throughout the decade Villard crusaded with "infections moral indignation" for the full range of liberal causes. He continued as editor until 1932 and then wrote a weekly column, "Issues and Men," until 1940.[26]

While *The Nation* had changed rather abruptly when Villard took over, *The New Republic* had shifted its emphases more gradually. Croly remained as editor until early 1930, although

Bruce Bliven and George Soule assumed major responsibility for the journal after Croly's stroke in October 1928. But even while Croly was active as editor, there were changes in personnel and philosophy. Randolph Bourne and Willard Straight died in 1918 and Walter Weyl in 1919. Walter Lippmann left the journal in 1921 and Philip Littell in 1923. Alvin Johnson, who had become an editor in 1915, assumed in 1926 the more peripheral role of contributing editor.[27]

These staff changes perhaps made it easier for Croly to put somewhat less emphasis on politics and more on culture, education, psychology, and religion. His earlier hope that political action might provide shortcuts to reform atrophied. Thus while Villard met the challenge of the 1920s with an intensification of his earlier approach—with shrill, unyielding attacks on corruption and conservatism—Croly shifted his ground somewhat and put his faith in a deeper, more long-range program of reform.

These changes in politics, society, and in the journals themselves were reflected in the educational commentary carried by the journals during the 1920s. The chapter that follows will describe and explain *The Nation*'s and *The New Republic*'s enthusiasm for the worker education movement, in which liberals invested so much hope during this decade. A second chapter will break from the topical format of most of the book and explain the particular role played by one journalist, Agnes de Lima, in publicizing and critiquing progressive education. This will provide background for a third chapter which analyzes—from the standpoint of the journals—the alleged anti-intellectualism of progressive education. These chapters may extend historical perspectives on American liberalism, its journalistic expression, and its relationship with educational developments during the 1920s. And they will serve as further reminders that the journals continued their important function of providing forums in which leading liberal thinkers could express their hopes for the future and show how education could assist in building that future.

7

A New Means for Liberals

American liberals found little cause for optimism in the post–World War I era. After a war "to make the world safe for democracy," the world was clearly less safe, and the war had provided a grisly reminder that humans were less rational and more beastly than humanitarians had believed. The conflict and the Red Scare that followed demonstrated forcefully to liberal intellectuals that humans were not yet able to live humanely and peacefully with their fellows.

For Herbert Croly, the war itself had provided sufficient proof that current social arrangements—family life, political and economic structures, and educational processes—were not developing decent human beings. Throughout the 1920s Croly called on liberals to reexamine the social environment, to correct weaknesses, and to support any movements that seemed likely to help rebuild civilization on a more humane basis. Croly and other liberal journalists, disillusioned to varying degrees with conventional politics, eagerly looked for positive trends,

This chapter takes its title from Eduard C. Lindeman's title for the lead article of a supplement on adult education that appeared *TNR* 54 (22 February 1928): 26. Lindeman was "Croly's closest intellectual companion during the last years of his life" (David W. Levy, *Herbert Croly of "The New Republic": The Life and Thought of an American Progressive* [Princeton: Princeton University Press, 1985], 281).

life-giving movements in which they could invest their influence and energy.[1]

To thoughtful and observant liberals, one such hopeful trend was the movement for adult education, and specifically for worker education, which grew rapidly during the 1920s. The journalists associated with *The Nation* and *The New Republic* considered this development of enough importance so that they promoted, interpreted, and criticized it, and some even went beyond their roles as journalists and participated in it as teachers and organizers. The response of liberal journalists to the worker education movement provides additional perspective on their continuous efforts to articulate a reformist role for education. And it gives another glimpse of the kind of society they hoped and worked for: one in which an enlightened and socially oriented labor movement would wield real power in promoting Croly's "promise of American life."

Adult education, in various forms and by different names, had been a part of American life for many years.[2] Chautauquas, Lyceums, Americanization classes, and correspondence schools had reached thousands of American adults over the years. But after World War I adult education had become more widespread, more varied, and more organized. Reformers, appalled at the ease with which America had been dragged into Europe's war, and dismayed at the nation's failure to work effectively for a just peace, saw an intensified need for adult citizenship education. And the same forces that imposed immigration restriction in 1917, 1921, and 1924 encouraged the growth of literacy education and Americanization classes for adults. By 1926, ventures in this field were substantial enough so that—with the help of the Carnegie Corporation—a national coordinating organization, the American Association for Adult Education, was formed.[3]

One of the newer departures within this broad field was the workers' education movement. Such education, in the form of apprenticeship and vocational training, had, of course, a long history. But the type of workers' education that caught the attention of American liberals during this period went far beyond this narrow job-oriented kind. It came to include, in varying proportions, education for union leadership, for social and political effectiveness, and for individual cultural development.

American workers' education of this broader type had

roots—though tenuous ones—even in the prewar period. Mr. and Mrs. Walter Vrooman who, in association with Charles Beard and others, had helped found Ruskin College in Oxford, England, had also been, upon their return to America, instrumental in the development of a labor college in Trenton, Missouri. In 1906 the Socialists had opened the Rand School of Social Science in New York City. *The Nation* had commented favorably on the work of the Boston Trade Union College, founded in 1915.[4] But such ventures were isolated and fragmentary, and a genuine movement did not exist until the founding, with the help of Charles Beard, Arthur Gleason, A. J. Muste, and others, of the Worker's Education Bureau in 1921. This organization provided the impetus for further growth, and through the usual means of conferences and publications, promoted workers' education as a partial strategy for social and industrial reform.[5]

In a single year, 1921, the Brookwood Labor College and the Bryn Mawr Summer School for Women Workers began, and the Labor Temple in New York City instituted classes for workers. From these small beginnings, the next decade saw a significant expansion of workers' education. As C. Hartley Grattan has written, "The nineteen-twenties appear very definitely to have been a period when new departures in workers' education were the order of the day, a current of intense seriousness in what is sometimes thought to have been a frivolous decade."[6]

Articles, editorials, and reviews in *The Nation* and *The New Republic* showed growing liberal interest in workers' education. From 1914 to 1918 the indices of the journals cited only two items under adult and workers' education. From 1918 through 1928 *The Nation* listed seventeen such items and *The New Republic* thirty-eight. But from 1928 through 1940 a sharp decline set in, and a total of only ten items appeared under these headings.[7]

How may one explain the growth and new departures in workers' education during the 1920s? In answering this question one may also find some of the reasons for the enthusiasm of the liberal journalists for the movement. It is important to note first that much American effort in this area was patterned on foreign—particularly British—antecedents.[8] Historians of American workers' education have recognized the movement's indebtedness to British models. The same vast forces of industrialization and urbanization that encouraged American workers' education had been felt and responded to years earlier in Europe. And some labor leaders and intellectuals hoped that workers' education might, in the European tradition, steer the American labor movement in a more class-conscious, politically active direction.[9]

Liberal journalists, British and American, wrote extensively on the British Workers' Education Association (WEA) and labor colleges, both in terms of their impact in England and their hoped-for effects on American labor and politics. As early as 1919 *The Nation* had carried an article that explored in some detail the history, purposes, and methods of the WEA. Later in the decade, R. H. Tawney and Harold Laski, both *New Republic* contributing editors who were active in British workers' education, wrote articles explaining and promoting the British model.[10]

But if England provided part of the pattern for American workers' education, American conditions presented the impetus for it. Much adult education had developed directly out of the movement for the Americanization of the immigrants. The connection between Americanization and workers' education was particularly clear in the case of classes sponsored by the International Ladies Garment Workers' Union. This union, dominated by first- and second-generation Jewish workers, developed—starting with efforts to teach English and citizenship to its members—one of the most extensive and effective educational programs of any American labor organization.[11]

Another impulse behind the development of labor education during the 1920s was the growing recognition by unionists and their intellectual allies that new economic, social, and political conditions necessitated a broader role for the labor movement. Just as the 1920s were a discouraging decade for liberals, they were also, as Roger Daniels has written, "clearly the 'lean years' for the whole labor movement."[12] After a period of dramatic growth during World War I, union membership began dropping following the recession of 1921–1922. From a high of 5,000,000 members in 1921, union rolls fell to fewer than 3,500,000 in 1929.[13] In a period of overt federal hostility toward labor and its causes, many union leaders saw the need to go beyond simple "business unionism" and to prepare workers for broader political and social action. James Maurer, socialist president of the Pennsylvania Federation of Labor and the first president of the Worker's Education Bureau, wrote in *The*

Nation in 1922 that workers' schools were needed because of "the necessity of labor's having to deal with bigger and more complex issues than heretofore."[14]

An intriguing aspect of workers' education during this period is the fact that unionists like Maurer and liberal intellectuals like Croly converged on it from quite different directions. Some representatives of labor saw that they had previously been too engrossed in collective bargaining and other parochial economic matters, and so began to promote workers' education in the hope that it would push labor toward a more effective political role, as had been the case in England.[15] Croly, however, gave increased attention to education in general, and workers' education in particular, partly out of disillusionment with failed efforts in political action. In simplest terms, education was seen by some unionists as a means of making labor less exclusively economic, and by many intellectuals as a way of making liberalism less narrowly political.

Croly and Villard were disenchanted with the major political parties, and both supported third-party candidates during the 1920s.[16] They turned to labor as one instrument of social progress, and hoped that revitalized unions might become the nucleus for a new political grouping.[17] They shared Dewey's view that "organized labor should be a great force in social reconstruction."[18] It is not surprising, then, that liberal journalists should join their general interest in adult education and their hopes for the labor movement into a specific concern for workers' education.

■

As they gave their support to the nascent workers' education movement, the liberal journals faced a fundamental question: Should such education be an instrument of union goals alone, or should it be the agent of broader social purposes? Intellectual encouragement for union educational experiments was not without its price, and always involved the possibility that these outsiders would try to broaden, dilute, or divert the mainstream of labor's efforts. A. J. Muste, the director of the Brookwood Labor College, noted in *The Nation* the calls for a workers' education movement that would "conceive of itself as an instrument being shaped by the trade unions for their own purposes."[19] But liberal journalists like Croly and Villard, not directly involved in the labor movement, claimed a broader perspective. Their backing for any social program was contingent on their conviction that the activity could serve as the agent of general reformist goals.[20]

The real issue here was, of course, the purpose of workers' education. Such a burgeoning movement was bound to attract a variety of adherents, all hoping to make it the vehicle of their particular objectives. Given the newness of this amorphous development, the journals were not prepared to promote a particular position on this issue; various writers for *The Nation* and *The New Republic* gave different emphases to individual, union, and cultural goals. As a 1921 editorial in *The New Republic* put it, "the old conflict between cultural and utilitarian ends is waged as violently in the workers' colleges as in the orthodox educational institutions of the country," and the editorial noted uncertainty over issues such as "whether the conception of a class struggle should be accepted or not" in workers' education classes.[21]

C. Hartley Grattan noted that there was a "fairly long tradition of educational activity on the 'left' where social reform gets badly mixed up with ideological particularism."[22] But worker educators were pulled in other directions as well. Besides feeling the political-ideological tug from the left, they were subject to short-term business unionist pressures from the right, while cultural aims were urged upon them from the sidelines by some of their intellectual allies.[23]

Arthur Gleason merged several of these issues—and oversimplified them—for *New Republic* readers in his approving statement that "some of the American workers are demanding that education directly feed the life of the union. This is different from a disinterested culture quest and from a propagandist drive."[24] With the issue stated in such pejorative terms, few liberals were so narrow as to defend either culture or propaganda as goals for workers' education. But writers for the journals were willing to propose stronger elements of both for labor schools. Jean Flexner, while approving the general orientation of Muste's Brookwood Labor College, was critical of the unrelieved "purposive atmosphere of the place." She asked *New Republic* readers: "Is it consistent with labor's social ideals and ultimate goal that this education should be concerned only with production, distribution, and organizational activity—not with consumption and enjoyment of the things to be produced?"

She answered her own question by proposing that Brookwood "season life" with such nonutilitarian subjects as music, drama, literature, and art.[25]

But men like Arthur Gleason, activists in workers' education, felt that such "frills," however desirable in the long run, would have to wait:

> Worker's education will probably continue to be a pretty practical affair, as long as enormous masses of workers are unorganized, as long as great unions, like the 'Miners,' can be scabbed in the richest coal districts. . . . The American labor movement is young in an annoying world. American workers' education therefore will probably be militant rather than cultural, for a generation or two.[26]

In both journals the pattern seemed to be for labor insiders, directly involved in workers' education, to promote instruction for short-term union goals and to postpone culture and "uplift"; the outsiders and critics grudgingly accepted this as a temporary expedient but hoped that the time might soon come when workers' education classes could move away from such purely utilitarian instruction.[27]

In addition to this dialogue on the culture versus utility issue, there was a related one on education versus propaganda. But on this topic there was considerably less difference of opinion, with most writers following the line set forth by *The New Republic* in 1923, rejecting propaganda from ideologists on the left or from business unionists on the right. In an editorial on "The Object of Worker's Education," the editors aligned themselves with those "who discriminate sharply between education and propaganda." They criticized the Garland Fund for supporting only a "radical program" that would, in the words of its trustees, "instill into the workers the knowledge and the qualities which will fit them for carrying on the struggle for the emancipation of their class." But the editors were even more forceful in their denunciation of Samuel Gompers for his "silly and contemptible" attack on the Fund. While the Garland Fund, headed by Roger Baldwin, could not transcend the interests of the working class, Gompers and his myopic cronies could not see beyond the short-term interests of the conservative American Federation of Labor.[28]

This attempt to call down a plague upon both houses did not

go unchallenged. Norman Thomas, a trustee of the Garland Fund, questioned the editors' emphasis on a disinterested, autonomous role for labor education, and asked: "Is not education a legitimate instrument" of class emancipation? Like the editors, Thomas wished to preserve the distinction between education and propaganda, but he warned against the pointless activities that often take place in the name of education. He retold the story of the American woman who had "hung in reverence upon every word that fell from the lips of G. B. Shaw." This eager disciple was supposed to have said: "Oh! Mr. Shaw, how I love that man! He is the man that made me think. Think, think what? Think? Oh, nothing particular, only Wonderful, Beautiful, Eternal, Thought, Thought, Thought."[29]

The issue this dialogue raised was a complex one. Certainly none of the liberal journalists proposed programs that might lead to the vapid emptiness of people like Shaw's admirer. Rather, they called for workers' education programs that adhered to standards of scientific method and objective truth. Thus the editors of *The Nation* commended the policy statement issued in 1921 by the Bryn Mawr Summer School for Women Workers: "The School shall not be committed to any dogma or theory, but shall conduct its teaching in a broad spirit of impartial inquiry, with absolute freedom of discussion and academic freedom of teaching."[30]

With this concern both for truth and for the interests of workers, it was not surprising that someone among this group of good Deweyan pragmatists would feel impelled to resolve the dilemma by creating a category inclusive of both propaganda and free inquiry. James Maurer did just that in declaring in 1922 that the purpose of a labor school was "propaganda for sound, independent thinking." And that, he added with well-founded suspicion, "is radical enough to condemn it in the opinion of certain interests."[31]

What the liberal journalists were proposing for the workers' education movement was a role much like their own: friendly to unionism, allied with it as a social force, but not irrevocably tied to specific organizations or factions within it. Worker's education should be sufficiently removed from deep involvement in union politics so it could provide labor with much-needed criticism and perspective. *The New Republic*'s editors were particularly emphatic on this point. They vigorously resisted the tendency of labor to "subordinate education, just as so many governments have done and so many ruling classes would like to do, to the aggrandizement of class interest and power." They supported those workers' education programs which would train leaders capable of "transcending a merely pugnacious psychology and a sectarian program." For them, education was "an independent and precious social activity with which a non-revolutionary social agitation did not need and could not afford to tamper."[32]

The Nation's editors expressed a similar hope that workers' education might "lift enough of the workers above the noise and dust of the strife of trade unions for advantage and of factions for power, and enable them to see what must be done for the sake of that future of which labor should be the chief builder."[33]

The editors were expressing here an essentially Deweyan conception of education as an instrument of social goals—yet as more than an instrument. Education grew out of social needs but could transcend its origins and develop objectives of its own broader than those of the institutions which supported it. With this view of education it is not surprising that liberal journalists resisted the tendency of workers' education to become exclusive—to find its support only within the unions, or even worse, within particular conservative labor groupings.

Thus, in 1921 *The New Republic* declared that because of different opinions regarding goals and methods it was a "wholesome sign that workers' education is at the same time being undertaken under auspices other than those of the trade unions themselves."[34] *The Nation*'s enthusiasm for joint union-university ventures like the Bryn Mawr Summer School denotes a similar outlook. Near the end of the decade, in 1928, *The New Republic* reaffirmed this position during a conflict between Brookwood Labor College and the American Federation of Labor (AFL). The conservative leaders of the AFL found Brookwood too radical, too critical, and too independent to merit their further support. But the Federation's withdrawal of financial aid to the College brought forth from John Dewey a withering three-page attack on this "scholastic lynching." Dewey took particular aim at Matthew Woll, an old-line business unionist, who was instrumental in pushing through the cutoff of funds. In his article, which was supported by an editorial in the same issue, Dewey rejected the charge that Brookwood was propagandizing, condemned the "inert character of the present labor movement," and vigorously argued the need for autonomous institutions like Brookwood. He declared that such labor schools "should train leaders who think independently and should thereby help in ushering in a social order free from exploitation."[35] They should, in short, fulfill the reformist function that Dewey advocated for all educational institutions.

One could, of course, dismiss this dispute as something of a tempest in a teapot. Brookwood was a small school that survived only sixteen years, and the issue under discussion was but one development in its history. But the event did provide a clear example of the liberal journalists' support for independent, critical workers' education not beholden to specific unions or to particular labor factions.

■

The journals' editors and writers, in their attention to workers' education, were particularly interested in the goals and effects of the movement, and with the institutional support behind it. Their concern for the internal working of labor schools—with teachers, students, and methodology—was expressed less often, but sometimes took an interesting twist. Journal comment in this area was usually highly favorable, praising labor education for its sense of relevance, its realism, and its progressive methodology, and it frequently made its point more strongly through invidious comparisons with effete, traditional, middle-class education. Such comparisons appeared in *The Nation* as early as 1919, when Herbert Horwill praised the British Workers' Educational Association as presenting a "spectacle of intellectual energy and enthusiasm which finds no parallel among the leisure classes."[36]

Jean Flexner, in the American context, was even more specific: "The Brookwood student can be most simply described by contrasting him with the undergraduate in the 'bourgeois' college—the inexperienced, amiable, impressionable dilettante, who drifts with open and colorless mind through a kaleidoscope of courses to emerge without deep convictions or definite objectives."[37]

The New Republic, in pointing to the same phenomenon, gleefully reported the pleasure felt by a teacher of working girls in contrast to the despair she experienced when instruct-

ing the "somnolent daughters of plutocracy." The editors concluded that there was less of a problem in educating the masses
than in enlightening the "great sodden middle class."[38]

This enthusiasm for the apparent liveliness, relevance, and
psychological soundness of workers' education is hardly surprising. Unions and their educational allies were conducting
their classes (perhaps more out of necessity than conviction) on
progressive Deweyan lines. The liberal journalists, most of
whom were Dewey's disciples in educational matters, were thus
pleased to see his theories receiving practical validation. Deweyan rhetoric runs through journal commentary on workers'
education during this period. Eduard C. Lindeman, for example, praised C. D. Burns's *The Philosophy of Labor* for its recognition that labor education might become "the force which
will evoke, clarify, and instrumentalize the worker's point of
view." Two years later he wrote in reference to the whole adult
education movement that "liberalism can become effective only
when it derives from a valid learning process which is continuous, co-terminous, with life itself."[39]

The Deweyan emphasis was particularly evident in the case
of Herbert Croly. Shortly after Croly's death in 1930, George
Soule wrote an appreciation of him that makes clear Croly's
Deweyan conviction that education was more than a simple
matter of transmitting information; rather, it was a process of
expanding the range of meanings that people attach to experience. According to Soule, Croly held that "it was useless merely
to preach people into acceptance of articles of faith. People
could be convinced and vitalized only through interpretation of
their own experience." He quoted Croly's assertion that adults
needed to regain "both their craving for experience and their
ability to attach meanings to it."[40]

Dewey was for long periods a contributing editor of both *The
Nation* and *The New Republic*, and through their pages he expressed his views on many political and educational issues, including workers' education. But his progressive, pragmatic
spirit was evident also in editorials and articles on labor education by Croly, Villard, Maurer, Muste, Kallen, Lindeman, and
others.[41] Such writers saw that the new pedagogy was particularly applicable to adult and workers' education, partly because adults had many rich life experiences to interpret.
Workers did not need to be inducted into social, economic, and

political reality—this they already felt and knew. What they needed was the opportunity to interpret this reality with the aid of psychology, history, and other disciplines. The relationship of learning and life—of school and society—was very real in workers' education, and it is clear that the closeness of this relationship accounts for much of the liberal intellectual enthusiasm for the movement.[42]

■

Workers' education may be seen, then, as one particular expression of the pragmatic impulse in education. As interpreted by liberal journalists, it should be reformist in goals, eclectic in institutional support, and progressive in methods. It was thus entirely reasonable that Croly, Villard, and their colleagues should give the movement their support and criticism. However, the association of liberal journalists with workers' education differed somewhat from their relationship with the progressive education of children and youth. In the latter area they functioned largely as promoters, interpreters, and critics; their involvement with elementary and secondary education was somewhat limited and generally indirect.

But in adult and workers' education the liberal journalists had something to offer; here they could become directly involved. Thus Croly took an active part in the founding of the New School for Social Research and gave particular attention to the Labor Research Bureau, which was associated with it.[43] Alvin Johnson, a *New Republic* editor intermittently until 1922 and a *Nation* editor in the 1930s, was the second director of the New School, succeeding James Harvey Robinson.[44] George Soule, who wrote for both *The New Republic* and *The Nation* (and who later became a *New Republic* editor), taught at Will Durant's Labor Temple School. Carl Van Doren, literary editor of *The Nation*, was a member of the same faculty. R. H. Tawney, H. N. Brailsford, and Harold Laski—all *New Republic* contributing editors during the 1920s—were influential leaders of the British workers' education movement. And Eduard C. Lindeman, who was one of America's leading adult educators during this period and who directed research for the Worker's Education Bureau, was a contributing editor of *The New Republic*. The point is evident: in the area of workers' education, the liberal journalists were what Michael Walzer has called "connected critics," or, in Croly's phrase, "participating agents who were also observers."[45]

In view of this active involvement in and support for workers' education, how may we explain the declining attention given to the movement by liberal journalists after the 1920s? Part of the reason clearly lies in the fact that liberal intellectuals lost their optimism concerning the effects of progressive worker education on the larger labor movement. After a period of tolerance for socially conscious workers' education, AFL President William Green and his supporters took, in the late 1920s, several steps to bring the movement into line: they withdrew support from Brookwood, censored publications of the Worker's Education Bureau, suspended the annual meetings of the Bureau, and promoted education through universities rather than through the labor colleges.[46] Dewey saw the withdrawal of assistance to Brookwood as part of a trend that could lead to workers' education "made safe for the political machine of the Federation." This trend continued, and liberal intellectuals found the official, bureaucratized AFL workers' education programs no longer worthy of attention or support.[47]

A broader explanation may be found in the growth of the union movement itself in the next decade. During the New Deal, particularly following the passage of the National Industrial Recovery Act in 1933 and the Wagner Act in 1935, unions grew rapidly in membership and influence. While continuing, and in some cases expanding workers' education programs, some unions now gave them a lower order of priority. Labor experienced major victories in politics and at the bargaining table and learned that such progress was not dependent on the slow processes of workers' education. As Brian Simon has suggested, union organization and political success thus contributed to the failure of socially oriented worker education.[48] And, as Richard Dwyer has noted, to meet the immediate needs of growing unions, education programs stressed "tool courses," which provided practical training for union leaders rather than a curriculum focused on social change.[49] Also, financial stringency brought about by the Depression forced the closure of some of the more radical labor colleges. Given the general drift away from the socially oriented workers' education to which they were committed, it is not surprising that the attention of the liberal journalists should have moved on to other matters.[50]

In the case of *The New Republic*, the death of editor Herbert Croly in 1930 may also help explain decreased attention to workers' education. His direct, personal concern for the movement was not felt to the same degree by the members of the editorial board who succeeded him. But even had Croly lived, it is probable that *The New Republic*, like *The Nation*, would have shown a less active interest in workers' education. After the Depression struck in 1929, intellectual journalists and other liberal activists felt that the overpowering economic problems faced by the nation could not wait for the incremental improvements promised by education. And, with the victory of Franklin Roosevelt in 1932, immediate political progress seemed more possible. During the 1920s much liberal political action had appeared futile; now, at long last, success in this realm was attainable. Liberal journalists could again feel that—as in the days of Theodore Roosevelt and the prewar Wilson—they had a significant relationship to power.[51] In simplest terms, as the journalists' political interests again increased, their specific educational concerns declined.

Reflecting in 1929 on the workers' education movement, A. J. Muste wrote: "Many labor organizers were enthusiastic. All the intellectuals were in a glow, feeling that once more the world was going to be saved. It was one of those golden dawns."[52] But the dawning of the New Deal, and of labor's accompanying political and economic progress, dimmed the interest of unions and of liberal intellectuals in the gradual workings of a socially oriented workers' education movement. As is so often the case, short-term success undermined opportunities for the long-range rethinking and restructuring that were so urgently needed in the liberal movement for social change.

8

Agnes de Lima and Progressive Education

All social movements require a range of people and institutions to generate their ideas and practices and to disseminate, interpret, and critique them. In the case of progressive education, a few great figures like John Dewey served in all these roles. Over his long and influential career he wrote some of the masterworks of progressive education, such as *Democracy and Education* (1916) and *Experience and Education* (1938); he also carried his ideas into the public arena through many topical articles and reviews in journals like *The Nation* and *The New Republic*.[1]

Other writers, with Randolph Bourne as the best early example, served primarily as disseminators and interpreters of progressive education. From 1914, when Bourne wrote "In a Schoolroom" for the first issue of *The New Republic*, until his death four years later, he published eighty-seven pieces in that journal, many of them dealing with educational matters. Bourne wrote a number of perceptive analyses of American education—both "horror stories" about the old formalistic schools and hopeful reports on some of the newer progressive developments.[2]

During his final illness, Bourne was cared for by his close

friends Agnes de Lima and Esther Cornell; he died in de Lima's arms on 22 December, 1918. De Lima was a researcher, activist, feminist, and socialist who had become friends with Bourne during the 1914–1917 struggle to introduce the Gary Plan to the New York schools.[3] She was in many ways a representative progressive woman. Born in 1887 into the family of a prosperous Latin American banker, she had become radicalized at Vassar College, which she had attended over the objections of her chauvinistic father.[4] Helen Horowitz has written of Vassar during this period: "Faculty, such as Herbert Mills and Lucy Salmon, actively engaged in the questions of the day and trained generations of reform-minded students."[5] De Lima studied economics with Dr. Mills and history with Dr. Salmon and also took courses in Labor Problems and Socialism, Charities and Corrections, Social Psychology, and the one education course offered by the college.[6] She was also a member of the Vassar College Settlement Association.[7]

After graduation, de Lima moved to New York City, where she lived for a time in a settlement house and was employed by such progressive groups as the Bureau of Municipal Research, the Russell Sage Foundation, the Public Education Association, and the Women's Municipal League. She acquired a master's degree in social work in 1912 and in 1914 served as official investigator for a study of the San Francisco schools.[8] These experiences extended and deepened her political education and helped give her a breadth of knowledge which was later useful in her journalistic career.[9]

De Lima worked for the Public Education Association of New York City and engaged in other educational activities for a few years after Bourne's death; starting in 1922, she became a serious journalist, writing sixteen articles and reviews—all but three dealing with education—for *The Nation* and *The New Republic*. Several of these articles were gathered into a widely read and much-quoted book, *Our Enemy the Child*.[10]

De Lima deserves attention, along with Dewey, Bourne, and others, as one of the writers who explained, interpreted, and critiqued progressive education for the liberals and activists who read those journals.[11] Through her articles and reviews we can see how one progressive woman responded to the many educational experiments being carried on—especially in New York City—during the 1920s. And we can assume that like-minded liberals, both editors and readers of the journals, received at least part of their picture of progressive education from de Lima.

■

Randolph Bourne had been on the payroll of *The New Republic*, receiving checks each week for his contributions.[12] De Lima did not have such a regular arrangement, but there was an informal understanding that the pages of the journal were open to her whenever she wished to write an article, and the editors would occasionally ask her to reply to the educational comment of other authors. Given the "patently sexist" environment of *The New Republic*, neither de Lima nor any other woman was during this period an insider on that journal.[13]

De Lima wrote all but one of her contributions to *The Nation* and *The New Republic* during the five-year period from 1922 through 1927. A review of these articles will give an impression of how the liberal readers of *The New Republic* and *The Nation* continued to learn about progressive education. It will also help explain the range of de Lima's interests, permit the identification of some of the recurrent themes in her educational writing, and provide background for an assessment of her role as an educational journalist.

During 1924 and 1925 de Lima visited a variety of schools and published the results of her inquiry in nine articles—six in *The New Republic* and three in *The Nation*. She began the series in February 1924 in *The New Republic* with a description of Helen Parkhurst's Dalton Plan, through which learning was individualized in laboratories or workshops. De Lima's enthusiasm for the program was clear, but she noted that the changes were ones of method, not of objectives: "Unless the curriculum is carefully adjusted to the child's needs, the plan might become the emptiest of cramming processes with the premium put on the amassing of information." She concluded that this reform in method might, however, prepare the ground for deeper reforms, more in keeping with emerging trends in psychology.[14]

De Lima followed this article two months later with another *New Republic* piece in which she described Elisabeth Irwin's experimental program, which was affiliated with New York City Public School 61, the Public Education Association, and the Children's Aid Society. (This later became The Little Red

School House, the subject of a second book by de Lima, published in 1942.) De Lima explained Irwin's philosophy, procedures, and special attention to the needs of neurotic children and noted the emphasis on encouraging children's speech and the deliberate delay in introducing reading and writing. She was heartened by the fact that such an experiment could take place in the public schools, concluding: "We cannot doubt . . . that Miss Irwin is on the track of an educational reform of immense importance. The fact that such an experiment can be carried on with the cooperation of the public educational authorities is one of the most encouraging signs of the times."[15]

De Lima published her next three reports that spring and summer in a *Nation* series titled "The New Education." The first article continued the theme of her last *New Republic* piece. She described progressive experiments in the public schools, summarized some of Elisabeth Irwin's work, and communicated the findings of an experimental school in Montgomery County, Missouri. She cited research showing the superiority of test scores in the experimental school over those in traditional schools—a comparison that was recurrent in her articles. But in spite of her enthusiasm, de Lima was not uncritical of these progressive developments. She noted that "certain textbooks about the project method show how formalized the best of methods can become in unimaginative hands." And she warned that "the present 'mental-age-grading' experiments in New York may degenerate into merely another mechanical device." In spite of her doubts, she closed with the hope that "the time is not far distant when a child need be neither feeble-minded, physically handicapped, dull, nor overbright to receive the benefits of teaching consciously designed to meet his needs instead of the maintenance of a more or less venerable tradition."[16]

The second article in this series began with a categorization of educational reformers that neatly anticipated Lawrence Cremin's 1961 division of progressives into "scientists, sentimentalists, and radicals."[17] De Lima identified first the "technicians" who focused on "the measurement of intelligence, of classroom achievement and improvement in method." A second group demanded "modern schools to fit children to play a worthy part in the modern world." A third viewed "education as an organic process which changes and develops as the child himself changes and grows." De Lima described the Horace Mann and Lincoln Schools and the Ethical Culture School as representatives in varying ways of the first two groups, noting that at the Ethical Culture School children were "not excluded because of race, religion or color" and that scholarships helped to "cut down economic barriers." She reported that "the avowed purpose of the school is to train ethical leaders, 'reformers' of society, and its officers are proud of the fact that a larger proportion of its graduates than of any other school are engaged in teaching, research, or some type of social service. The ideal of service to society is held constantly before the pupils by means of formal ethics instruction as well as by numerous activities on behalf of the community."

De Lima described the activities of Patty Hill at the Horace Mann School, noting that her work "had profoundly affected the course of kindergarten and primary education throughout the country in the direction of a freer and more democratic type of organization." She reported that Miss Hill had recently been "attempting to apply the principles of behaviorist psychology to curriculum making" but warned of the danger, which Miss Hill acknowledged, that "the very explicit aims set down by her group will be used not as a means of wider freedom but of more repression. Unhappily the moralists and disciplinarians manage to function, no matter what instrument is put into their hands."

In describing the Lincoln School, de Lima gave particular attention to Harold Rugg's integrated social studies curriculum, which was "designed to help the student to understand and deal intelligently with the problems of contemporary life." But she closed by noting "the predominance of the teacher" in the elementary school, concluding that the children were "being prepared for a future society by means contrived and imposed upon them by their elders. In appearance they are accordingly sober, constrained, polite and even occasionally somewhat bored." Clearly, for de Lima, in some of the experimental schools the new education was still too much like the old.

De Lima's final article in *The Nation* series began by reporting that the Teachers Union of New York City was supporting the establishment of an "experimental center in the public-school system." She noted that the models for the proposed union program included the City and Country School, influenced by behaviorist psychology, and the Walden School, inspired by analytic psychology. She described the differences and similarities between the two schools, and again made the point that children in the experimental schools learned the three R's more effectively than did their peers in traditional schools. And she concluded that the success of these schools was evident: "In one sense, neither Miss Pratt's nor the Walden School is experimental. These happy, vitalized children whom one observes are proof enough that what these schools are achieving is of supreme social worth."[18]

The editors referred to de Lima's series in an editorial two weeks later, reflecting her perception that "most of the new ideas in education emanate from teachers and other persons professionally concerned with their subject." They went on to cite a study by some of "the victims" of education—Dartmouth students who had criticized their college education in terms similar to those used by de Lima in critiquing traditional schools: students in higher education were "spoon-fed" and were made "passive" and "dependent" on their instructors. The students proposed fewer lectures, better materials, more work in small groups, less testing, and more short papers. The editors concluded: "We shall wait with interest to learn what teachers think of these suggestions. To us they seem as hopeful as any that have appeared."[19]

During the preceding spring, de Lima had visited a fourth-grade class in a New York City school. Late that year, in the *New Republic* article in which she described her visit, she said that "both school and class were selected at random, the visitor merely choosing the first school she happened to come across after going into an unfamiliar part of town." De Lima described a class in which students were "frozen into immobility. . . . The teacher's voice was hard and metallic and her face lined with a multitude of little seams of nervous irritation. Police duty is hard work, when it means keeping forty-six children caged and immovable in a tiny room five hours a day, five days a week for ten months a year."

The classroom was as depressing as the teacher: "In this cramped and arid space was not one thing to call forth the slightest creative impulse of the children who were doomed by law to spend the sunniest hours of their lives there. All they could do was sit up rigid and 'tall,' while the teacher doled out irrelevant and uninviting bits of knowledge in the name of 'education.'"

In spite of all this, de Lima was sympathetic with the teacher's plight. "Miss Perkins seemed as aware as anyone else of the futility of this performance. Still, was she not as trapped as the children? . . . She must drive relentlessly ahead, in appearance only more free than the driven." But the basic problem was that was that this classroom was not unique and that de Lima's report "would probably have been little different, no matter what school or class she had visited."[20]

De Lima read widely in the educational literature of the period and wrote for this same issue of *The New Republic* a review of seven books by various authors. She had drawn on some of these books in her articles and repeated in the review the now familiar point that students in experimental schools were "learning as well if not better than those in the traditional school." De Lima quoted approvingly from Gertrude Hartman's *Home and Community Life*, noting its demand that schools "must set up an environment which requires social cooperation," but said that "one must seriously question whether acquaintance with the mechanics of civilization, even if acquired young, will usher in the millenium." As a civil libertarian, she also criticized Otis Caldwell and Stuart Courtis for their expectation, "expressed quite sanguinely, that teachers of the future will be examined as to their social and civic orthodoxy before they are licensed to teach."[21]

The following week de Lima reviewed for *The New Republic* Caroline Pratt's *Experimental Practice in the City and Country School*. She criticized the usual educators' "flood of jargonated oratory which is a great deal more confusing than enlightening" and said that by comparison, Pratt's book was "an informing and thought-provoking exposition of what goes on in an experimental school." She pointed out that students in Pratt's school were "mastering the tools of reading and writing by methods at once novel and sound" and gave particular credit to teachers who were keeping records needed for educational research: "Such copious note-taking as these records involve is arduous work for the teachers, but it is from such records, vivid and concrete, that we can study education in the making, count our gains, and make the necessary revision which will insure future progress."[22]

Following the publication of "Any School Morning" the previous fall, some teachers had complained to de Lima that it had been unfair of her to select a class at random for her observation, so she asked "one of the most enlightened and progressive" principals in the city to identify his best fourth-grade teacher. She spent half a day in the teacher's class and published her observations in the spring of 1925 in *The New Republic* in an article titled "The 'Best' of School Mornings." She described a class of forty-two students in which the teacher was "warm and human," where children responded positively to her attention, and in which brighter students coached the slower ones. However, she also reported on the too-frequent changes of activity, the sometimes "perfunctory" student participation, and the general passivity of the class, but again went out of her way to blame the system, not the teacher: "It is worth while to ask just how much in the way of creative experience can be afforded to children by any teacher, no matter how technically skilled or graciously human, who suffers under a fixed course of study, an overcrowded class, a room void of any materials save blackboards, desks and books, and the tradition of the teacher as the active, directing agent, and of the pupils as the docile and receptive ones."

De Lima also cited an event in New York City that convinced her that instructors were "more aware of the necessity for change than . . . their superiors," noting that—in response to a superintendent's request—teachers had recently suggested five hundred changes in curriculum and methods, only two of which had been supported by the superintendent.[23]

De Lima continued to respond to the large number of educational books being published at the time. Her final piece in the series that led to *Our Enemy the Child* was a 1925 *New Republic* review of nine such books. She criticized Bird Baldwin and Lorie Stecher, "apparently inspired by the philosophy of an older school," who were "opposed to letting the child 'just grow.'" She again noted test results that favored the students in experimental schools. She praised Ovide Decroly, whose "fundamental principle, like that of Dewey, is that children learn through living, and living not according to some prearranged adult formula, but on their own level of needs and interests." She criticized James Hosic's treatment of the project method as "thin and pedagogical," and reapplied some of her earlier critiques by noting that under Hosic's scheme, "the same old subject matter is to be retained, and the same objectives, but through a sugar coating of 'purposeful activity' the learning process is to be facilitated and the dreariness of drill overcome."

De Lima made a similar criticism of a study by Charles Spain: "It is this preoccupation with subject matter and units of the course of study that is over emphasized in too much of the discussion of so hopeful an educational movement as the platoon school." And she joined her antielitism with her proteacher stance in the statement that "Elizabeth Banks's arraignment of England's abominable caste system in education . . . ought to prove needed ammunition to the Labor Party, especially as she wisely gives due credit to the enlightened work of teachers in the county council schools."

She praised Isaac Kandel's history of recent education, but objected to its narrow focus: "We must regret that of necessity progress is seen through the lens of Teachers' College . . . and so hopeful a development as that of the experimental school is scarcely touched upon." She closed by quoting one of her heroes, William Kilpatrick, on the misuse of educational measurement and the lack of attention to educational objectives: "It has been the more disheartening because that part, being chiefly formal and mechanical, was easy to be seized upon by the mechanically minded and by them treated as if it were in effect the whole."[24]

Readers of *The New Republic* or *The Nation* received from these articles a comprehensive and insightful description and interpretation of contemporary progressive schools, particularly those in New York City.[25] Each of the journals had about thirty thousand subscribers, including many educators, during this period.[26] So teachers and other readers had the opportunity, at least, to be unusually well informed about what was going on in experimental schools as well as to receive the benefit of de Lima's criticisms of those schools. But in order to reach an even broader audience, de Lima decided to revise and extend her articles and to publish her findings in book form.

Continuing her intense period of educational study and writing, de Lima quickly transformed her articles into a book titled *Our Enemy the Child*, which *The New Republic* published in its series of dollar books. The author noted in her introduction that three chapters had appeared in *The New Republic* and that parts of others had been printed in that journal and in *The Nation*. There was some additional material, for example on the labor movement's role in education, but the book faithfully reflected the themes, the tone, and the emphasis of the articles. De Lima used the same three categories in analyzing experimental schools and made clear her preference for the organic group that focused on child development. Her commitment to child study, which was at the heart of child-centered education, was apparent in the dedication to her daughter: "To Sigrid, aged three and a half, from whom I have learned more about education than from any pedagogue or any book." She criticized those schools which tinkered with methods but that kept the same old "fact-cramming" objectives. She decried the excesses of the educational testers, but used their scores to support the claims for superior instruction in experimental schools. She defended those teachers who were the victims of traditional schooling and praised those who were valiantly participating in educational research and experiments.

De Lima placed herself in the progressive Deweyan mainstream with a denunciation of "such absurd antitheses as school and society, or child and community." While critical of narrow social and political objectives for schools, she held out the hope that child-centered and reformist objectives could be compatible: the task of the new schools was to move away from "the problem of adapting the child to the static or so called progressing world about him . . . and make a developing prime mover in progress out of the child himself."[27]

One of the book's enthusiastic reviewers reflected de Lima's synthesis of child-oriented and socially relevant education, noting that the book ended with "pen pictures of the world the children would make if they were allowed freedom of creation in their own right." Another echoed de Lima's hope for the new schools that "this enriched environment and freedom of expression will belong to all the children of the country and not be reserved for children of privilege in the private schools." Other reviewers were equally positive, one predicting that readers would find "exciting reading in this description of various experimental schools in which a stimulating environment and freedom for the child to use his creative powers are set over against 'police duty.'"[28]

The book was widely read and was popular enough so that *The New Republic* reprinted it in 1930, listing it first among its reprints, and noting that ten thousand copies had been published. (This series, incidentally, gives some indication of *The New Republic*'s interest in education during this period. Eleven of the twenty-eight books, several of which grew out of articles in the journal, dealt with education, youth, or parents.)[29]

Our Enemy the Child has received considerable attention from later writers, especially educational historians, partly because it includes some of the few published descriptions of what actually went on in progressive classrooms. It has been cited in books by (among others) Harold Rugg and Ann Shumaker (1928), Lawrence Cremin (1961), Sol Cohen (1964), Patricia Graham (1967), Robert Elias (1973), Clarence Karier (1986), and Larry Cuban (1984).[30]

Assessments of the book since 1961 have been mixed. Lawrence Cremin, in *The Transformation of the School* (1961), wrote: "The activities of these private progressive schools of the twenties are vividly described by Agnes de Lima in *Our Enemy the Child* (1926) and by Harold Rugg and Ann Shumaker in *The Child-Centered School* (1928). . . . More than de Lima, Rugg and Shumaker found elements to criticize." Cremin added that "radicalism even tended to disappear from the pedagogical formulations of many political radicals," citing *Our Enemy the Child* as an example. Sol Cohen described the book in 1964 as a "full-length progressive tract." Patricia Graham, in her 1967 history of the Progressive Education Association, made more forcefully than Cremin some of the same comparisons and critiques. While acknowledging *The New Republic*'s perceptive coverage of educational matters during this period, and giving special notice to de Lima's articles, she described *Our Enemy the Child* as "wholly uncritical," and—pairing it with Rugg's and Shumaker's book—said that "neither is very analytical." She wrote that the best treatments of the issues surrounding child-centered schools were in de Lima's and in Rugg's and Shumaker's books, but added that "both books are essentially descriptions of practices in 'progressive schools' and fail to evaluate seriously the new movement, although the Rugg and Shumaker book makes a brief attempt."[31] More recently Larry Cuban has drawn on *Our Enemy the Child* in his analysis of progressive education. He described de Lima as "a passionate advocate of child-centered schools . . . who believed that progressive classes in experimental schools would die if placed within public schools."[32]

In fairness to de Lima—and in order to clarify the role of liberal journalism in the progressive education movement—some response to these judgments is in order. A careful review of *Our Enemy the Child* shows that de Lima included the same critical assessments of the new schools as in her articles. She continued to be generally supportive of child-centered education and directed most of her criticisms at the scientific and reformist branches of progressive education. In reference to the reformers, she said that "a word of warning is not amiss in view of the over emphasis on socialization which one meets everywhere in current educational discussion. Because modern social life has become so complex and the interdependence of human beings so diverse, we have come to believe that we shall somehow solve the problem by plunging people into social situations at the age of eighteen months." We may qualify Cremin's judgment that radicalism "tended to disappear" from her educational writing. It did not disappear, but rather took the form of reminders to other radicals not to interfere with childhood education by the premature imposition of social goals. Like Dewey, de Lima was confident that sound progressive education, without imposition or manipulation, would develop students with a healthy predisposition toward social change.[33]

De Lima was even more negative about "the habit maker, the pedagogue or supervisor who has got up in advance an inventory of desirable habits . . . and sails into the nursery school room with score and note book to see whether or not they are being acquired."[34] But she also criticized—albeit gently—some of the developments within the child-centered strand of progressivism: "Many of the newer institutions tend to regard some psychological principle as more sacred than the child." Some educators were "magnifying the bogey of 'emotional fixation' and 'complexes' to absurd proportions." Toward the end of the book she wrote that some of these schools "perhaps carry this psychoanalytic interest—particularly in their vocabularies—to an extreme."[35]

The bulk of de Lima's criticism, however, was of schools that were insufficiently child-centered. She constantly denounced schools that had altered methods but not purposes; she noted the tendency of formalism and repression to survive amidst new techniques; she reminded her readers that the curriculum existed for the child, not vice versa. But this was criticism from within the movement; these were reminders to fellow progressives that the new education would succeed only by being fundamentally different from formalistic traditional schools.

Cuban's statement that de Lima believed that progressivism "would die" in the public schools should also be qualified. De Lima did say that "while many of these freer principles are being taught in teacher training schools, and are here and there reflected in isolated classrooms, it is unlikely that we shall see their very rapid extension to the public schools. . . . The

obstacles against their general adoption seem insurmountable."
But, after describing the obstacles, she concluded more optimistically that "although the actual number of 'progressive'
schools and radical experimental centers is still small, modifica-
tions in line with their teachings are gradually finding their way
into school systems. As such ideas gain wider acceptance, we are
likely to hear less about the difficulty of applying them under
public school conditions."[36]

De Lima was thus not being conservative or pessimistic, but
rather was reminding her fellow liberals to be realistic concerning their expectations from progressive education. Schools
could have a long-range role in social change, but this would
not be promoted by naive and premature efforts to turn young
children into reformers; similarly, progressivism could gradually penetrate the public schools, but the difficulties of the effort were not to be underestimated.

De Lima's self-assigned role was to build support for progressive education, to insure that it was understood and appreciated, to promote its improvement through criticism, and to
encourage its diffusion to the public schools. On the last page
of *Our Enemy the Child* she wrote: "Many of the experiments we
have been discussing are being tried out under public auspices.
All of them might be, and their number indefinitely increased,
once the philosophy that underlies them was held to be valid."[37]
Her task was to see that this philosophy was perceived and
understood by her liberal audience, and she undertook it in-
ductively (again, appropriate for a Deweyan), by describing,
critiquing, and generalizing from those schools which embodied this new philosophy.

During the 1920s the liberal weeklies, acknowledging the hostile political environment in which they worked, shifted much
of their attention to cultural and social matters, including education. De Lima's articles may be seen as part of an effort by the
journals to look below the level of immediate political activity
and support those movements which—like progressive education—held out the hope that a long-range transformation of individuals and society might be possible.[38]

Writing about the muckraking period, Richard Hofstader
said: "It is hardly an exaggeration to say that the Progressive
mind was characteristically a journalistic mind, and that its
characteristic contribution was that of a socially responsible reporter-reformer."[39] Agnes de Lima was the epitome of the "so-

cially responsible reporter-reformer," and her "journalistic mind" had been formed during the period Hofstader described. Through her liberating studies at Vassar and at the New York School for Social Work, her work with reform and research organizations, and her association with Bourne and other radicals, she had acquired a critical point of view and a set of journalistic skills that enabled her to function as a lively and insightful interpreter of the new education.

Partly because of her rich and varied preparation for her writing career, readers of the liberal journals had an unusually good opportunity to follow and understand developments within the progressive education movement. De Lima's articles explained the origins and context of the movement, described some of the variations within it, and provided useful reminders about the limitations as well as the excesses of the experimental schools.

Educational reform movements rely on a variety of people for their efforts. While acknowledging the work of philosophers, activists, and educators, we should not lose sight of the important function served by those who explain, interpret, and criticize educational developments. Agnes de Lima often described herself as "just a journalist."[40] She need not have been so modest; she was a careful, perceptive, observant writer who communicated clearly and persuasively. Journalists like de Lima played a useful role in helping the readers of *The New Republic* and *The Nation* understand developments in America's schools and in keeping alive a vision of a humane educational system in a more just society.

9

The Eggheads and the Fatheads

In a retrospective review with the charming title "The Egg-heads and the Fatheads," Stephen Whitfield in 1978 noted that Richard Hofstadter's 1963 book, *Anti-intellectualism in American Life*, had "failed to ignite the controversy of his other big books or to send younger scholars into archives the master so sedulously avoided."[1] It is unfair to criticize the master for avoiding the archives. Hofstadter assimilated and interpreted a vast array of material in researching and writing his Pulitzer Prize-winning book. But an examination of archival material in the liberal journals may extend Hofstadter's analyses and help to balance his judgments concerning some American educators, particularly John Dewey.

Hofstadter defined anti-intellectualism as a "resentment and suspicion of the life of the mind and of those who are considered to represent it; and a disposition constantly to minimize the value of that life."[2] He surveyed the origins and effects of anti-intellectualism in religion, politics, and business, and—in the longest section of the book—traced the depressing history of educational anti-intellectualism, with special attention to progressive education and its bastard offspring, life adjustment education.

Other historians, both before and after 1963, have analyzed anti-intellectualism and its expression in schooling, particularly in progressive education. Hofstadter acknowledged his debt to Merle Curti and other scholars, and drew particularly on Lawrence Cremin's *Transformation of the School.*[3] In that book, Cremin asserted that some progressive educators used Freudian insights in such a way as to shift the focus of the school almost entirely to nonintellectual, or indeed, anti-intellectual concerns.[4]

In a book published a year after *Anti-intellectualism,* Sol Cohen identified the Public Education Association (PEA) of New York City—and particularly Elisabeth Irwin's Little Red School House—with anti-intellectual trends during the 1920s. He claimed that the PEA's concern over such problems as mental hygiene, delinquency, and nonpromotion led it to "minimize courses of study, eliminate academic standards or set them at the lowest level, and educate the public school staff in the principles and precepts of mental hygiene." He reported that before World War I, the PEA took a generally social-reformist position on education; later, when it shifted to a more child-centered orientation, it became "no longer merely indifferent to the school's role in the training of intelligence, but hostile to it."[5]

More recently, Diane Ravitch, although acknowledging Dewey's "humane, pragmatic, open-minded approach" to education, reinforced the charges of some earlier historians, stating that "progressive educators rejected . . . the belief that the primary purpose of the school was to improve intellectual functioning."[6]

This is a persistent issue, worth the continued attention of historians and educators, so it is appropriate to turn back to Hofstadter as the key figure in this historical controversy and see what effect the use of some different source material might have. In a chapter titled "The Child and the World," Hofstadter assessed John Dewey's responsibility for child-centered and life-adjustment education and their anti-intellectual elements. While recognizing that Dewey increasingly came to deplore the child-centered excesses of some of his disciples, the author maintained that Dewey's refusal to outline specific goals for education (other than "growth") led to confusion, and that "the effect of Dewey's philosophy on the design of curricular systems was devastating." He added that "Dewey did American education a major disservice by providing what appears to be authoritative sanction for that monotonous and suffocating rhetoric about 'democratic living' with which American educationists smother our discussions of the means and ends of education."

Hofstadter did not claim that Dewey himself was anti-intellectual; he was not examining the intent of Dewey's work but its effect: "Having once put the child so firmly at the center, having defined education as growth without end, Dewey had so weighted the discussion of educational goals that a quarter century of clarificatory statements did not avail to check the anti-intellectual perversions of the theory."[7]

In spite of the vigor of such statements, Hofstadter's overall treatment of Dewey was not unsympathetic. Dewey was seen not as the villain of the later antiprogressive tracts of Max Rafferty and Hyman Rickover, but as in some ways a tragic figure.[8] There was in Hofstadter's critique a tone of sorrow that Dewey was not a writer of greater clarity and incisiveness who might have anticipated and prevented some of the misinterpretations and misapplications of his educational ideas and thus saved the progressive education movement from the excesses that contributed to its downfall and continued bad repute.

In analyzing Dewey's role in progressive education, Hofstadter drew on eight of his books, ranging in time from *My Pedagogic Creed* (1897) to *Experience and Education* (1938). But, had Hofstadter also considered Dewey's journalistic writings and those of his major interpreters, he might have seen more clearly Dewey's early and forceful efforts to refute anti-intellectual mutilation of his ideas.

An examination of educational commentary in *The Nation* and *The New Republic* during the 1920s suggests a more complex picture than Hofstadter presented in his sweeping overview. It shows that the two leading liberal journals, both with long-standing interests in educational matters, provided a forum for thoughtful dialogue on progressive education and its child-centered elements. And it demonstrates that John Dewey, Boyd Bode, Joseph K. Hart, and others issued repeated warnings against anti-intellectual expressions of child-centered education.

One irony to be noted in all this is that Dewey and the other thinkers who wrote for these journals were, by any reasonable standard, intellectuals. Thus we have, to the degree that they were guilty as charged, what Christopher Lasch has called the "anti-intellectualism of the intellectuals." Lasch's study, *The New Radicalism in America*, did not focus on educators as a group, but it did consider a number of people associated with the liberal journals, particularly *The New Republic*, including Dewey, Croly, Lippmann, and Bourne. And Lasch concluded that at least some American intellectuals felt impelled to flee from what they saw as their own sterile, overcivilized intellectuality to seek the nonrational and the primitive in art, music, literature, politics, and education.[9] Richard Pells also has claimed that during the 1920s the writings of the *New Republic* group "expressed a certain anti-intellectualism, a discomfort with theory and abstract social analysis that sometimes verged on self-hate."[10]

The Nation and *The New Republic* were proponents of progressive education and gave considerable attention to (though not consistent editorial support for) the child-centered elements of that movement. In view of the continuing historical interest in anti-intellectualism and the recurrent educational concern over issues of excellence, certain questions are relevant: To what degree (if any) did the liberal journals provide a forum for anti-intellectual statements on education? Did the editors themselves take positions that provided aid and comfort to anti-intellectual forces? In short, did Lasch's "anti-intellectualism of the intellectuals" extend to the educational commentary carried by America's two leading liberal journals?

The first question is easily answered. In the pages of *The Nation*, then under the editorship of Oswald Villard, anti-intellectual statements are rarely found.[11] *The New Republic*, however, still under the leadership of founding editor Herbert Croly, was more culturally liberal and more attuned to new educational developments than was *The Nation*, and thus gave more space to proponents of the new psychology and its child-centered educational expression.[12] And amidst these child-centered statements were some, particularly those written by Elisabeth Irwin and her admirers, that were at least superficially anti-intellectual.

In a 1924 *New Republic* symposium on the elementary school, Irwin wrote enthusiastically of the kind of schooling in which "the conception of education as being of the intellect soon fades into the background." She recognized, however, that such a statement raised an important question:

> If, then, the new school is to take this off-hand view of the intellectual life of the child, what is education all about? It is not primarily a process of imparting information; it is not first of all a method of teaching reading and writing and thereby ridding the country of illiteracy. It is to provide situations in which a child can experiment with life, can express himself creatively, can orient himself in his own world.[13]

Seven months earlier Agnes de Lima had passed on to readers of *The New Republic* Irwin's startling statement that "no child under eight should be expected to form letters less than a foot high, and even then no high standard of perfection should be imposed." De Lima added matter-of-factly that "the nerve strain is too severe."[14]

That same year Irwin and Louis Marks published *Fitting the School to the Child*—a description and defense of their child-centered experiment in Public School 61. De Lima, in a sympathetic review of the book, quoted the authors' statement that: "What education chiefly needs is that we shall take more for granted in regard to the child's intellectual development and take more thought about teaching him the art of happy and productive living."[15]

Irwin herself made the same point even more forcefully two years later in a plea that six-year-olds not be taught to read: "If I had my way I'd turn them all out with balls and bats, hoops and jumping ropes and let them be as illiterate as nature made them for at least another year or two." Irwin's readers may have been surprised by the statements that followed. She had noticed that: "Bright children usually learn to read of themselves with very little help before they are eight, and the task of the modern school becomes one of luring them from this field into activity." But such an approach brought anxious questions. Irwin reported that she was often asked: "Do you prevent your children from learning to read when they want to?" Her reply was: "Not by main force do we prevent them, but if we can make reality more enticing and participation in active enterprises more interesting, we feel that we have succeeded better than if we leave them bent double over the Book of Knowledge."[16]

But statements such as these were rare in *New Republic* articles and reviews—and even scarcer in the editorials carried by that journal. Occasionally in the heat of dispute with educational conservatives the editors would oppose a "return to the 'intellectual' standpoint of the older type" of education. (But the placement of "intellectual" in quotations suggests their doubts about how intellectual such education actually was.) Or they would express the opinion that in the high school the "field of choice should not be limited to the so-called intellectual pursuits." But the words that followed may have disturbed some of the journal's educated readers: ". . . nor should any prejudice be exerted in their favor."[17]

Statements such as those, standing by themselves, certainly suggest that anti-intellectual views had penetrated the educational thinking of some *New Republic* writers and editors. But context is all-important here. A further look indicates that in most cases the writers believed that the newer approaches to education would eventually result in greater, rather than less, intellectual development.

Irwin, for example, in her article "Personal Education," followed critical comments on intellectual education with a list of stages: "First of all a child functions physically, then emotionally, and then intellectually. In the traditional school this order is reversed and therefore the child does not function at all. He is educated in the passive voice." An organic education would support the child's natural growth patterns and thus result in greater development in all areas:

> If the first few years of children's lives are devoted to self-initiated activity, to free use of their hands, their bodies, and their imaginations without much regard to what they learn or to the actual quality of what they make, it automatically happens that their standard of performance goes up. Their intellectual curiosity awakes and they themselves wish to be taught the techniques that the traditional school is so eager to give them. Such children learn to read because they want to; they learn to reason because they have to; they learn arithmetic because they need it.[18]

De Lima, one of Irwin's most enthusiastic interpreters, made

the same point in "Education Moves Ahead," in which she reviewed several educational books, including Irwin's and Marks'
Fitting the School to the Child. She asserted: "Children who are 'let
alone,' who are not forced into uncongenial tasks and held to
them by the lash of the schoolmaster, or by his black marks, are
. . . acquiring not merely more general information and a vastly
richer sense of the world, but they can read, write and do arith-
metic in advance of their grade."

She cited evidence on this point from Ellsworth Collings's
study of an experimental school in Missouri, which demonstrated that "children, under such a regime, acquire the 'common facts and skills'—the three R's—better than in the traditional school."[19]

This theme—that the new education not only provided for
children's physical, emotional, and esthetic needs, but that it
equalled or surpassed traditional schools in intellectual or academic development—appeared in numerous articles in the
journals during the 1920s. Thus Irwin asserted that if children
exercised their "intelligence upon the problems of their miniature world," this would induce a "hunger for information and a
thirst for intellectual adventure that will demand the aid of
books." Lawrence Morris claimed that "by shoveling information into children, the traditional schools fill their heads with
unrelated knowledge and deaden intelligence. Miss Pratt [di-
rector of the City and Country School], by assuming that childhood *is a part of life instead of a preparation for it,* awakens
intelligence." De Lima's articles in *The Nation* asserted that in Irwin's educational scheme "the three R's are adequately taken
care of, though not in the ordinary stultifying fashion." And
Evelyn Dewey gave readers of *The Nation* the same assurance,
noting that at the Children's School "the children keep ahead
of the conventional school curriculum."[20]

Throughout these statements is the belief that—to compli-
cate an aphorism—schools could have their academic bread
and eat their child-centered cake too. Or, as Alvin Johnson put
it in reporting that the Walden School was able to surpass traditional academic standards: "The school is ready to pay Caesar
in full the things that are Caesar's."[21] (This had the neat effect
of casting the traditional school in the role of Caesar, thus as-
signing a more exalted status to the progressive school.) An important point in all this is that no writers stepped forward to
defend a version of child-centered education which was un-

abashedly anti-intellectual. The various authors promoted an education in which schools could (to add yet another proverb) seek first the kingdom of childhood and freedom, with the blessed assurance that all else (test scores and college admissions) would be added unto them.

Some writers for the journals would not let the child-centered enthusiasts off so easily. In 1929 Jean Temple, a former teacher at the Walden School, emphasized in her *New Republic* review of Rugg and Shumaker's *The Child-Centered School* the authors' critique of the lack of intellectual discipline in the new schools: They "feel that the experimental school fails to train in critical intelligence, in those estimates, appreciations, and eneralizations which are essential to either understanding or direction of the problem presented by modern culture."[22]

A year later *The New Republic* carried several authoritative analyses of child-centered education and its alleged failure to provide for optimal intellectual development. By the time these articles appeared the stock market crash had occurred, the Depression was settling over the country, and the socially oriented reformist educators were starting to reassert themselves more vigorously. Boyd Bode of Ohio State University wrote the first article in a *New Republic* series on "The New Education Ten Years After." His contribution was an incisive critique of both "the doctrine of specific objectives" and "the doctrine of 'freedom.'" By the former he meant the pseudoscientific, utilitarian pedagogy identified with Franklin Bobbitt and W. W. Charters. Bode noted the absence of any reformist elements in this "scheme," which was "naturally predicated on the requirements of society as now constituted." He concluded: "A more poverty-stricken conception of education than this it would be difficult to imagine."

Bode was less hostile to "the freedom theory of education," but noted that its claims to true Deweyan lineage were not persuasive. This theory, "though always facile in quoting Dewey to its purpose, seems never to have acquired an understanding of Dewey's conception of freedom. According to Dewey, freedom is achieved through the exercise of intelligence, whereas the less discriminating of his disciples understand him to mean that intelligence is achieved through the exercise of freedom."[23]

Freedom, then, was not something to be found when adult stimuli and coercion were removed; it was to be created through the development of a disciplined intelligence.[24] And

for the development of such intelligence "a body of scientifi-
cally-organized matter is of inestimable value, not only as a resource in later life, but as a basis for present thinking. . . . The
lack of concern for the scientific organization of subject matter
that is shown by the newer movements in education is an ominous fact. It tends to justify the suspicion that they seek to
achieve the ends of education by a kind of magic."

It is clear that Bode had not been seduced by the beguiling
rhetoric of the new Rousseauans. Their pedagogy was lacking
in reformist vigor, had "no adequate mission or social gospel,"
and failed to give sufficient emphasis to "the place of intelligence in human affairs."[25]

The second article in the series, by Joseph K. Hart, provided
another profound critique of the excesses of the child-centered
movement. Hart's concern centered on two related problems—
the lack of personal integration achieved by many progressive
school graduates and their inability to relate effectively to
others and to society in general. Like Bode, Hart saw an excess
of purposeless freedom and a shortage of intelligent direction:
"It seems certain that the progressive schools have been successful in their emotional rebellions against the 'stupidities' of
the academic schools, but not so successful in the intellectual
task of establishing these freer methods as a positive instrument
of personal education in a social world."[26]

Following statements of the child-centered position by Margaret Naumberg and Caroline Pratt, John Dewey presented the
final article in the series—a vigorous, authoritative examination
of the question "How Much Freedom in the New Schools?"[27]
Dewey posited a dialectical swing from the thesis stage of formalistic education to its antithesis in the child-centered schools,
which had produced a "one-sided emphasis—that upon pupils
at the expense of subject matter." He was not satisfied with the
shift from the old formalism to the new chaos, and held that the
solution was not to discard or deemphasize content, but to develop "a new subject matter, as well organized as the old . . . but
having an intimate and developing relation to the experience of
those in school."

Like Bode, Dewey believed that a new curriculum, well
taught, could enhance children's freedom by preparing them
to shape their environments and to direct their own lives. The
way for the new schools to increase their effectiveness was to

develop "the rational freedom which is the fruit of objective knowledge and understanding." Dewey thus outlined the task of the child-centered school—to go beyond the existing stage of "casual improvisation and living intellectually from hand to mouth." The schools would have to develop experimentally a subject matter which would include "preparation for the social realities—including the evils—of industrial civilization."

As Dewey's writings consistently attest, intelligence and knowledge were instruments, not ends in themselves. Intelligence had evolved in order to help humans cope more effectively with their environments.[28] Thus Dewey stressed not only the need for new knowledge and for intelligent people to use that knowledge, but the social ends to which it should be put:

> A truly progressive development of progressive education could not be secured by the study of children alone. It requires a searching study of society and its moving forces. That the traditional schools have almost evaded consideration of the social potentialities of education is no reason why progressive schools should continue the evasion, even though it be sugared over with esthetic refinements. The time ought to come when no one will be judged to be an educated man or woman who does not have insight into the basic forces of industrial civilization.

This analysis led Dewey to define out of the progressive education movement those institutions which ignored the pressing need for sound social knowledge: "Only schools which take the lead in bringing about this kind of education can claim to be progressive in any socially significant sense."[29] This was not a defense of neutral intellectuality or disinterested scholarship. Rather, it was a forceful objection to the social waste involved in producing esthetes, dabblers, and triflers. Society desperately needed people with deep social insights and skills if human problems were to be solved, and Dewey firmly believed that the schools could help produce such people. Thus Dewey, like Bode, tied the twin values of reformism and intellectualism inextricably together.

It is clear, then, that Dewey, Bode, Hart, and other writers for the journals vigorously defended an intellectual, reformist role for the new education. But what of the editors themselves?

A "reader's-eye-view" will indicate the editors' positions on this issue. During the 1920s, the readers of either journal (but especially *The New Republic*) were kept well informed about developments in progressive education—including some of the disputes within the movement. *New Republic* readers, if they followed the articles and reviews by Elisabeth Irwin and Margaret Naumberg, may also have noted the ostensibly anti-intellectual elements in their educational programs. But they may also have been impressed by the more philosophically rigorous defenses of intellectualism and reformism that issued from the pens of Hart, Bode, and Dewey.

Dewey was, from 1922 to 1937, a contributing editor of *The New Republic*—evidence that he was considered by the regular editors as closely aligned with the general policies of the journal.[30] Dewey's articles (cited above) give at least a partial indication that Dewey himself was free from the taint of anti-intellectualism. But what of Croly and the other editors? Do their editorials bespeak a fundamental anti-intellectual bent? An examination of the context of editorial statements shows that a rather complex answer is required.

In the 1923 editorials cited previously, the snide comments on intellectual studies can be read not as anti-intellectualism but as defenses of the expanding role of the high schools and as critiques of a narrow academic curriculum. In each case, the editorial was in part a response to statements by Henry S. Pritchett of the Carnegie Foundation. As Ellen Condliffe Lagemann has shown, Pritchett was appalled by the growing masses of youth attending American high schools and by the immense expense this entailed for the nation.[31] He felt that many of these young people should not be in high school, since some were ill-prepared to profit from traditional academic studies and had forced the schools to lower standards and to expand the curriculum to include vocational training and other watered-down fare. His solution was to return to educational fundamentals and to let nonacademic pupils drop out entirely or enter special trade schools.[32]

In the editors' minds, Pritchett had raised what was basically a social-class issue. They saw the consequence of Pritchett's proposals as a restriction of the high school to the more prosperous classes and a dumping of lower-class children either onto the labor market or into vocational schools that would serve to freeze existing class lines:

The notion that schooling should end for all but the ablest and most fortunate at twelve or fourteen years of age is a monstrous survival of everything that we as Americans are committed to getting away from. It represents an abdication of social intelligence and nurture; a surrender of society to blind chance with the odds all on the side of those favored by fortune.[33]

Like Dewey, the editors saw the sources of educational problems as lying beyond the school: "A transitional and often incoherent society has reflected itself in a transitional and often incoherent education." And they agreed with Dewey that the way out was neither to return to the old subject matter nor to abandon content altogether. The solution was to discover new fundamentals in education appropriate to "the needs of those who attend." Educational and social imperatives called for "faith in humanity and faith in inquiry and continued experimentation. Social snobbishness, fear for the pocket of the taxpayer and complacent assurance that fundamentals are already known renders a disservice."[34]

The consistency of the editors' convictions on this point is indicated by the fact that their editorial, "The High School and Democracy," which accompanied *The New Republic*'s supplement on the high school eight months later, was essentially a reprise of this earlier statement. The editors cited some of Pritchett's same remarks and rebutted them with several of their previous points.[35] And this time they had George Counts's evidence on class discrimination in high schools with which to undergird their assertions. Counts had concluded his groundbreaking 1923 article by stating:

The ancient tradition of secondary education as class education, though repudiated in theory, is still reflected in practice. The establishment of the public high school was a great achievement, but it has not as yet included the equalization of educational opportunity among the classes. Beyond the age of economic self-support, since education means leisure and since leisure is costly, education remains in no small measure a function of family ambition and fortune. Through the social inheritance inequalities are thus passed on from generation to generation. In the struggle for the equalization of educational opportunity important battles have been won, but for the nation as a whole the fight itself is only well begun.[36]

The editors were, however, perceptive enough to realize that teachers and administrators, who had to work amidst the pressures of the new mass high school, were often inclined to sympathize with views like Pritchett's. They were the ones who suffered when the high school becomes a "kindergarten for adolescents" and who wondered "how long the experiment of democracy must continue to involve individual and social waste and inefficiency." The way out, however, was not to choose between educational democracy and instructional excellence, but to keep the young in school, help them to select appropriate educational paths, and then to insure that "the years of choice shall be followed by years of more strenuous application of standards of workmanship, whether in intellectual or technical efforts."

Like many *New Republic* and *Nation* editorials on education, this one ended on a reformist note. The editors insisted that "the chief derelictions of the high school are due to the false standards of the community." Society maintained a social and economic class structure that impelled parents and children to try to use the schools as ladders of individual mobility. But the real solution was to create a true industrial democracy in which class lines and privileges would be wiped out—and "the high school should itself be a powerful engine in bringing industrial society to this equilibrium."[37]

When the editors did appear to veer close to the abyss of anti-intellectualism, they were in fact engaging in antiformalism, antiacademicism, and anticonservatism. They fought efforts to restore the high school as a class-bound academic hothouse. As with thinkers like Bode, Hart, and Dewey, their defenses of democracy and of social intelligence formed a seamless whole.

Richard Gilman's original 1963 *New Republic* review of *Anti-intellectualism* says that Hofstadter's section on education has "about it too much of the smell of the archives, from which nothing new or revelatory comes."[38] This survey of material from a decade of liberal journalism may carry a different archival aroma emanating from the dusty, crumbly library volumes of *The New Republic* and *The Nation*. But it can only redress the balance somewhat. It suggests that Dewey as journalist is a needed source as we assess his essential ideas and impact. As a contributing editor and writer for *The New Republic,* Dewey reached thousands of educationally oriented readers. And he made a valiant effort to correct—as they appeared—misinterpretations and misapplications of his theories. With the help of good editors, he made his points clearly and crisply.[39]

Gilman notes that Hofstadter "attempts to rescue Dewey from his more egregious misinterpreters while fixing a certain degree of blame upon him."[40] But if blame must be assigned, this examination of the liberal journals may help to shift a measure of it away from Dewey and onto those child-centered educators who were moving from Deweyan reformism to Freudian and Jungian child-centered education.

Hofstadter not only gave a limited interpretation of Dewey's work; he also, as Merle Borrowman pointed out in a perceptive review, gave "too much credit to the older system of secondary schools and colleges."[41] These institutions were not the centers of intellectual rigor that one might imagine from Hofstadter's description of the slide into progressivism. Hofstadter was to some degree guilty of the two charges Michael B. Katz leveled against Diane Ravitch. Katz said that Ravitch promoted the "notion that the goals of American schools once were primarily cognitive rather than social, affective, or, in nineteenth-century terminology, moral." And he reported Ravitch's "odd assertion that the schools really did adopt the progressive agenda in the years after the Second World War."[42] There is increasing evidence that progressive education, particularly the Deweyan reformist variety, had only a limited impact on American schools either before or after World War II. As early as 1956, Merle Curti wrote:

> The contention that Dewey's followers have subtracted intellectual values from our schools fails to take into account certain relevant facts. It assumes that progressive education has actually swept the country, which is hardly the case. And even what passes for progressive education is often the outer shell rather than the substance of Dewey's philosophy. Critics often fail to see that Dewey did not reject reason: he tried to sharpen rationality by urging that assumptions be tested and verified, and that experience be relived and critically reconstructed in terms of new situations.[43]

Support for Curti's assertion concerning the limited impact of progressive education may be found in books and articles by Arthur Zilversmit, David Tyack, Larry Cuban, and other scholars.[44] But we need not go as a far as Michael Katz, who has written, "Progressivism did not fail to work a fundamental transformation in American schools; it did not even try."[45] The evidence from the liberal journals suggests that Dewey and his more knowledgeable interpreters had a clear picture of the intellectual deficiencies of traditional education as well as a firm reformist stance against anti-intellectual dilutions of the new education and that, in fact, they tried very hard through their multiple roles as educators, journalists, and political activists to make a fundamental and progressive transformation of the traditional school.

In his 1985 John Dewey lecture, Richard Bernstein, one of Dewey's most faithful modern interpreters, reminded his listeners: "Nothing would be more unpragmatic—a violation of the pragmatic spirit of Dewey—than the suggestion that a return to his texts is sufficient to gain illumination and guidance for confronting our problems and conflicts."[46] It is not sufficient, but it is clearly helpful. For it was from a careful reading of those texts that Bernstein was able to write, in 1966, the following judicious statement:

It has become fashionable to criticize American education for being unduly influenced during the last fifty years by Dewey's ideas. But it would be more accurate to say that insofar as our schools have failed to develop the tough-minded habits of intelligence, they have failed to be influenced by what is most basic in Dewey's concept of the function of education in a democratic society.[47]

As the nation entered a new and more frightening decade, *The Nation* and *The New Republic* held to their liberal belief in humankind's rationality and educability. If they were less optimistic and naive on these matters than they had been before World War I, they still kept the hope that educative journalism and creative education might yet be worthy and effective instruments of a better social order. And they maintained a vision of a rational society and a relevant education that gave heart to reformers and liberals during those depressing years.

PART III

Active Liberalism Revives, 1930–1941

10

Liberals Move Left

Amidst the conservatism, complacency, and delusive prosperity of the 1920s, the economic warnings of American liberals had been all but drowned out by a barrage of boosterism. But the massive collapse of the stock market in late 1929 initiated a decade of depression that exceeded even the pessimistic prophecies of the liberal Jeremiahs. After the crash, the nation slid rapidly into the most severe depression in its history. Neither Congress nor President Hoover could stem the tide of economic disaster that swept over the country.

Hoover could hardly be held fully responsible for a depression based on years of economic mismanagement. But he could be—and was—blamed for his inadequate and ineffectual response to the crisis. His life had been marked by many successes, but he was now unable to adapt to the huge challenge of the Depression. As Robert McElvaine has suggested, "It may well be that Herbert Hoover simply had the misfortune of being in the right place at the wrong time."[1] Though he went farther than any earlier President in using federal power to try to

---

The phrase "active liberalism revives" comes from John Dewey's article, "The American Intellectual Frontier," *TNR* 30 (10 May 1922): 303. The description applies more appropriately to the decade of the 1930s.

stabilize the economy, the demands of the situation far exceeded Hoover's meager responses.[2] And whatever Hoover's
precise degree of responsibility, the American people were in
no mood to assess it calmly. As Stewart Holbrook wrote, "They
had already elected him President of the United States, and
now they elected him father of the Depression."[3] In November
1932, people flocked to the polls to turn him out of office by a
popular vote of 22,800,000 for Roosevelt against 15,750,000
for Hoover.[4]

Franklin Roosevelt, whom the electorate had chosen to replace Hoover, was at best an unknown quantity. Although he
was identified with the liberal wing of the Democratic party, his
campaign utterances were often vague and contradictory.[5] In
fact, the editors of *The New Republic*, though vigorously opposed to Hoover, could not bring themselves to support Roosevelt. To these liberal intellectuals, the Democratic platform
was a "mass of inconsistencies, a puny answer to the challenge
of the times." The candidate and party were "an untried jockey
on a very lame horse."[6] *The Nation* made similar assessments of
Roosevelt. He had displayed "weak and vacillating leadership,"
and his campaign maneuvers showed that he had joined the
"old guard of political sharpers." Under these circumstances,
both journals, though they recognized that he had no chance of
victory, urged their readers to support the Socialist candidate,
Norman Thomas.[7]

Thus the liberal weeklies entered the 1930s, as they had the
1920s, still estranged from the majoritarian politics of the Republican and Democratic parties. In spite of their skepticism,
however, the weeklies were at first pleasantly surprised by
Roosevelt's vigorous attack on the Depression. But when it became apparent that the early New Deal measures were not
going to provide basic solutions to America's problems, both
journals returned to the attack.[8] Until 1936 they continually be-
rated the administration for its unwillingness to make fundamental changes in the economy and for its cautious, tepid
responses to the crisis.

Thus the weeklies moved resolutely leftward. The combined
effects of the Depression, a drastically altered political situation, and the claimed success of the Russian Five Year plans
made a move toward collectivism seem eminently realistic. And
these external changes were intensified by transitions within
the journals themselves. On 1 January 1933, Oswald Villard re-

signed his editorship of *The Nation*, though he continued to contribute a weekly column until 1940. An editorial board led by Freda Kirchwey assumed direction of the magazine.[9] As the restraining hand of Villard's more conventional liberalism was lifted, *The Nation* spoke out increasingly for collectivist solutions to America's problems. And in its strongly antifascist foreign policy, it was often—particularly from 1935 to 1939—allied in the Popular Front with the Communists.[10] Although Villard deplored the increasing radicalism and interventionism of *The Nation*, he should not have been surprised. As early as 1927, R. L. Duffus had noted that in selecting personnel for the journal, Villard had "purposefully chosen men who were more radical than he was." He also reported Villard's jocular complaint that whenever he found it necessary to leave the *Nation's* offices for brief periods, "the staff goes Bolshevist."[11]

Like many liberals, *The Nation's* editors were shaken and confused by the Moscow Trials of 1935–1938, but not until after the Hitler-Stalin Pact in 1939 did the journal break decisively with the Popular Front. This decade of sympathy with Communist causes was distressing to many readers. As late as February 1940, Henry Wallace felt it necessary to suggest that the journal be "as critical of the doctrines and doctrinaires of the left as it has always been, and properly, of the doctrines and doctrinaires of the right." In the same issue, Norman Thomas expressed his opinion that the journal had abandoned its earlier critical standards "in favor of the 'democratic frontism' so popular among intellectuals." But he was happy to note that since the Hitler-Stalin Pact he had seen "something of a return of the magazine to its old critical standards."[12]

The New Republic, too, underwent internal changes that accentuated its leftward shift. Croly's stroke in 1928 and death in 1930 brought to an end his forceful editorship of the journal.[13] He also was succeeded by a collective editorship: Bruce Bliven, George Soule, Malcolm Cowley, Robert M. Lovett, and Stark Young assumed direction of the journal, with Bliven as the guiding force. The weekly was edited more democratically than it had been under Croly, and there was less uniformity between the editorials and other sections of the paper.[14] Thus while Bliven and Soule were writing articles and editorials promoting a democratic collectivism, Malcolm Cowley was, in the words of Alfred Kazin, taking "the literary side of the *New Republic* in the direction of a sophisticated literary Stalinism."[15] In fact, while the journal editorially supported Thomas for President in 1932, Cowley and Edmund Wilson (the previous literary editor) backed William Z. Foster and James Ford, the Communist candidates.[16]

There was, however, one major difference between the journals. While *The Nation* joined the Communists in adopting a collective-security policy against the threat of fascism, the *New Republic* editors maintained a noninterventionist foreign policy until 1940.[17] But in spite of this difference, both journals expressed sympathy for Soviet Russia, attacked the failures and excesses of capitalism, supported extensive national planning, and gave a hearing to authors who proposed Communist solutions to American problems. Such policies opened *The New Republic* to charges from Benjamin Stolberg that it was "merely a 'liberal' echo of the *New Masses*." But a more balanced view was reflected by *Time* magazine, which in 1941 referred to it both as a "pinko weekly" and as moving "straight along its New Deal course."[18] In fact, from 1936 to 1939, *The Nation* and *The New Republic* managed to live up to both these descriptions. This was the heyday of the Popular Front, when even the Communists, out of their fear of fascism, were backing Roosevelt.[19] The journals thus found themselves for a few years in the position of being able simultaneously to support Roosevelt against his conservative enemies, snipe at the New Deal for its limitations, and enjoy the unity on the left that the temporary moderation of the Communists made possible. The fact that Roosevelt in the "second hundred days" in 1936 appeared to move his administration leftward and forced the enactment of some progressive legislation made it easier for both the Communists and their liberal allies to support him.[20] By placing themselves within Roosevelt's camp, but on its far left fringes, liberal journalists took positions such as Heywood Broun's: "I am an ardent New Dealer but with the reservation that in my opinion Mr. Roosevelt and his policies are by far too conservative."[21]

In spite of this move toward collectivism, Bliven, Kirchwey, and their colleagues still had much in common with Croly and Villard in continuing to be idealistic, nonideological, and pragmatic. The apparently paradoxical step they had taken—which Villard opposed and Croly probably would have resisted—was to enter into a working alliance with doctrinaire Communists.[22] In spite of their participation in the Popular Front, however, Bliven and Kirchwey never permitted their journals to become uncritical allies of the Communist party, and never supported its candidates for major office. But the shattering experience of the Depression did have a profound impact on them. It deepened their convictions concerning the failures of capitalism and heightened their sympathy for what they persisted in calling "the Russian experiment." Bliven's later characterization of American liberals of the 1930s can well be applied to both journals: "The innocents of those days were certainly naive; they were gullible; they were very slow to face the changing facts of history. It is also true however that they were miles away from supporting dictatorship, rule by torture and the building of a whole society on falsehood."[23] In spite of their leftward drift, Lillian Symes's comment in the 1920s applies as well to the 1930s. She declared that the two journals had "taken their revolution vicariously."[24]

Knowledgeable observers agreed that *The Nation* and *The New Republic* continued to wield, through their intellectual readership, a power greater than mere numbers would indicate. One cannot, of course, prove that readers were actually swayed in their ideas or actions because of what they read in the journals. But one can show that some important people believed themselves to have been so influenced. *The New Republic*'s twenty-fifth anniversary in 1939 and the *The Nation*'s seventy-fifth a year later gave American leaders the opportunity to testify to that effect.

To celebrate its twenty-fifth birthday *The New Republic* gave a party for its staff, writers, and friends. In attendance, according to *Time* magazine, were "free traders, isolationists, progressive educators, single taxers, practicing Marxists, disillusioned Marxists, poets, professors, publishers, all who believe themselves to be liberals, all who thus claim to fit into a category that nobody has satisfactorily defined."[25] The journal also received letters bearing the good wishes of many influential people. Messages came from persons active in government, like Henry Wallace, Harry Hopkins, and Harold Ickes. Ickes, who had subscribed since the first issue, declared that *The New Republic* had served liberals and progressives as "a steady beacon, a staunch friend, and an ever-ready defender of enlightened causes." He added, "I think I speak for all of us liberals when I say that I do not know what we would have done without the stimulation of the *New Republic*." Speaking for writers and editors were Sherwood Eddy, Stuart Chase, and a host of their colleagues. Eddy described the journal as "a national institution," and praised it for being "always fresh, vigorous, stimulating, independent, progressive; always liberal, sometimes radical." And true to the spirit of the decade, he added: "I would rather see you always radical and sometimes liberal."[26]

When *The Nation* celebrated its seventy-fifth birthday it carried a similar series of letters from opinion leaders. Messages were received from President Roosevelt, George Norris, Josephus Daniels, and others active in government. Daniels praised the "independence, fearlessness, and ability of the *Nation*," and described it as "an influential agency in an era when leadership without strings is the hope of a drifting world."

Editors and writers also attested to *The Nation*'s influence and importance. Among those sending their good wishes were William Allen White, H. V. Kaltenborn, and Norman Thomas. White was lavish in his praise, claiming that *The Nation* had been his "guide, philosopher, and friend." He added: "For me it has interpreted the news and often even its opinions are news." Kaltenborn, one of the period's most influential news commentators, asserted that "the *Nation* should be required reading for every opinion-maker."[27]

■

After the crash, as David Seideman has noted, *The New Republic* "transformed itself overnight to meet the new circumstances. Its normally desk-bound writers journeyed into the field to investigate the rumblings of discontent." *The Nation* also sent reporters and editors on the road to cover the impact of the Depression and Hoover's faltering response to it.[28] Both journals described the effects of the economic disaster on jobs, wages, housing, politics, culture, and, of course, education.[29]

The editors, writers, and readers of the journals continued to express their concern about educational matters. Many in the group, as in the earlier periods of the journals' histories, were professors, teachers, and students, and some were active in educational associations and activities. Most of them saw schools and colleges as institutions of central importance in the development of a better society. Thus the liberal journalists explored the impact of economic contraction on many aspects of education—on public and private schools, on colleges and universities, on school budgets, on educational opportunities for depressed groups such as blacks and southern whites, on students, and particularly on teachers and professors.

The stock market crash occurred in October 1929, but since school budgets for 1929–30 had already been established, educational spending for that year held up well in most parts of the country.[30] But in some areas where tax structures were weak and municipal finances shaky, the schools began to suffer almost immediately. *The Nation* noted in February 1930 the difficulties in Chicago, where teachers and other public employees were going unpaid and the city could not afford to buy coal to heat the schools. A month later "The Drifter" reported that over half the schools in one Georgia county had been closed because funds for teachers' pay had been exhausted.[31]

School budgets declined only slightly during the next academic year, but in 1931–32 per pupil spending dropped by over 5 percent, and the next year by another 10 percent.[32] In February 1933, *The Nation* noted that in 4 states over half the rural schools had shut down, that 60 cities had closed their evening classes, and that 145 communities had abandoned their kindergartens.[33] Villard reported from Oregon that many rural schools in that state had closed for the year at Christmas.[34]

During the 1933–34 year, the schools hit bottom. While enrollments reached their peak for the decade, the number of teachers, average teacher salaries, total expenditures, and per pupil costs reached their lowest points.[35] A *Nation* editorial reported on this alarming situation, noting that while the Depression had forced the closing of only forty schools by November 1932, eighteen months later the figure had soared to forty thousand.

One ominous development was, to *The Nation*'s editors, the fact that in some cities educational budgets were being cut more drastically than spending in general. In Chicago, for example, the school budget for 1933 was slashed by about 35 percent, while the average cut in municipal spending was only about 10 percent:

Because the children could not answer back, because their parents perhaps did not realize the gravity of the situation, and because the school teachers were helpless in the face of direct threats to their jobs, local budgets have made cuts in the school funds out of all proportion to the general budgetary cuts.[36]

The journals angrily predicted the educational disaster sure to befall the country unless the budget-slashers were stopped, but both decried also the damage being done in specific areas and to particular groups. In 1935, for example, *The New Republic* carried an article by Harold Ward on "The Poverty Belt"— the area of the southern mountains now labeled Appalachia. Ward reported that in 1930 the area had suffered from adult illiteracy rates of 10 or 12 percent. Schools were having difficulty rectifying the situation, for in many areas fewer than a quarter of third-grade pupils reached high school. And those tragic statistics could not have improved during "five years of acute depression."[37] The same issue of *The New Republic* carried a review by Martha Gruening of Ella Enslow's book, *Schoolhouse in the Foothills*. Miss Enslow had taught for some time in the Tennessee backcountry and reported on her experience as "teacher, attorney, financier, nurse . . . and preacher to the community." Conditions in the southern mountains were bad enough in normal times, but Miss Gruening was most disturbed that "five years of depression and two of drought, meant half-starved children coming to school or staying away because they hadn't clothes or shoes to come in."[38]

Another group whose educational opportunities were particularly hard-hit were blacks. *The Nation*, true to the traditions of its founder, E. L. Godkin, took a particular interest in their problems. The journal had long supported equal education as a path to progress for blacks, and now its writers lamented the special difficulties the Depression made for black schools. In an analysis of the effects of the economic downturn on teachers, Eunice Langdon described the problems of unemployment, of nonpayment of salaries, of crowded classes, of inadequate materials, and of actual hunger and deprivation that assailed instructors throughout the country. And she added that it was "a safe assumption that in those states and counties which normally spend from three to sixty times as much on their white as on their colored schools, the sufferings of the Negro school teachers and of the Negro school population have been proportionately heavier."[39]

Three years later, Villard gave the problem more searching attention in an article titled "Slumbering Fires in Harlem." The previous March there had been a serious riot in Harlem, and Mayor LaGuardia had appointed a commission to investigate its causes. Villard's article, essentially an interpretation of the commission's report, gave substantial attention to school conditions. No elementary schools had been built in Harlem since 1924, during the period of greatest black in-migration. Many southern black schools had been closed since the onset of the Depression, and some parents had "recklessly shipped their children to friends or relatives or even speaking acquaintances in the North in the hope that they would be taken in and educated." Such children added to overcrowded conditions in which schools were forced to conduct double and even triple sessions. More than half the grade schools had between forty and fifty students in each class. Villard told of one boy whose teacher "discovered that he was half-fainting from hunger and had not had sufficient food for three days." Such cases dramatized a situation in which schools were not only directly affected by economic stringency, but also affected indirectly, as the families of their students suffered unemployment and hunger.[40]

It was evident to the liberal journalists that the Depression was hitting hardest at the educational opportunities of those groups, like blacks and southern whites, at the bottom of the economic heap. But this fact did not diminish the editors' concerns for the state of higher education. Both journals considered themselves as organs of intellectual liberalism, whose chief base was the university. And both assigned college-trained intellectuals a role in reform out of proportion to their limited numbers. Thus *The New Republic* wrote in 1933:

> Unemployment and destitution of the intellectual worker have a graver significance than the plight of a class. In this world, where factories, schools, hospitals and even political parties and labor unions cannot be operated without the knowledge of experts, we rarely visualize their real importance. They hold the key for the functioning of our complicated world. They interpret past events and draw the lines for the future. Invention, education, propaganda, organization, come through them to the masses.[41]

In February 1933, just at the end of Hoover's term in office, *The Nation* was vigorously resisting the efforts of state agencies to cut the budgets of colleges and universities. The editors were particularly indignant when a liberal institution like the University of North Carolina came under attack. Under the leadership of Frank Graham it had become a university that "in the productivity of its scholars, in its public spirit, in its service to its State, is certainly unexcelled by any similar institution." Nonetheless, the budget bureau of North Carolina was proposing a 20 percent cut in appropriations, which would have meant a total decline of 56 percent from 1929. The editors advised North Carolina authorities to follow the example of New York's Governor Herbert Lehman, who had recently refused to knuckle under to business efforts to cripple the "great educational machine" of his state.[42]

This editorial set the pattern for much of the journals' comment on the Depression and higher education: it coupled a defense of universities with praise for their champions and indictments of the conservatives who threatened to cripple them financially.[43] But the liberal weeklies occasionally carried more dispassionate analyses of the problems of higher education. During 1933 and 1934 *The Nation* ran one of the longest series in its history—thirteen articles on the Depression and the professions. In the third article, William Thomas considered the impact of the Depression on college instructors and pointed out that by 1932 the Depression had "caught up with the universities," particularly the tax-supported institutions. He provided figures on numerous universities, noting that general funds had declined between 1931–32 and 1933–34 anywhere from 6.9 percent to 53 percent.[44]

Later in that same school year, Villard took a trip through the western states, visiting a number of colleges and universities along the way. In March 1934 he wrote from Oregon on "The Plight of Higher Education." He reported that at the University of Oregon, enrollment had dropped by a third, some faculty salaries had been halved, and the library lacked funds even for important new books. Villard was impressed, however, by the determination of students to continue their education in the face of deprivation, and spoke of one "whose work improved enormously when it was arranged that he could get one square meal a day." He declared that "somebody ought to call President Roosevelt's attention to the dire distress of so many of our schools of higher learning, which ought to be the most cher-

ished institutions in our entire national life." And he concluded
with his usual coupling of pacifism and reformism:

> It is an infernal outrage in this national emergency to ap-
> prove a bill for the expenditure of $500,000,000 for war-
> ships when the price of even two battleships expended
> upon our universities would bring hope and cheer, yes,
> decent sustenance, to students and teachers on a thousand
> campuses. Can there be any question which expenditure
> would really make for the true preparedness of this coun-
> try for the tasks and dangers and infinitely difficult prob-
> lems of the future?[45]

But the journals' concern for colleges and their students did
not stop at the point at which graduates received their degrees.
In a depressed labor market, many graduates found that their
hard-won degrees led straight to unemployment. An editorial
in 1933 called attention to the difficulty experienced by recent
college graduates in finding work. New engineers, teachers,
doctors, lawyers, and other professionals found little call for
their services. The editors saw clearly how this "professional depression" related to the general economic situation: "Over-
production of trained minds among millions of illiterates,
destitute physicians among hundreds of thousands who die
without medical care, is neither more nor less a paradox than
having too much bread, too many shoes, too much of everything when people go hungry and in rags."[46]

The Nation was similarly angered at the situation and agreed
that it was "wasteful and degrading to train scholars and professionals for posts which they will not be able to find." But it
took issue with Harvard president James Conant's proposed solution—a cut in college enrollments. It could not agree that the
time had come for a "planned contraction" in the universities.
Instead, the editors believed that:

> The fate of American university graduates must be inte-
> grated with a program of expansion throughout American
> society. Our "surplus" of graduates is a measure of the
> chaos in our economy rather than a sign that their services
> are not needed. Dr. Conant's recognition of the problem is
> courageous; his solution is as dangerous as it is evasive.[47]

The graduates themselves were not totally passive in this situation, and some of the more radical among them took collective action to deal with the problem. Under the leadership of Joseph Lash of the City College of New York, an association of unemployed college alumni was formed. The liberal weeklies occasionally reminded their readers of their plight by printing correspondence from such groups. *The New Republic* carried a letter from Lash's organization inviting interested persons to a Washington conference on the problem. The letter made the quite unwarranted assertion that "college graduates and the professional classes in general have been the group most severely affected in this depression," but then went on moderately enough to call on the federal government for "significant unemployment relief and . . . more permanent remedial measures."[48]

The Roosevelt administration did undertake some programs, such as the National Youth Administration, which benefited students, colleges, and professors. And as broader New Deal programs began to ease the economic situation by 1936, employment prospects for graduates began to improve. *The New Republic* then briefly abandoned its doom-saying and reported that "a much larger proportion of young people going out from schools and colleges now are able to find employment."[49]

But this uncharacteristic optimism was short-lived, and it soon became clear that even the best efforts of the New Deal would not alleviate the situation sufficiently. The economy went into a recession in late 1937, and the following June *The New Republic* was again lamenting "the season when several hundred thousand college graduates are pushed off into the open ocean. The icy plunge was always frightening, but in recent years there has been an added trouble—the sea of employment hasn't nearly enough room for them." The continued existence of this problem was an indictment not only of the general political and economic system but of the colleges and universities that should provide society with criticism and innovative ideas. Thus the editors proposed a more extreme version of Conant's suggestion:

> It might be a good thing for the universities to get together and resolve that it is foolish to go on educating young men and women for whom the world has no use; that it would

be better to shut up shop for a while and turn their staffs and endowments loose on the problem of why the world does not take fuller advantage of what they have to offer.[50]

For the liberal journalists, one of the most irritating aspects of the situation was the blithe way many educational institutions succeeded in ignoring both the state of the economy and the embarrassing questions being raised about the viability of the whole American enterprise. *The New Republic*, concerned about the lack of opportunity for college graduates, asked whether the universities could "just shrug their black-gowned shoulders and say it is not their business."[51] It was disappointed that American education was "still based, in the main, on the rags and tatters of the education deemed appropriate for the English landed gentry of several centuries ago." This anachronistic education, further weakened by attacks on academic freedom, produced appallingly few students "who understand the sickness of our society and are prepared to fight for a cure."[52]

Villard, too, was angry at the failure of educational institutions to grapple with the problems raised by the economic crisis. He recalled that during the World War it had not been "considered ridiculous then to rebuild the whole life of the universities and colleges around the business of teaching youth to go overseas and slaughter fellow human beings." He proposed that now, in similar fashion but for better ends, "the entire life of the university should be built around the existing economic crisis; that the first function of such an institution should be to keep the students and faculty currently aware of the momentous changes that are going on in our economic, social and political life."[53]

But Villard's was a voice from outside the educational world, as well as from an older generation. More poignant, because it came from one of the "victims" of schooling, was the testimony of Jon (later John) Cheever. During his junior year at Thayer Academy in Massachusetts, Cheever was expelled because of his low grades. Then, at the age of seventeen, he wrote one of the most personal articles on education that journal had carried since the days of Randolph Bourne. He reproduced, in the words of the editors, "the atmosphere of an institution where education is served out dry in cakes, like pemmican." He described the fatuous headmaster, the conformist faculty, the dessicated curriculum. And he derided the social and economic blindness which characterized the institution during the first year of the Depression.

> Our country is the best country in the world. We are swimming in prosperity and our President is the best president in the world. We have larger apples and better cotton and faster and more beautiful machines. This ·makes us the greatest country in the world. Unemployment is a myth. Dissatisfaction is a fable. In preparatory school America is beautiful.[54]

Cheever's piece added a student's perspective to the articles and editorials through which the journals responded to the effects of the Depression on America's schools and colleges. The weeklies reminded their readers of the range of difficulties experienced by educational institutions of all types and in all parts of the country. They worried readers about declining educational budgets, overcrowded schools, and shortened school terms. They decried the special impact of the Depression on higher education and on the most vulnerable groups. And they noted the irony of a situation in which schools and colleges tried to ignore the financial disaster that was undermining their effectiveness.

But such a summary should not overshadow the depth of emotion the journalists had on this issue. Their feelings were indicated in a *Nation* editorial that asserted that "nothing could be more dangerous for the future of the country than the failure to maintain even our present inadequate educational standards."[55] This expressed a solid commitment to education and a concern for its preservation and improvement. But it was tepid in comparison with the rhetoric unloosed by the editors against those school boards and their conservative business allies who used the Depression as an excuse to cut educational budgets:

> Of all the disastrous consequences of the depression, this assault on the coming generation's chance to secure a modicum of education is the most damnable. These would-be tax slackers are public enemies who, while patrioteering at every opportunity, are themselves as unpatriotic a brood as exist in our society. They should be scourged from their positions of authority and influence by a wrathful public

opinion, and education should not only be restored to its former place, but lifted to a new level of efficiency, dignity, and freedom.[56]

■

Not surprisingly, as the liberal weeklies developed changing policies on politics, economics, foreign policy, literature, and the arts, they evolved different positions on issues in the world of education. The chapters that follow will emphasize three points.

First, the weeklies gave particular attention to the effects of the Depression on educators, denounced conservative economic and political attacks on teachers and professors, and encouraged unionization for educators. As part of their Popular Front positions, both journals avoided and delayed criticism of Communist influence in the American Federation of Teachers (AFT) but finally—after the Hitler-Stalin Pact—called for elimination of Communist influence in that union.

Second, the journals welcomed the increasing activism and militancy of college students, gave particular support to radical campus journalists, called for a united front among student groups and—as in the case of the AFT—finally spoke out in favor of an autonomous student movement not under the control of Communist ideologues.

Third, both journals supported new federal initiatives for youth, particularly the Civilian Conservation Corps (CCC) and the National Youth Administration (NYA). They called for expansion of these programs, denounced militarism and censorship in the CCC, and resisted conservative efforts to bring the NYA under control of the educational establishment.

These issues were deeply entangled with other educational concerns as well as with larger social questions. The journalists were not providing *ad hoc* commentary on discrete topics, but were applying to educational issues the more radical positions they were taking on broader political and intellectual matters. But while assuming a more radical stance on specific organizational developments, the journals continued to maintain their historic progressive commitment both to the reform of education and to education as an instrument of reform. And in so doing, they continued to hold forth a vision of the kind of society they hoped might emerge from the ravages of the Depression.

11

From Campus to Breadline

The Depression, which wreaked destruction in so many areas of American life, had a severe impact on schools and colleges, and on the teachers and professors who staffed them. Although, as noted in the previous chapter, the effects of reduced tax revenues and financial stringency were not felt immediately in all districts and institutions, they eventually took their toll throughout the country. As schools and colleges cut expenditures, they slashed away at teachers' jobs and salaries, which were the largest items in most educational budgets.[1] The effects on educators may be described in directional terms: they were pressed downward in security, income, and sometimes even in economic class, and in response many chose to move leftward in political thought and action. Robert McElvaine has written that "the Depression made the interests of working-class Americans more apparent to them and led many in the middle class to identify with those below them."[2] The liberal journals made it clear that this was happening to numerous American teachers and to their intellectual allies.

The shift of some educators toward the left, toward political involvement and toward unionism, while basically an outcome

This chapter takes its title from the title of an editorial in *TNR* 75 (17 May 1933): 6–7.

of the Depression, was accentuated by a new "Red Scare"—
a wave of teacher oaths and attacks on already limited academic
freedom.[3] As teachers became more militant in response to
economic pressures, local and state officials responded with
repressive legislation and loyalty oaths, stimulating further
teacher activism.

In all this, educators did not become the passive, acquiescent
victims of outside pressures. If economic constraints or conservative political coercion were forces over which they had little
control, their responses were at least in part voluntary ones.
They might, for example, like many other alienated and aggrieved groups, have moved to the political right and followed
Father Charles Coughlin, Gerald L. K. Smith, or other demagogues.[4] But instead, many chose a radical response: to become
members of the American Federation of Teachers (AFT) and
to push that union to become more aggressive and militant.

The National Education Association (NEA), perceived by
many teachers as a company union, barely held its own during
the 1930s. In 1932 the NEA enrolled 21.1 percent of America's
teachers. After some losses, it slowly rebuilt its numbers until by
1938, 22.3 percent of America's teachers were members. Between those same years, however, the AFT more than quadru-
pled in size, from a minuscule .08 percent to 3.4 percent of the
teaching force. And throughout the period—partly because of
its power in a few large cities—the AFT exercised an influence
out of proportion to its small numbers.[5]

As unionized teachers became more numerous, active, and
militant, they received the support—and later the criticism—of
The Nation and *The New Republic*. The weeklies gave particular
attention to the economic and political pressures on teachers
and to their varied responses: political action, support for remedial legislation, and unionization. The journals shifted from
general support for teacher unions (as part of their basic
prolabor stance) to a class-conscious sympathy for militant and
fellow-traveling groups, and finally to a break with, and vigorous opposition to, Communist influence in the American
Federation of Teachers. Underlying these superficially shifting
positions were the journals' consistent policies of supporting reformist objectives for education and of promoting active coalition-building with educators, unionists, and others in pursuit
of these goals.

As the Depression deepened, articles, editorials, and letters all dramatized for readers the predicament of elementary and secondary teachers. A *New Republic* editorial reported in May 1933 that there were fifteen thousand teachers seeking positions in New York City alone. And those with jobs were only marginally better off than the unemployed, as a quarter of a million teachers were scheduled to receive salaries below the meager minimum set by the National Recovery Administration for unskilled workers. That same year Eunice Langdon noted in *The Nation* that conditions in the poorer parts of the nation were even worse, with Alabama, for example, owing its teachers seven million dollars by 1933.[6]

But there was a more tragic human story behind these cold statistics. Langdon reported the case of a sick and crippled Chicago teacher who, in desperation over his situation, killed himself. "His widow, left with three children, stated that he had not been paid for eight months, that his property had depreciated, groceries which his family needed could be bought only on wage assignment, and worry had aggravated his illness." When Chicago teachers were finally paid three-fourths of a year's salary, one reported his sense of relief: "For the first time in four painful years my mailbox will cease to be cluttered; I'll not be afraid to answer my doorbell any more; the hard-boiled collectors that have hunted me relentlessly will at last be appeased."[7]

The Unemployed Teachers Association (UTA) wrote to both weeklies concerning the plight of its members. By 1932 the unemployed teachers of the city could "no longer withdraw into a false haven of pride and gentility; their need is too desperate and pressing." The school board was combining classes and increasing class size, moves that would "not only create more difficult tasks for the teachers employed, but also lower the quality of education for the children."[8] But perhaps the letter that most touched the hearts of the editors (or at least of the circulation manager) was one from a teacher to *The Nation* reporting: "I get more good from it than from any other paper with which I have ever come in contact," and informing the editors that he had borrowed on his life insurance in order to subscribe to the journal for two years.[9]

The journals gave similar coverage to the difficulties of college faculties. William Thomas reported in *The Nation* that by the summer of 1933 "wholesale dismissals" of instructors had occurred at several institutions. The University of Pittsburgh had dropped more than one-eighth of its faculty, and Cornell

had released forty-four staff members in one year. For the fortunate ones who had retained their positions, salary cuts up to
45 percent had been instituted.[10] Of particular concern was the
fact that "equality of sacrifice" was not the pattern adopted by
the colleges. Institutions found it easiest to proceed on the "last
hired, first fired" system, so those at the lowest ranks were most
likely to be let go. Thus "in nearly every case the people most
severely affected by the retrenchment are those least able to
stand it."[11]

Robert Conklin pointed out in 1936 that the blacklisting of
the University of Pittsburgh by the American Association of
University Professors (AAUP) could have little effect because
"dollars are scarcer than teachers." There were many "trained
and experienced college teachers either totally unemployed or
teaching in Relief Administration projects for $21 a week." The
college held all the power, and AAUP pressure could hardly
hope to affect the University. Conklin expected "Pittsburgh to
close down about the same year that the Standard Oil goes
bankrupt and the Communists elect a president."[12]

These various pressures—joblessness, delayed salaries, pay
cuts, and increased workloads—alone would have been enough
to impel educators to seek more active means of defending
their interests. But when such economic hardships were combined with attacks on academic freedom and teacher loyalty,
the move to organize and protest took on added momentum.
This was particularly true when educators could identify the
same conservative forces as responsible for both situations. The
Depression provoked teacher militancy; this in turn promoted
conservative efforts to force teachers back into their traditional
subservient roles. As some teacher organizations began challenging orthodox economic beliefs, conservatives—who often
got Americanism, capitalism, and democracy inextricably
scrambled in their minds—demanded loyalty oaths to bring
restive teachers back into line. And conservatives who were experiencing setbacks at the polls sought to build bastions of tradition and conformity in the schools. These attempts to impose
orthodoxy on teachers took a number of forms, including the
enactment of teacher oaths, loyalty investigations, the firing of
radical instructors, restrictions on union activity, and attacks on
liberal textbooks.[13]

The journals, true to their tradition of defending free
thought, denounced these measures, particularly loyalty oaths,

which were the most publicized symbol of the new wave of repression. In 1935 *The Nation* reported the findings of the American Civil Liberties Union that the number of states imposing such oaths had grown in four years from six to twenty, and that behind the new laws were the Hearst press, the Daughters of the American Revolution, veterans' groups, fraternal lodges, and business associations.[14]

The weeklies gave particular attention to the fight against teacher oaths in such politically important states as Massachusetts. *The New Republic* pointed out the irony in a law that required instructors to swear allegiance to the constitution of Massachusetts, a document that guaranteed "the right of revolution—not once, but twice!" With tongue in cheek the editors added: "When we realize that the infamous members of the Massachusetts State Legislature are actually forcing thousands of innocent young teachers, male and female, to swear loyalty to these subversive sentiments, we get so mad we see blue. Is the State Legislature subsidized by Moscow gold?"[15]

The Nation, too, criticized—though more seriously—teacher oaths in Massachusetts and other states. It saw the oaths as exhibitions of "infantilism by our state legislatures" and regretted the decision of Harvard instructors to drop their fight against the oath. While university faculties, relatively protected in their exercise of academic freedom, might find the oath "too ridiculous to be worth resisting," teachers in small towns were much more vulnerable. College liberals should not drop their opposition, because, "since the teachers who have most to fear from red-baiting organizations are in no position to combat the oath, the responsibility obviously falls on the few whose positions are most secure."[16]

But loyalty oaths were only part of the challenge facing teachers. In 1934 *The Nation* alerted its readers to the beginning of a "renewed campaign to force teachers in schools to hew to the line of orthodoxy." The editors offered several items in evidence: six Toledo teachers had been warned that they would lose their jobs "unless they recanted their radicalism." (One had used a book by New Dealer Rexford Tugwell.) A principal had been dismissed in North Carolina for writing a novel that exposed school conditions. And teachers' college presidents in California had supported pledges of loyalty for students as well as for instructors. A month later the editors announced that the New York City Board of Examiners was instituting procedures for screening out subversive teachers. The steps taken were so alarming that the editors denounced them as a "virtual system of espionage."[17]

The attacks on freedom in the colleges came, according to the weeklies, from the same sources as those in the schools: from militarists, patrioteers, businessmen, and the yellow press. In 1931, while Hoover still presided over America's slide into economic chaos, Norman Thomas wrote a case study of the problems of one typical university. Thomas, leader of American socialists and a contributing editor of *The Nation*, saw Ohio State as a "splendid laboratory for the study of what has been called the 'hire learning' in America." The lineup in the case of Professor Herbert Miller was one readers were familiar with: on the side of the liberal angels was Miller, who had opposed compulsory military training, promoted advanced views on race relations, and expressed a sympathetic interest in Gandhi's fight for Indian freedom; on the other side was the conservative president of the trustees, Julius Stone, a leading Columbus industrialist, banker, and publisher.

According to Thomas, Stone and his allies ran the university as a "disguised economic dictatorship," which expected its students to be "docile Babbits in embryo, its university president to be a high-grade office manager, and its faculty to conform or get out." Under such a regime, the university could not rise above its usual level as "that annex to the stadium which we call the college campus in America."[18]

Throughout the decade journal readers were treated to such vigorous attacks on reactionary trustees and administrators and to praise for faculties and students who resisted pressures toward orthodoxy. George Counts was lauded in *The Nation* in 1935 for his exposure of the latest phase of "Hearst's perennial red-hunt."[19] In that same year, *The New Republic* denounced Rensselaer Polytechnic Institute for its dismissal of Granville Hicks, who—while an admitted Communist sympathizer—was "one of the shining lights of the English department." Such events were evidence that "the whole situation regarding civil liberties daily grows more tense."[20] The editors were similarly indignant at the failure of City College to reappoint Morris Schappes to the faculty. Schappes was an outstanding teacher and writer, but was a founder of the City College Teachers Union and had addressed a rally of student peace strikers, so was thus an embarrassment to the college administration.[21]

There were also instances in which the two main causes of protest—economic hardship and attacks on academic freedom—were explicitly joined. *The Nation* in 1935 alerted its readers to "Trouble in Paradise"—a situation in Westchester County where a 10 percent pay cut was imposed on teachers and where two instructors were dismissed for agitating to have their pay restored.[22] And Blanche Hofrichter of the Classroom Teachers Groups wrote to *The Nation* that the New York City superintendent, whose budget "carries on the policy of overcrowding classes, of ignoring the fifteen thousand unemployed teachers, and of taking no notice of the effect of five years of crisis on the health and well-being of the children," was also supporting a loyalty oath for teachers.[23]

Most of this was familiar material to regular journal readers, but during the 1930s three elements were at least partially new: first, the sheer quantity of material on teachers' problems—evidence of the effects of both depression and repression; second, where the journals had previously supported liberals and home-grown radicals, they now defended Communists and fellow-travelers as well; and third, although since 1918 both journals had backed teachers' unions, they were now supporting reality as well as rhetoric. The AFT was gaining members and assuming a new militancy, and the journals became deeply involved in the ideological struggles in the organization. Journal support for militant unions, along with the general liberal drift to a united front with Communists, led first to sympathy for Communist groups in the AFT and then, at the end of the decade, to hostility and resistance to such factions.[24]

The two journals tried to strengthen alliances of workers, intellectuals, civil servants, educators, racial minorities, and others who had been hurt by the Depression. Editorials, articles, and letters reminded these groups that they had grievances in common and that only coordinated political and economic action would enable them to better their condition. Teachers were urged to support political candidates who would aid their cause and to punish those who hurt them, to demand federal assistance when states and municipalities failed to meet their responsibilities, and to organize strong unions that would give them real power in their dealings with school committees, trustees, politicians, and the public.

Because of local peculiarities of politics and educational finance, the Chicago schools were among the first to suffer seriously from the Depression.[25] Many teachers lost their jobs, while those who kept their positions were plagued by large classes, pay cuts, and delayed salaries. After school staffs had gone unpaid for almost a year, the editors of *The Nation* in 1933 praised those teachers who had "staged an educational program of their own consonant with the modern 'learn by doing' formula." This had included a march by five thousand teachers on the city's banks, and another demonstration where teachers pulled down a flag which flaunted the now-ironic slogan of the World's Fair—"A Century of Progress." Unfortunately, the educational program was a two-way process, as the editorial noted that the teachers had received "an object lesson in civics from policemen's nightsticks."[26] When the teachers were finally given part of their back pay, *The Nation* carried an article by a Chicago teacher who declared that the teachers' own efforts, including the "thousands of letters, telegrams, and post cards to President Roosevelt did more than anything else" to get the loan passed.[27]

Letters to both journals called for further action of this sort. The Unemployed Teachers Association demanded that political parties support the maintenance of school budgets, relief for unemployed teachers, and reductions in class size, and announced meetings to protest "economic retrenchment in education."[28] The Classroom Teacher Groups called for pressure on New York's Governor Lehman and state senators to get them to provide needed school aid. And Eunice Langdon tied the whole program together in calling for "equalization of the tax burden . . . State and Federal aid . . . the strengthening of teachers' associations everywhere and determined action against false 'economies' . . . if the schools and the teaching profession are to be saved from disaster."[29]

But to the liberals associated with the journals, the major need was organization. Robert Morss Lovett, a member of *The New Republic*'s editorial board, presented an extravagant conception of the role of educators, claiming that "under democracy, even more than under communism, the teachers are the only crew that can work the ship of state." He advocated a reformist role for the schools, but noted that such a role could become a reality only "through an enlightened, radical and militantly organized teaching force, conscious of its power and its responsiblities, [and] capable of gaining the support of public opinion against the representatives of vested interests."[30]

The logical place to look for leadership in organizing educators should have been the National Education Association (NEA), the country's largest teacher organization. The liberal journals had, however, never put much faith in the NEA, which they saw as conservative and bureaucratic. But during the 1930s, as the NEA became occasionally more aggressive, the journals saw intermittent glimmers of hope for the organization. *The New Republic* observed at the 1936 NEA convention signs that teachers were beginning to realize their "humiliating position" under the thumbs of conservative school boards. The following year *The Nation* reported from the superintendents' convention that educators who ten years before had been a "peculiarly inert and submissive body of citizens" were now, "perhaps because of their experience with professional heresy-hunters . . . beginning to show courage and social intelligence."[31]

These were straws in the wind but did not represent the fundamental change in attitudes and organization the times required. The NEA might be somewhat more progressive than in the past, but it had not moved far enough to satisfy the liberal journalists. Their basic position was well summarized in a 1938 *Nation* editorial: "The N.E.A. . . . has proved a slow moving group, embodying all the inertias of the American social system. It is to American education what the A.F. of L. is to American labor. It has neither the educational vision of the Progressive Education Association nor the social militancy of the American Federation of Teachers."[32] *The New Republic* agreed with William Gellerman that progress for educators required "the formation of strong teachers' organizations, allied with labor and working groups, to offset the effects of the American Legion and its allies."[33] A decade earlier both journals had looked to labor education to join workers and educators in the promotion of their common interests; now the general union movement, embracing both blue-collar and professional workers, presented similar opportunities.[34]

For the liberal journalists, support for unions of teachers and professors was nothing new. During the 1920s they had promoted "industrial democracy" in the schools through teacher unions. But such unions made little progress during that decade, and in the 1930s the journals had the welcome opportunity of supporting a movement that seemed full of promise for success.

In 1931, on the fifteenth anniversary of the New York Teachers Union, *The Nation* extended its congratulations to the organization for its "consistently progressive educational and social program." The union was a welcome ally in a number of causes: it had supported improved educational programs and had fought witch-hunts, militarism, political control of the schools, and discrimination against minority teachers. The editors said that, although administrators might object to teachers' unions, "the close association of teachers with labor groups is a wholesome thing."[35]

The *New Republic* expressed similar sentiments. A 1936 article noted the impressive growth of the AFT from five thousand members in 1931 to twenty-four thousand in 1936. This was seen by the authors as part of a larger movement in which white-collar workers—musicians, journalists, and even ministers—had formed unions to protect their interests. Later that same year the editors reported on the convention of the AFT, noting that membership had soared and that special efforts were underway to organize college faculties and Works Progress Administration teachers. Under the new leadership of Jerome Davis, the editors looked for further gains by a teachers union "united, militant, and facing forward."[36]

The organization of college faculties met with considerable success, and by 1936 sixteen out of the two hundred AFT locals were on college campuses.[37] In forming unions, college instructors had the enthusiastic support of liberal journalists. In 1934 Villard asserted that college teachers "ought now to organize in unions, following the example of editorial writers and reporters." In proletarian rhetoric rather startling from a patrician liberal, he asked: "Is not this hour of revolution the time for them to demand representation upon the boards of trustees, to acquire some voice in how much freedom there shall be upon the university campuses and what shall be taught and not taught? Mr. Roosevelt declares that he is freeing industry from innumerable shackles. Why not strike a few from the wrists of university professors?"[38]

Journal advocacy of teacher unions was not, of course, an isolated phenomenon. *The Nation* and *The New Republic* were vigorously supporting the growth of the broader union movement throughout the country. With the encouragement of the Roosevelt administration, and bolstered by such measures as the Norris-LaGuardia Act (1932), section 7a of the National Industrial Recovery Act (1933), and the Wagner Act (1935), union membership was growing rapidly. The aggressive efforts of the Congress of Industrial Organizations (CIO) also gave a boost to union membership, which increased from under 3 million in 1933 to over 8 million in 1939.[39]

Communists were among the most active organizers and officers in some of the new and growing unions.[40] They were particularly effective in the American Federation of Teachers, especially in New York City and Philadelphia, and succeeded from 1936 to 1939 in taking virtual control of the union.[41] Thus even though, as Robert Iversen has written, "the control was not absolute," it was the Communist party's "most significant success in the A.F. of L."[42]

New York Local 5 of the AFT was plagued with factionalism for years, inspiring Abraham Lefkowitz, a leader of the anti-Communist group, to say: "Between the bankers and the Communists, we're having a hell of a time."[43] In October 1935, many of the non-Communist members resigned to form the New York Teachers Guild, leaving Local 5 firmly in the hands of the Communist group.[44] Throughout the controversy both factions used the pages of *The Nation* and *The New Republic* to try to build support for their positions. In 1935, for example, *The Nation* carried statements both by Lefkowitz and by the United Committee to Save the Union, representing the Communist elements. The Committee accused Lefkowitz and his group of red-baiting and the sin of dual unionism, and announced that his charges would be "refuted in the daily press and in the columns of liberal periodicals."[45]

Although the journals did not at this point attempt to answer Lefkowitz's accusations categorically, for a period of several years—as part of their popular front position—they first downplayed Communist influence and then supported pro-Communist factions, both in the AFT and in other unions.[46] In 1936 both journals praised the AFT convention's refusal to follow the advice of the American Federation of Labor (AFL) and eject Local 5. In early 1939, when the AFT was rocked by a struggle between pro-Communist and anti-Communist factions, *The New Republic* carried an article by AFT president Jerome Davis, denouncing attacks on his organization by a "miscellaneous assortment of sharpshooters stretching from the Dies Committee all the way to John L. Childs of Teachers' College, Columbia University." Davis declared "with complete assurance that the charges of communist control" of the AFT were untrue. In any case, he said, the union need not be concerned about the political activities of its members, and he asserted that "every teacher has the right to be a Republican, Democrat, Socialist, Communist, or support any other party."[47]

The editors found Davis's argument persuasive. To them the AFT was a "power for enlightenment and American principles," which deserved the "loyalty and united action of all its members." They believed, with Davis, that the Federation was "an efficient and progressive trade union, not led or influenced by Communists." This editorial absolution called forth a vigorous response from George W. Hartmann of Columbia University, who offered considerable evidence of Communist control of the union. He noted also that a number of outstanding liberals, including John Dewey, Harold Rugg, Louis Hacker, and John Childs, had resigned because of Communist factionalism, and called attention to George Counts's recent *Social Frontier* article exposing Communist damage to the union.[48]

Hartmann noted that the AFT's struggle with Communists was not an isolated phenomenon, but part of a larger battle in which the entire labor movement was engaged. And he rejected the "superstition of many liberals that any critique of Stalinist tactics means that one is an agent of the Dies Committee." He closed with the hope that "Dr. Davis, The New Republic, or anyone else who is disposed to 'whitewash' the present Union administration in New York will first make a thorough and independent inquiry" into the situation.[49]

But neither *The Nation* nor *The New Republic*, committed as they were to maintaining the united front, was disposed to undertake such an investigation. The journals carried letters from John Childs, Leo Huberman, and others on both sides of the dispute, but failed to deal seriously with the issue of control of the local by Communists and their allies.[50]

■

The timing of the Hitler-Stalin Pact could not have been worse for the Communists and fellow-travelers in the American Federation of Teachers. The Pact was signed on 23 August 1939 while the AFT was holding its annual convention, and was probably what gave anti-Communist George Counts his narrow margin of victory over Communist-supported incumbent president Jerome Davis.[51] Amidst the liberal shock and embarrassment over the Pact, the journals completely ignored this important event in the union's history. Not until the Pact and its aftereffects had begun to reorient their whole political perspective did the journals slowly begin to take the offensive against Communist influence in the AFT and in the labor movement generally.[52] And only after the anti-Communists had begun to achieve some success in their struggle with the Communist faction in the AFT did the journals offer them belated words of encouragement.

In early 1941 *The New Republic* admitted at last that several AFT locals had been "dominated by the Stalinists, whose activities had been designed to aid the Communist movement, whatever the effect might be on the organization." The editors had come to realize that "it is impossible for a working trade union to continue with a large minority which is unscrupulously resolved to serve only the purposes of a single foreign country, even at the risk of destroying the union." And they cited in defense of their position the testimony of a group that included John Dewey, Reinhold Niebuhr, and John Childs—who, after several years of struggle against the Stalinists, may have had mixed feelings about the support finally offered them by *The New Republic*.[53]

The Nation now also jumped with equal enthusiasm onto the anti-Communist bandwagon, and approved the action of the AFT executive council in seeking expulsion of the Communist locals: "If a majority of the members of the union sustain the council, the A.F. of L. will with one sweeping gesture have rid itself of a growth which has been sapping it internally and exposing it to attack from without."[54] And when the Communist locals were finally expelled, both journals expressed their satisfaction at the outcome. *The New Republic* hoped that the shift away from Communist influence might continue and that "within a few months the A.F.T. will be in a position to assure the people of the United States that no part of its organization is dominated by fanatical foes of democracy and the democratic process." *The Nation* agreed that the previous Communist domination had been "intolerable" and that the expulsion of the offending locals was clearly justified.[55]

There was of course the possibility that the newly awakened journals, in order to expiate their past political sins, might demand harsh and even undemocratic treatment for their former Communist allies, but this did not occur. Both weeklies insisted that the purge of the Communists should be carried out fairly and that the rights of innocent teachers should be protected. *The New Republic* welcomed the "democratic action that puts the final decision where it should be, in the hands of the whole membership." *The Nation* proposed that the union set up a committee to weed out "party-liners," and when the union adopted just such a policy, declared that "the desperate remedy seems to us justified" and hoped that it would effectively keep out the Stalinists without hurting those members who were above suspicion.[56]

Both journals insisted that purging the Communists was a job for the union itself. The editors criticized the Rapp-Coudert Committee of the New York legislature, which, among other offenses, had seized lists of union members. This was an act of intimidation intended not just as a blow at the Stalinists but as "an attack on the union itself." When the probe reached New York City colleges, *The New Republic* proposed that the city Board of Higher Education establish a committee of respected educators to investigate not questions of belief—as indicated by party membership—but individual "performance in objective and creative teaching."[57]

This proposal appealed to liberal AFT officials like union vice-president Mark Starr, who wrote: "I only hope that we can set up the group of scholars suggested by you and not leave the investigation to the mixed motivation and dubious methods of such a political body as the Coudert Committee."[58] Starr's praise for *The New Republic*'s position suggests that in the eyes of some of their former allies the liberal journalists had come home again. They were, after a drift to the far left, back in the familiar position of opposing doctrinaire positions at both ends of the political spectrum. They had rejoined men like Dewey, Childs, and Starr, who had maintained all along that the true liberal—to be consistent and effective—must oppose Stalinism as vigorously as fascism.

In April 1941, *The Nation* printed a letter from Max Kline which puts much of this controversy in perspective: "Your recent comments on Communists and Unions were amusing and irritating. You wrote on March 1, for example, that "until two weeks ago this blight (i.e., Communist influence in the Teachers Union) was treated pretty much in the spirit of Mark Twain's remark about the weather. Everybody talked about it but nobody did anything."

Kline then reviewed the efforts, going back to 1932, of men

like himself and Dewey to rid the AFT of Communist factionalism. He reminded the editors of the founding of the Teachers Guild in 1935 when efforts failed to wrest control of Local 5 from the Communists. He then asked the logical question:

> Now, between 1933 and 1935, did we get the support of the *Nation*, the *Post*, and other organs of liberal opinion? Quite the contrary. It was explained in those journals that we were impatient with minority opinion, that we were seeking to retain power by undemocratic methods, that we were "red-baiting," etc. The *Nation*, with its tremendous influence among liberals, could have assisted us in our struggle against the well-organized program and unscrupulous tactics of the Communists in our union. But in those days the *Nation* and the *Post* were catering to the party line.[59]

Kline might well have included *The New Republic* and extended the time period to 1939. In any case, the editors made no response to his charges. In fact, neither journal so much as mentioned what was glaringly apparent to Kline and others— their dramatic shift from backing a united front with the Communists to support for the expulsion of Communist-dominated locals from the AFT. The editors may well have been embarrassed that an alliance between communism and nazism in Europe should have caused the breakup of a liberal-Communist alliance in America. Or perhaps they assumed that the reason for their shift away from sympathy for communism was too obvious to require discussion. At any rate, men like Kline no doubt felt quite justified in asking, in effect: "Where were you when we needed you most?" and in expressing irritation at *The Nation*'s unexplained return to a policy of democratic liberalism.

Thus, with some understandable carping from those who had kept the liberal faith, the journals belatedly joined people like Dewey who had much earlier seen through communism's democratic facade. But how shall we explain the journals' earlier fall from liberal grace—their tenacious conviction that "you can do business with ideologues"? On the domestic front, both journals sought during the Depression to maintain pressure from the left on the Roosevelt administration, and in so doing were quite willing to join forces with all those, including Communists, who seemed to share their views. In the foreign sphere, the liberals had an abiding horror of the fascist dictatorships that successively took power in Italy, Germany, and Spain. While the democracies wavered in the face of the fascist threat, the liberal journalists believed that Russia was providing the only effective opposition. *The Nation* and *The New Republic* were occasionally critical of denials of liberty in Russia, but managed to convince themselves that life was better than under the tyranny of the czars, and that Russia was gradually transforming itself into a prosperous liberal state.

This was the larger context in which American liberals pursued their united front effort in the 1930s.[60] And such considerations had particular force in the journals' policies on labor. The organization of both blue-collar and professional workers seemed at long last possible in the 1930s. *The Nation* and *The New Republic* had little faith in the ability of old-line leaders in the AFL to organize the unorganized, and the break with the CIO in 1936 seemed evidence enough of the failure of the conservative unionists. By contrast, the Communists were proving to be very successful labor organizers. They were able not only to bring workers into the unions, but to form them into militant, effective units in the organizations. In 1938 *The New Republic* admitted that within the unions, because of Communist "zeal and ability, the number of offices that they hold is out of proportion to their numerical strength."[61] After its break with the united front, *The Nation* made a similar, though grudging, admission. In a comparison neither group would have welcomed, it referred to the Communists as the "Tammany Hall of the labor movement," and added that "they have the discipline, the zeal, the central boards of strategy, and above all the political axes to grind" to be effective.[62]

But this suggested the problem in the journals' positions. While praising the Communists for their organizing ability and holding that labor needed the Communists for that reason, the journals ignored the other half of the equation: that the Communists needed and used the unions for their own purposes as well. For several years the journals seemed to feel that the Communists were just strong enough to help the unions, but not quite powerful enough to injure them. Thus, on 24 August 1939 (in an issue that went to press before the Hitler-Stalin Pact), *The New Republic* had declared that "no important part of the labor movement is now in danger from the Reds." If labor leaders made "use of a few Communists for union work, we may be sure it is because the persons in question are able and conscientious trade-unionists who do not allow party politics to interfere with their jobs."[63]

William O'Neill has noted ironically that "on no point were liberals more sharply divided than over the need for unity."[64] The liberal journals had a deep anxiety over disunity on the left and hesitated to denounce the Communists for fear of strengthening the hands of conservative forces. Thus, in early 1939 *The New Republic*, in opposing AFL vice president Matthew Woll's attack on the AFT, asked: "Isn't it time for intelligent people to realize that the red bogey is useful only to blackshirts and brownshirts and their allies?" *The Nation*, out of a similar fear of the fascist right, was also reluctant to draw lines between left-wing groups. Its editors argued against taking a first step against Communists for fear that this might lead inexorably to a fourth step to reaction. Thus, while admitting that unions might well be watchful of various brands of factionalism, the editors felt that the current campaign against Communists was perilous. For "once you begin attacking Communists as such, your next step . . . is to attack progressives for 'following the line.' The step after that . . . is to attack all progressives. And beyond that looms a reactionary trade-union movement."[65]

With such a domino theory of politics, it is understandable that the journals would emphasize the similarities of Communists to other groups. The editors of *The New Republic* sought in 1938 to make the attack on Communists appear absurd by declaring them no less worthy of union benefits than "Republicans or New Dealers or Townsendites or adherents of Father Divine."[66] Such a statement perhaps gives as much insight as any into the positions of the journals: they trivialized the Communist threat to the unions. The Communists were at best a militant organizing force and at worst a factional irritant. But at any rate they were seen as no more of a danger to unions than were members of major parties or bizarre political and religious sects.

By 1941, however, *The New Republic* could admit, concerning the AFT, that "the widespread reports of Communist domination in these locals, going back many years, have enormously weakened the movement for trade unionism among teachers." And *The Nation* could refer to the need for protecting those union "innocents, who are the easiest prey of the 'militant'

Communists."[67] If the journalists had any feeling that the terms "naive" or "innocents" might earlier have applied to themselves, they did not betray it. They had followed their liberal lights where they led, analyzed with good journalistic sense the economic and political pressures on teachers, and called, reasonably enough, for vigorous organizations to advance the interests of educators. But they had dissipated their energy and some of their influence among educators and others by failing to oppose those factions in the AFT that were less interested in educational reform than in supporting Russia's tortuously shifting foreign policy.

There is irony enough in the picture of liberals fleeing from fascists into the arms of authoritarians of the left; that irony is deepened when the failure to defend liberalism occurred in education—the field in which free inquiry and expression are most fundamental. When the Stalinist enemies of free thought were clamping their hold on an influential group of American teachers, *The Nation* and *The New Republic* were painfully slow to come to the aid of the beleaguered non-Communists in the union. The liberal journals, which had usually shown sound insights into a variety of educational developments, missed the opportunity in the 1930s to promote a truly independent and free teachers union. In all their educational concerns over the years, this was doubtless their greatest failure: that for a time during the Great Depression, *The Nation* and *The New Republic* sacrificed the interests of unions and educators to what they saw as the imperatives of international politics.[68]

12

Revolt on the Campus

James Wechsler, who became a liberal hero in 1953 for his defense against Joseph McCarthy's attacks on freedom of the
press, once wrote that "all newspapermen like to believe that
they were born with the scent of printer's ink about them."[1] If
Wechsler had a genetic predisposition toward journalism, he
thought he might have inherited it from his paternal grand-
father, Rabbi Moshe Wechsler, who had edited a Jewish newspaper in his native Hungary, and who, after migrating to
America, worked for the first American Jewish daily and went
on to start his own crusading paper, *The Jewish Times*. James
Wechsler later speculated: "Possibly then, that is how the fra-
grance of the print shop was transmitted to me."[2]

James Wechsler wasted no time getting into journalism. At
the age of eleven, in summer camp, he became editor of *The
Chicopee Chirp*. He recalled modestly: "I was the only aspirant
for the post and the renown associated with it was a sublimation
for my deficiencies at bat."[3] His rebellious tendencies first became noticeable when he was fired from the editorship of *The*

Revolt on the Campus (New York: Covici-Friede, 1935) was the title of James Wechsler's
study of student activism. The book was considered of sufficient historical significance
that it was republished in 1973 with a new introduction by the author (Seattle: University of Washington Press).

Stadium, the student newspaper at New York's elite Townsend Harris High School, for sneaking past the faculty censors a front-page editorial denouncing the power-hungry teachers.[4]

So it was understandable that, as a precocious sixteen-year-old freshman at Columbia University, Wechsler would in 1931 join the staff of the Columbia *Spectator*. And, given his energy, intelligence, and commitment to journalism, it was not surprising that at the end of his junior year he would become the editor. In that role and through the various activities to which it led, Wechsler became a central figure in the campus revolt of the 1930s. Much of the history of the student movement of that period and of its relationship to liberal journalism can be traced through Wechsler's experiences and writings.

Wechsler's career in college journalism began when America was in the grip of its worst depression, and he and his fellow writers could not ignore what was happening around their urban campus. In November 1931, one of the *Spectator* editors visited New York City soup lines and, to bring the reality of the Depression home to students, noted that among the hungry he had found "graduates of the leading universities—some members of the class of 1931, and others of classes not much older. . . . Yet these men a short while ago left college filled with ambitions of a type so high that only a newly graduated and naive senior could conceive of them."[5]

An "Ode to Higher Education," published in another college paper at this time made the same point more briefly:

> I sing in praise of college,
> Of M.A.'s and Ph.D.'s,
> But in pursuit of knowledge
> We are starving by degrees.[6]

Depression at home and the growing specter of fascism abroad led Wechsler to combine his journalism with activism. The most politically effective groups on campus were the Communists, so—like a number of his fellow undergraduates—Wechsler joined in the strikes and rallies they helped organize. By the spring of his junior year he had joined the Young Communist League, and in his senior year, as editor of *The Spectator*, he achieved some notoriety for his well-publicized left-wing views.[7]

Weschsler was the most prominent of the student activists

of this period, but he was far from alone. During the 1930s many American college students abandoned the self-indulgent campus ethos of the 1920s and threw their energies into a bewildering array of groups and causes.[8] Some of their new organizations went through a cycle that was replicated in many leftist groups during this period: from initial organization, to growth and militancy, through a "popular front" stage, to Communist domination, and finally, in late 1939, to the collapse of the popular front and, in some cases, to the dissolution of the organizations themselves.[9]

The Nation and *The New Republic,* continuing their long-standing interests in both journalism and education, followed these developments closely. And their responses to the student rebellion paralleled their reactions to the union movement. In the early 1930s they cheered from the sidelines as students took the first tentative steps toward forming aggressive and socially conscious organizations. In mid-decade they supported the popular front with the Communists in the American Youth Congress and the American Student Union. And finally, after the Hitler-Stalin Pact, they applauded as youth organizations broke the hold of the doctrinaire Marxists and moved back into the mainstream of pragmatic liberalism.[10]

The support given by the liberal journals to the student movement, particularly at the beginning of the decade, was stated in terms of reformist objectives. *The Nation* and *The New Republic* were continually seeking allies in their fight for progressive causes, and thus encouraged various groups, including youth organizations, to work for economic justice, peace, racial progress, and more realistic and effective education.[11]

Some of the earliest journal editorials on this subject focused on educational institutions and processes. The weeklies were pleased to see students protesting against the irrelevant education that was offered to them in most colleges. Thus in May 1931, the editors of *The Nation* praised a Yale undergraduate publication, *The Harkness Hoot,* for its caustic critique of academic rigidity and conservatism and for exposing the "paucity of intellectual and social interest" in the college. This might be seen as a rather parochial matter, but the editors placed it in a larger context:

The indictment has importance far beyond the academic limits of Yale. It matters a good deal to our national life that a great university . . . should seem to its thoughtful undergraduates to have done so little to develop the proper function of a university and subordinated intellectual enrichment to academic formalism, grandiloquent notions of organizing the incongruous, and material display. The revolt of youth against the education that is offered to it is a warning of intellectual discontent which no university can afford to ignore, for unless such evils as have been courageously exposed at Yale are done away with, the revolt is likely to carry far and wide.[12]

Such criticisms of the conservatism of the colleges were common in the journals. Just two weeks earlier, for example, *The Nation* had observed that "the percentage of ignorance among our graduates is high enough to maintain a good working Republican majority."[13]

Obviously, academic irrelevance and the other ills that aroused the ire of student editors and liberal journalists did not disappear, and the "revolt of youth," the journalists predicted was underway. The rebellion did not, of course, restrict itself to the internal problems of the colleges. It soon became a political force, seeking not only educational change but economic, social, and racial reform as well. And this broader movement naturally received vigorous encouragement from the liberal journals.

In June 1931, *The Nation* indulged in its perennial polemic on the occasion of college commencements. The editors noted the stirrings of liberalism and criticism among students but feared that as usual most of the "degree-bearing host" would go into business or the professions, become apathetic and conservative, and leave the country worse off than they had found it. America's great need was for a "stalwart, aggressive, self-conscious youth movement. It needs a sense of solidarity among its young intellectuals, its novelists, poets, dramatists, critics, artists, and scientists, not merely for the advancement of learning or various forms of art, but for the betterment of a dull, unthinking, and leaderless people."[14]

The editors' hopes for student activism were soon realized. In 1932, the Communist-dominated National Student League (NSL) joined the field with older organizations like the National Student Federation (NSF) and the socialist Student League for Industrial Democracy (SLID).[15] Radicals like Sherwood

Anderson, Roger Baldwin, Max Eastman, and Michael Gold used the correspondence columns of *The New Republic* to drum up adult support for the new group.[16] *The Nation*, drawing on articles in the Yale *Daily News*, backed the action of the Yale NSL in joining the picket line in a New Haven foundry strike and denounced the efforts of a dean to discourage such involvement. The editors noted the educational implications of the situation, commenting that Yale was "doubtless offering courses in sociology and economics. Where is there a better place for a direct application of the theories being taught in the classroom than in the town where the college is located?"[17]

But it was the militancy and social consciousness of the student groups, rather than their sometimes doctrinaire programs, that held the most appeal for the liberal journalists. In 1934 *The Nation* carried an analysis of the whole student movement, from its conservative to its radical fringes, which was somewhat critical of the divisive tactics of the Communist groups. The author, Seldon Rodman, predicted correctly that such tactics would be self-defeating: "The orthodox Marxist romanticizes the industrial worker and fails to understand the psychological prejudices of the American from any class. The strange terminology and sentimental internationalism, the rigid adherence to doctrines no longer fresh or modified realistically to fit modern conditions, make it impossible for them either to appeal to the reason of new human material or to fire the imagination."[18]

But in spite of such critiques, the pressing desire for unity on the left encouraged some writers for the journals to support a united front of Communists and socialists. James Wechsler, who had graduated four months earlier from Columbia, wrote for *The New Republic* in October 1935 a plea for the emerging American Student Union (ASU). Reflecting the new popular front line, he said that the ASU was trying to bring together socialists, Communists, and others in a "common front on palpably acute issues." This joining of radical forces seemed to Wechsler "utterly sensible," for "when war and reaction are the order of the day, those dedicated to averting them are coming to realize that questions of ultimate social reorganization must not remain barriers."[19]

Wechsler's journalistic experiences had helped him become a rapid, fluent writer, and during the summer of 1935, following his graduation from Columbia, he wrote his first book, *Revolt on the Campus.* The book was published that fall and was recognized, both at the time and later, as one of the key documents of the student movement of the 1930s.[20] Support from liberal journalists was indicated in the introduction by Robert Morss Lovett, a member of the editorial board of *The New Republic*. Lovett noted that three developments had inspired the revolt that Wechsler analyzed: the reaction against World War I; the "example of the Soviet Union"; and the Depression. He mildly criticized Wechsler for being unfair to some college administrators but said that the book should be taken seriously by "those of us who have had the responsibility of college teachers during these late crucial years." He denounced violent efforts to suppress the student movement and said that "undoubtedly a responsibility rests upon those of us who welcome the campus revolt as a hopeful sign for the future, to discourage practices which have no objective except provocation to disorder and reprisals."[21]

The New Republic carried a review of the book that accurately summarized the topics Wechsler covered: "protest against war, compulsory military drill and gag-censorship; against racial discrimination and industrial oppression." The reviewer, Edgar Johnson, said that Wechsler wrote "with a skill and forcefulness that make it a brilliant and often impassioned piece of reporting." He observed that Wechsler included "a few doctrinaire distortions," but that it was nonetheless "a brave, generous-hearted and intelligent job." And he concluded that "the cross-section it gives of American youth struggling for its beliefs, often in defiance of genuine risks and dangers, should inspire all liberals—and sometimes arouse their shame."[22]

When the American Student Union actually got underway in December 1935, Robert Morss Lovett and *Nation* editor Freda Kirchwey agreed to serve on its Advisory Committee.[23] And *New Republic* editor Bruce Bliven wrote the preface for the first book published by the new group, *War Our Heritage*, by Wechsler and Joseph Lash, the socialist executive secretary of the new organization.[24] Thus the liberal journalists demonstrated in several ways that at this point their support for a united front with activist students outweighed any fears they might have had of Communist factionalism or domination.

Until his graduation in 1934, Hal Draper was the chairman of the socialist group at Brooklyn College, which he later described as "probably the most highly politicalized college in the country."[25] Looking back on that exciting period after thirty years, Draper recalled the issues that had fired the activism of the student groups: "(1) Anti-war activity and opposition to compulsory ROTC. (2) Violations of academic freedom and student rights on campus. (3) Issues involving economic aid to students . . . (4) Reforms of college administrations . . . (5) Aid to the labor movement [and] (6) Anti-fascist activity."[26] Focusing on these concerns, the student groups conducted a variety of projects, the best-publicized of which were the annual spring peace strikes. These mass demonstrations, drawing on disillusionment with World War I and on fear of another conflict, involved as many as 500,000 students on over 130 campuses throughout the country.[27] The liberal journalists continued to encourage such activities and to support their radical younger colleagues. But even at the height of the popular front movement there were signs that the leftist coalition was beginning to come apart.

During the summer of 1937, James and Nancy Wechsler took a group of college students on a tour of Europe, including a trip to Russia. The combined impact of the Moscow Trials and the disillusioning weeks in the Soviet Union led Wechsler and his wife to leave the Young Communist League four months after their return.[28] Following a brief but depressing period of unemployment, and after assuring the managing editor that he had broken with the Communists, Wechsler took a job with *The Nation*.[29]

Other student activists took longer to give up their Communist affiliations, but the Hitler-Stalin Pact of August 1939 helped many of them make up their minds. In December of that year Wechsler analyzed in *The Nation* those forces which had led to the establishment of the popular front and had given the Communists such power within it. The ASU, according to Wechsler, was "made possible by the coincidence of Communist realism and anti-fascist sentiment on the campus." The members of the ASU "agreed that the Union's most important mission was to arouse and organize critical student thought; and its preoccupations ranged from the Spanish war to curricular reform."

The power of the Communist groups in the ASU was explained not by their numbers but by their organization and militancy: "The Communist students act as a unified bloc in the elections of delegates; they hold important posts in the Union's district apparatus because they are willing to do the difficult and unrewarding postgraduate work of organization."[30] But by early 1941, the ASU, though still Communist-dominated, had been seriously weakened by defections. Both *The Nation* and *The New Republic* hailed the growth of a free, pragmatic, non-doctrinaire student movement. *The New Republic* admitted that "in the early years of the depression the Communists did a good job of helping young people to shake themselves out of their traditional lethargy, in college and out." But, they added, "the cost was high—a commitment to the Communist leadership of the ASU and the American Youth Congress." The Nazi-Soviet pact and the war had now motivated youth groups to break the hold of the Communists on their organizations.[31] Thus non-Communist youth groups such as the International Student Service (ISS) were, with the guidance of liberals like Alvin Johnson, beginning to attain the ascendancy. (Johnson, who had been associated with both *The New Republic* and *The Nation*, was chair of the ISS executive board.)[32] But, as in the case of so many other leftist organizations, only cataclysmic international events had encouraged the youth movement and its liberal journalistic allies to finally make the break with the popular front.[33]

It was clear to the journalists that the shifts within the youth movement were part of this larger pattern. Robert Spivack wrote in 1941: "Trends of thought and action among progressive young people are in many respects analogous to recent developments in the labor movement."[34] And the motivations of the liberal journalists were similar in their responses to both unions and student groups. They thought that the interests of society, of labor, of students, and of reform generally would be served by militant organizations. They hoped that student groups would be progressive forces within the schools and colleges and would help institutions develop more relevant curricula and programs. But they also wanted such groups to go beyond purely institutional, internal, educational matters. They encouraged them to extend their influence into domestic and international politics and to use their numbers and their organizational powers to fight fascism, racism, war, and depression.[35] And it was here that the difficulty began. Some of the liberal journalists assisted in the development of movements in which Communists soon gained the upper hand and in which they turned the organizations to the purposes of Russia's foreign policy rather than of education and reform. But finally, after the shocks of the Moscow Trials and the Hitler-Stalin Pact, the journalists encouraged the return of students and teachers to liberal, nondogmatic—but nonetheless militant— organizations.

■

Contemporary participants and observers as well as later scholars have attested to the crucial role played by student journalists in defining, developing, and promoting the "revolt of youth." From the right, William Randolph Hearst asserted that "Red Radicalism has planted a soapbox on every campus of America." In response, Saul Bellow and Isaac Rosenfeld placed Hearst's statement on the masthead of their Socialist Club newspaper at the University of Chicago, and obligingly titled the paper *Soapbox*.[36] Reporters for Henry Luce's conservative *Fortune* magazine visited a number of campuses in the mid-1930s and noted that "college newspapers are often far to the left of the undergraduate bodies."[37] From the left, Joseph Lash, national secretary of the Communist-dominated American Student Union, claimed in 1936: "The majority of college papers are edited by ASU people and utilize the ASU programs as the basis for editorial policy."[38] (*The Student Advocate*, the monthly paper of the ASU, was edited by Wechsler in 1936–1937 and then by Lash, and achieved a circulation of 30,000.[39]) Ralph Brax, in his 1981 assessment of the student movement, confirms that "while activists were a minority on most campuses, they comprised the editorial staffs of a disproportionate number of college newspapers."[40]

The editors of *The Nation* and *The New Republic* were impressed by the role of student journalists in the youth movement and gave them considerable attention and encouragement. Much of the material the journals printed about student activities was gleaned from the pages of student newspapers and magazines. The weeklies cited items from the Yale *Daily News*, the Harvard *Crimson*, the Columbia *Spectator*, *The Harkness Hoot*, the *Daily Illini*, and other campus periodicals and praised college editors for their vigorous support of radical causes. *The Nation* even included Columbia's James Wechsler in its "Honor Roll for 1934" for his "able and courageous journalistic attack on all forms of reaction at the university."[41]

This support for radical campus newspapers was, of course, just one aspect of the larger alliance liberal journalists were trying to forge with various groups, including the student movement. But it is not surprising that the personnel of *The Nation* and *The New Republic* should have taken a particular interest in the work of their young activist colleagues on campus publications. Some of them, like Bruce Bliven, Freda Kirchwey, and Robert Morss Lovett, had been campus journalists themselves.[42] They identified with college journalists and recognized the key role student editors could play in promoting activism in the colleges. The militant young journalists seemed to be in the forefront of the American radical movement. *The Nation* and *The New Republic* saw in student publications and in the movement they served useful instruments of social and educational progress.

As the liberal journalists became clearer about Stalinist threats to free inquiry and a free press, they then gave belated support to efforts by student journalists to throw off their ideological chains. James Wechsler, writing four months after the Hitler-Stalin Pact, reported that the Harvard *Crimson*, which previously had been sympathetic to the Communist-dominated American Student Union, had warned against a "whitewash of Soviet policy." And he criticized Communist abuse of Joseph Lash—the other leading young activist and journalist of the period—who could not accept the "mass mind-changing" required of loyal fellow-travelers and who had broken with his fellow radicals and denounced the Nazi-Communist pact.[43]

On 18 May 1940, *The Nation* reported that "James Wechsler, for two years a valued member of *The Nation*'s staff, has accepted a position as assistant labor editor of *PM*, New York's long-heralded, eagerly awaited afternoon newspaper. We are sorry to lose Mr. Wechsler, who in addition to his editorial duties has contributed several of the most striking articles printed in *The Nation* in the last two years."[44] Wechsler left *The Nation* bothered "by that ancient disease of liberal journalism—the feeling that we were talking to ourselves, and to those who agreed with us," and hoped that through *PM* he could reach a wider audience.[45] He struggled with Communists and fellow-travelers on that newspaper and in the Newspaper Guild and, following a brief period of military service, took a job with the liberal New York *Post*. He moved on to become editor, and used the editorial page for equally vigorous attacks on Stalinism and later on McCarthyism. This led to his celebrated appearance before McCarthy's committee and his impassioned counterattack on McCarthy for his thinly veiled attempts to inhibit press criticism of his committee.

These experiences led Wechsler to write his autobiography, *The Age of Suspicion*, and to reflect on his student experiences in the 1930s. In the prologue to the book Wechsler denied the inevitability of the idea—for which there was more than enough evidence during the McCarthy era—"that young radicals become old conservatives, as if this were an inevitable life pattern. . . . If it is true that some former communists have become more dogmatically rightist than the reactionaries they once spurned, if some have even become sympathizers of a domestic neo-fascism almost as intolerant, inhumane, and irrational as Stalinism, there are countless former communists who have unostentatiously embraced the calmer credo of democratic liberalism. They have tried to retain a sense of identification with the oppressed and the unfortunate. . . . And they have cherished the one piece of wisdom which the communist experience inadvertently imparts—an appreciation of the grandeur of the free mind and the wretchedness of the man who has abdicated his own reason."[46]

In 1973, when *Revolt on the Campus* was republished, Wechsler wrote a new introduction that continued to argue for responsible student involvement: "I know it has long been fashionable to assume that the activist undergraduate is some kind of a psychological freak; one might argue at least as convincingly that education is an unrewarding sedative if its model specimens are those who do not give a damn, or have acquired the spurious maturity of cynical disengagement. . . . In so far as we were moved then, as other young men and women are now, by an impulse 'to comfort the afflicted and afflict the comfortable,' I should like to believe that many of us were engaged in something more meaningful than ego-trips. Many of us were to move from those days of dogma toward a democratic humanism to which we still adhere. In doing so we have perhaps at least refuted the smug bromide that young radicals are hopelessly destined to become aged reactionaries."[47]

13

A New Deal for Youth

John Kazarian went broke while job-hunting in Los Angeles in 1933, so, like thousands of the unemployed, he joined "the starvation army"—the homeless wanderers who moved from town to town seeking work, a handout, a place to sleep. The Depression, although it hit hardest at the poor, also caught many educated middle-class people like Kazarian in its web.[1] But Kazarian made the best of a bad situation and turned his experiences into a graphic, depressing series of three articles for *The Nation*.[2]

Kazarian described the men, women, children, and families he encountered in his travels: a tough ten-year-old boy bumming cigarettes and bragging about his success as a panhandler; a twenty-five-year-old woman who had quarrelled with her family and was on her way to Florida hoping for a job as a waitress or secretary; a young construction worker with his wife and six-month-old baby hitchhiking from town to town looking for work; a "distinguished-looking man with pince-nez and white hair" who shared with Kazarian the newspapers that made up his "Hoover mattress"; a "red-faced Scotchman with

This chapter takes its title from that of Betty and Ernest Lindley's book on the National Youth Administration, *A New Deal for Youth* (New York: Viking, 1938).

blue eyes that looked sad and disappointed" who had been on the road for two years, but who had—out of embarrassment— kept his miserable situation hidden from his daughter.

Among the wanderers were many young people. Some had dropped out of school because their families could not support them; others had lost jobs or had never been able to find any. Kazarian met "B" when they were stacking used periodicals in the Salvation Army workroom in Richmond, Virginia. B's father, the family's sole support, had died the previous year, and his older brother was taking care of their mother. He was on his way to New York City. Kazarian asked "Why New York?" The young man replied: "What difference does it make where a fellow goes? One place is about as good as another for a man on the bum."

Kazarian encountered "A" at the YMCA in Wilmington, Delaware. "He was young, sensitive, intelligent." He told Kazarian: "If only I could get a job, so I wouldn't have to beg any more. Men like us aren't human beings. We're animals, just like rats, hunting for food and shelter while the law isn't looking. . . . If I have to bum people for my existence much longer I'm going to get in with some gang and get some cash. I'm not afraid if I'm with a gang."

Descriptions such as these were published by *The Nation* and *The New Republic*, and similar ones reached far larger audiences in newspapers and mass circulation magazines. They helped arouse in the American people—and in their political representatives—the classic responses of pity and terror: pity for the helpless victims of the Depression and terror at the threats of violence and disruption that these wandering thousands seemed to present.[3]

Among the earliest pieces of legislation Roosevelt sent to Congress was one that was "close to his own heart" and a direct reaction to the problem of unemployed and wandering youth: a bill for the establishment of the Civilian Conservation Corps (CCC).[4] The bill, which became law less than a month after Roosevelt took office, provided for the creation of conservation camps for unemployed young men between the ages of eighteen and twenty-five.[5] But the CCC program helped only those youth who could leave home and live in the camps, so two years later, Roosevelt created, by executive order, the National Youth Administration (NYA) to give work relief to high school, college, and graduate students, as well as some out-of-school youth.[6]

These two programs—the CCC and the NYA—were the New Deal's major efforts to deal with the specific problems of youth. As such, they had the overwhelming support of the country at large, and in particular of activist liberals who had long advocated governmental solutions to social and economic problems. It was natural that liberal journalists should support such federal programs. Unlike many more conservative Americans, the writers who spoke through *The Nation* and *The New Republic* had no reluctance to call on the national government to meet pressing social needs. Indeed, Arthur Schlesinger, Jr., has identified Herbert Croly, *The New Republic*'s founder, and John Dewey, longtime contributing editor, as two of the four intellectuals who helped develop the philosophy on which the New Deal was based.[7]

Thus the support the liberal journals gave to federal action for youth, as for other people in need, was more than an *ad hoc* response to the crisis of the Depression; it was an outgrowth of a basic political philosophy that welcomed collective solutions to national problems. That philosophy had found little public support during the conservative 1920s; now it was seen as relevant—in fact necessary—not only by liberal intellectuals but by many politicians and their constituents.

An exploration of liberal journalists' responses to the CCC and the NYA may help illuminate some of the relationships between New Deal programs and their supporters and critics. It may also clarify some of the continuing interaction between political liberalism and educational developments and show that liberals—while preoccupied with the massive economic problems facing the country—continued to see education as part of a larger program of reform. And, given the persistence of youth unemployment in America, with all its related problems of poverty and crime, it may help us see such chronic problems in helpful historical perspective.

The problems of youth were acute by the winter of 1932–33. Many young men had left the inadequate security of their homes and were wandering aimlessly seeking employment and excitement. They were seen not only as problems for themselves but as threats to the peace and order of the communities through which they passed. One of the objectives of the CCC, as a *New Republic* article put it, was to prevent such youth "from becoming semi-criminal hitchhikers."[8]

The CCC succeeded in getting large numbers of young men off the highways and railroads and out of the cities and into useful conservation work. One man recalled, "I literally came off a freight train into the CCC."[9] By the summer of 1932, 300,000 youth were in the camps. Two years later this figure had risen to over 500,000, and during the nine years of its existence, over 3,000,000 young men went through the program.[10] Because it dealt imaginatively with a serious and threatening problem, the CCC was one of the most popular of all New Deal programs. Roosevelt himself said, in an early assessment in 1934, that the CCC has "probably been the most successful of anything we have done."[11]

The liberal journals greeted this promising new effort with enthusiasm. Four days after the passage of the CCC bill, *The New Republic* criticized those pacifists, deflationists, unionists, and Communists who, from their divergent positions, had attacked the plan. (William Green, president of the AFL, had said the bill carried the threat of "fascism, of Hitlerism, of a form of sovietism.") The editors saw it as a promising program and complained only that it was too modest an effort, which would assist fewer than 2 percent of those out of work.[12] *The Nation*, too, applauded the program, and near the end of Roosevelt's first term singled it out as one of the best of the new government efforts, praising it especially for its work in soil and forest conservation. In 1935, Raymond Gram Swing, one of the journal's board of three editors, praised the CCC as "the bright jewel of the New Deal" and declared that "on the whole the C.C.C. is liked throughout the breadth of the land, and deservedly so." And in 1937, when Roosevelt asked Congress to make the agency permanent, *The Nation* called the CCC "indisputably one of the best relief agencies set up under the New Deal."[13]

The original plans for the CCC included no provision for educational work with the enrollees. In fact, the War Department, which supervised the camps, and Robert Fechner, director of the Corps, at first resisted efforts to establish an educational program. Col. Duncan Major, the War Department's representative on the CCC's advisory council, responding to a rumor that unemployed teachers would be assigned to the camps, said: "I have constantly fought the attempts of long-haired men

and short-haired women to get in our camps. . . . We are going
to be hounded to death by all sorts of educators."[14] But during
1933 and 1934, George Zook, U.S. Commissioner of Education, worked out an educational plan that was carried out by the
United States Office of Education under the aegis of the War
Department.[15]

Throughout its history the work of the CCC generally, and
its educational activities in particular, were hampered by an administrative structure that Tyack, Lowe, and Hansot have
called "a Rube Goldberg invention designed to calm the fears
of organized labor while still getting a program into place rapidly."[16] The Department of Labor recruited the enrollees; the
War Department ran the camps; the Departments of Agricul-
ture and Interior arranged the conservation projects; the Office of Education coordinated the education program; and
Fechner as director tried intermittently to exercise some administrative authority. In fact, the Army, under General Douglas MacArthur, held the ultimate power, with the concurrence
and occasional intervention of Roosevelt himself. Frances
Perkins noted Roosevelt's *ad hoc* and pragmatic administrative
style in quoting his statement that "the Army and the Forestry
Service will really run the show. The Secretary of Labor will select the men and make the rules and Fechner will 'go along' and
give everybody satisfaction and confidence."[17] Fechner was an
official of the International Association of Machinists who had
been appointed by Roosevelt "on the theory that that would
make organized labor well disposed to the project."[18]

C. S. Marsh was educational director of the CCC from December 1933 through late 1935, when he left following a conflict with Robert Fechner.[19] But the programs he began expanded under his successor, Howard Oxley. The educational
work carried out under these two men was quite diverse; it included elementary reading classes, a variety of forms of vocational training, and some instruction in liberal and cultural
subjects. Basic literacy training was a response to the fact that
many CCC men were—as one participant put it—"pretty much
on the side of not being able to read or write." During the life of
the CCC over forty thousand young men became literate
through the program. Other formal and informal teaching was
provided to give skills needed for work in the Corps and to help
enrollees find jobs after leaving the program.[20] During the first
four years, educational activity was voluntary, and attendance

at classes varied considerably. But in 1937 participation was made compulsory, and the largest enrollments were recorded during the next two years.

Given the speed with which the CCC had been established and the ambiguity within the Corps over the educational program, it is not surprising that problems arose. There was considerable bureaucratic in-fighting, and a conflict over goals, with men like Commissioner of Education Studebaker (who succeeded Zook in 1934) proposing a broader, more reformist program than was being offered in most camps. There was the question of the relationship of CCC programs to local and state educational agencies. And there was the problem of developing and maintaining some semblance of free inquiry in Corps classes.

The journals did not try to consider all aspects of the educational program in their coverage of the CCC. They ignored for the most part questions such as the Corps' relationships with existing educational authorities and instead concentrated their attention on matters of particular concern to liberals: education for conservation, reformist elements in instruction, military influence in the classes, and intellectual freedom in the program.

One of the primary functions of the CCC was to carry out conservation projects, and liberal journalists were quick to note that such work not only solved pressing resource problems, but that it had a useful by-product in conservation education, both for the Corpsmen and for the public. *The Nation*, in assessing the work of the program in late 1933, declared that its "educational effect upon the farmer"—in demonstrating methods of controlling cycles of flood and drought—was "not its least important one," and hoped that this might encourage farmers to believe that economic cycles might be regulated as well.[21]

Raymond Swing was also encouraged by the prospect that work in the Corps might make youth more concerned about the protection of American resources. He held out the hope that "if 200,000 young men pass through the camps every two years, in ten years a million young men would be educated conservationists, and in a few decades we should have a nation which for the first time was conservation-wise. That would mean that the American people at last had grown out of the piratical economy by which they spread over the continent." In teaching the younger generation about conservation, the camps could become "the finest practical university of elementary social economy ever established in this country." Swing was more impressed by the general educative effect of the program—particularly in conservation—than by its specifically instructional efforts, and predicted that "in a permanent C.C.C. the present somewhat extemporized system of education will need overhauling."[22]

Jonathan Mitchell, a contributing editor of *The New Republic*, made a thorough study of the CCC in operation and reported his findings in two 1935 articles. He said that the organization was meeting its employment and conservation objectives but that its educational work had been only a partial success. The instructional program had been handicapped by the running dispute between Fechner and Education Director Marsh.[23] Marsh was the kind of educator for whose ideas *New Republic* readers naturally felt some affinity. According to Mitchell, he had tried through CCC educational programs to "give a large part of the male youth of this country a conscious, realistic social point of view." His reformist outlook was evident in a "Handbook for Educational Advisers" in which he stated a Deweyan goal for CCC instruction: "To develop as far as practicable an understanding of the prevailing social and economic conditions, to the end that each man may cooperate intelligently in improving those conditions." He arranged for the production of inexpensive socially oriented textbooks for camp use, but these were suppressed by Fechner. In spite of bureaucratic apathy and hostility, however, Marsh succeeded in improving libraries and in hiring some outstanding educational advisers for the camps.

Mitchell saw two imperatives for the Corps: "Better central organization, and an ending of the enmity between Fechner's office and the educational division." The latter need could not be met simply by giving the new educational director increased authority. Mitchell proposed also that educational work be given a higher priority in the agency, for under existing arrangements all studying was done in the evening after a full day's work. In effect, the Corps was saying that the development of natural resources took precedence over the cultivation of human resources. Mitchell proposed that time during the day be made available for education as well as for work. The shift to a higher priority for education was slow in coming, however, and as late as 1941 Dorothy Bromley reported in *The New Republic* that in the camps "formal evening classes for youth employed all day in strenuous physical work have little appeal."[24]

Of more continuing concern to the civil libertarians associated with the journals was the problem—which Mitchell had noted—of intellectual freedom in the camps. This was no idle consideration. The assistant secretary of war, for example, had proposed that the CCC should make the participants into "economic storm troops."[25] In 1936 *The New Republic* reprinted from *The Social Studies* some advice carried in a handbook for CCC instructors. The manual recommended strategies by which teachers could steer discussions away from controversial matters. One approach was "to promise to bring up the dangerous issue at some future time. This will make it possible for the instructor to secure additional information before discussing it, and it also sets up the possibility of the topic being forgotten. A story to switch the interests of the class is a clever device for changing the topic."

"In a spirit of sweet cooperation," the editors added some suggestions: "If a C.C.C. class asks, 'How does it happen that so many people are hungry while surplus food is being destroyed?' let the instructor be prepared and immediately tell, not merely a story, but a dirty one. This will take the boys' minds off the subject, and the story probably won't be any dirtier than a true answer to the question would be."[26]

But such light treatment should not obscure the depth of liberal conviction on freedom of thought in the camps. Both journals carried letters from readers who objected to the CCC's dominance by the Army, which carried with it the "evils of regimentation."[27] And *The Nation* proposed editorially that the agency's connection with the War Department be severed, offering as partial justification the fact that the Army had "deliberately sought to censor the reading matter sent to the camps."[28] Such defenses of free inquiry in the CCC were logical applications of the journals' general positions in favor of academic freedom. If freedom in the pursuit of truth was sound policy in schools and colleges, it was equally necessary in other educational endeavors. And the journals were doubly vigilant when the attacks on free inquiry came, as they usually did in the CCC, from conservatives and militarists—the natural enemies of the liberal movement.

In the case of the CCC, as in so many areas, the journals performed both supportive and critical functions. They praised the agency as a hopeful, if inadequate, approach to pressing social and economic problems. They expressed special enthusiasm for the educational benefits offered by the agency—both to the public and to the young members of the Corps. And they were encouraged by the reformist emphasis some agency personnel tried to give to the educational program. But they did not let their enthusiasm blind them to the dangers in the CCC, and they proposed structural and personnel changes to weaken the forces of militarism and thought control that threatened a truly progressive educational program in the Corps.

■

The Civilian Conservation Corps was effective in coping with the problems of those youth who were able to enter the camps. But Franklin and Eleanor Roosevelt, Harry Hopkins, and other leaders were concerned also about the difficulties of the many young people—including women—for whom the CCC was not appropriate. It was important that as many as possible of these young people remain in school, in the short run, to keep them from competing with adults for scarce jobs, and in the long run, for the benefits their education would confer on them and on society.[29]

After 1932 hard-pressed students began dropping out of college in increasing numbers. As enrollments declined, the Federal Emergency Relief Administration began in February 1934 to extend financial aid to students in hopes that many might be able to continue their studies.[30] This was simply a stopgap effort, however, and in June 1935, by executive order, Roosevelt created the National Youth Administration (NYA) to conduct the program on a more permanent basis. The new agency gave work relief to youth both in and out of school and undertook a variety of projects, including vocational training and guidance, youth centers, and work for libraries and other agencies. Seven-eighths of the young people assisted were in school, and the others were employed on many different socially constructive projects.[31]

The educational work of the NYA differed from that of the CCC in two significant ways: first, education was a major priority in the NYA program; second, the NYA accomplished its purposes largely by enabling youth to continue their studies in established institutions. So, although it had a greater impact on formal education than did the CCC, it carried out few directly educational projects of its own.

Like the CCC, the NYA was plagued with a number of persistent problems. Aubrey Williams, the director, was often under attack as too radical, and conservatives resented his racial policies. At Eleanor Roosevelt's suggestion he had hired black leader Mary McLeod Bethune as an assistant and in various ways had made the NYA "a model of government assistance for blacks."[32] Some of the employment projects were poorly planned and supervised, and a number seemed to be little more than busy work. The Office of Education and the National Education Association resented the fact that the NYA often bypassed them in setting up its projects. And vocational training programs under the NYA were occasionally misused by unscrupulous employers.[33]

As with the CCC, the liberal journals responded selectively to the agency and its problems. Their analyses of the new program tended to overlook specific bureaucratic difficulties and to concentrate on the general inadequacy of the NYA, on its failure to respond realistically to the critical nature of the youth problem, and on the opportunities it presented to certain industries to use NYA youth as cheap labor.

When the NYA was first launched, the journals were prompt to applaud the promise held out by the new organization. *The Nation* declared that "the plight of young people is perhaps the most dangerous aspect of the present crisis" and defended the program by saying: "If democracy does not enlist youth, fascism will." And *The New Republic* praised Roosevelt and Hopkins for dealing forthrightly with the "staggering economic and psychological problems facing young men and women in the depression."[34]

During the eight years of the NYA's existence, *The New Republic* continued to hope for fulfillment of the promise the agency seemed at first to offer, and in this it was not entirely disappointed. After the agency had been in operation for seven months, Jonathan Mitchell reported that the NYA was assisting over 100,000 undergraduates, many graduate students, and nearly 200,000 high school pupils to continue their studies. Over 90,000 out-of-school youth were being helped through jobs in government, in research, and on recreation projects.[35]

In May 1936 Mitchell referred in *The New Republic* to "the relative success of Mr. Aubrey Williams' National Youth Administration." He noted that nearly all of the youth in the out-of-school work program were receiving instruction along with their work and that NYA personnel considered that the effort constituted, "at least potentially, a wholly new kind of popular university." Some of the more effective work-study programs could be considered as "education at its best."[36]

Two years later, John Chamberlain, in reviewing the Lindleys' book *A New Deal for Youth*, concluded that the NYA had a "record of relief money that has been well invested," and claimed that it had "done more to create a feeling of self-reliance in young Americans than anything since the Alger books." In spite of its inadequacies, "for a few hundred thousand destitute boys and girls, the N.Y.A. has meant work, self-respect, and the opportunity to continue their education on at least a part-time basis."[37]

In 1941, when the nation was shifting its attention from depression to defense, *The New Republic* again found reason to commend the NYA. In an editorial proposing greater reliance on the agency in vocational training for defense projects, the editors stated that "the National Youth Administration has the organization, the experience, the social intelligence and some of the equipment" to do the job. Its practical training program had operated on the principles of "learning by doing in the better sense." But though the agency could assist in the defense program, the editors insisted that the "non-defense activities of the NYA should not be crippled. The people on these projects are from low-income homes. Many of them vitally need the opportunity, the encouragement, the discipline, and the few dollars a month that the NYA provides."[38]

Such statements, however, appear to have exhausted the optimism of the journalists concerning the NYA. The agency never evoked from the editors and writers (nor from the nation at large) the enthusiasm engendered by the CCC, which, with its conservation projects, its healthy outdoor life, and its forest rangers, had a romantic appeal the NYA could not match.[39] It was easy to identify with the CCC as the modern expression of William James's "moral equivalent of war"; it was more difficult to evoke the same response to the NYA's less dramatic programs. The NYA enabled youth to continue fairly normal patterns of life and education. Keeping young people in school or in part-time jobs lacked the elements of adventure which, in the CCC, stirred the country's imaginative impulses.

■

Maintaining their pressure from the left on the administration, the liberal weeklies were often critical of the inadequate way in which government youth programs were carried out. In April 1936, nine months after the NYA was started, *The Nation* lamented the hopeless chances of the Amlie-Benson Youth Bill, which would have set up a substantial, well-financed program for youth. Such bold approaches were badly needed, and yet Commissioner of Education Studebaker was proposing only additional study of the problems of the young. The editors declared that this was not the major need: "Meanwhile ever more transients are riding our freight cars and new criminals are being made every day. Most important of all, an unemployed mass of young people form fertile soil for social despair and for all the reckless political movements that may lead to fascism. The Roosevelt Administration is making one of its most disastrous errors by failing to grapple with the problem of the desperate American youth."[40]

William Mangold, who wrote a regular *New Republic* column called "On the Labor Front," in 1935 questioned not only the adequacy of the NYA but also whether its programs in vocational guidance and training were even a sound approach to the difficulties facing youth. Admitting that enrollment in such programs might be "better than idleness," he nevertheless noted that there was little value in educating people for jobs that did not exist. The problem was basically one of employment rather than education, and "unless the government can also find real jobs the National Youth Administration will not help greatly in solving this fundamental problem."[41]

But it was contributing editor Jonathan Mitchell who, as he had done with the CCC, wrote the most comprehensive analysis of the problems besetting the NYA. Although the agency had been in operation only six months when he wrote "Without Work Experience" for *The New Republic*, enough time had elapsed so that Mitchell was able to identify those aspects of the program about which liberals would have doubts. The agency had been "inordinately slow in putting its limited program into operation." Like the CCC, it suffered from an administrative feud—this one between Harry Hopkins, director of the Works Progress Administration, and Harold Ickes, secretary of the interior.[42] This conflict was paralleled at a lower level by a "contest for jurisdiction" between NYA director Aubrey Williams (an assistant to Hopkins) and Commissioner of Education John Studebaker (who worked under Ickes).

Laboring under such handicaps, suffering from the "meagerness of its payments to individuals," and not reaching "more than a tenth of those needing help," perhaps not too much should have been expected from the new organization. But Mitchell nonetheless proceeded to indict the NYA for not providing a fundamental solution for "the youth problem." Its sins were largely ones of omission. First, although the effect of such programs was to hold youth in school until they were older, no effort was being made to face "the immense problem of changed curricula that will be made necessary by an increase in the school age, nor is it encouraging teachers to draft solutions of their own." Second, although vocational training programs involved both "misuse of government funds and exploitation of apprentice labor," the NYA was providing no leadership in developing projects free of such ills or in giving direction to vocational education in general. And finally, while the Federal Emergency Relief Administration and the NYA deliberately chose not to antagonize voting adults by letting youth compete for their jobs, it might be preferable to society that "young men and women, upon reaching adulthood, have first chance at jobs and marriage, even if they displace workers in middle age."

Perhaps Mitchell saw that the NYA was too new and too small a program to bear the weight of this broad social and educational indictment. The problems of youth had their roots deep in the economic and social structure and were beyond the ability of one new bureau to deal with. But that made the crisis no less pressing. Mitchell admitted in closing that probably the NYA was not equipped to deal with the fundamental questions he had raised but concluded that "if this is so then some other agency—either inside or outside the government—is urgently needed."[43]

Clearly, in putting forth judgments such as these, Mitchell was transcending the context of one government youth program and was using the NYA as a basis for fundamental critiques of the way America inducted the young into adulthood. In a constricted economy, society was offering youth incentives to remain in school. Yet it was doing little to see that schools developed programs more suited to the needs and interests of youth than those that had been inherited from an earlier era.

In an unjust and contracted economy, government vocational training programs, poorly financed and supervised, gave unprincipled employers further opportunities to exploit defenseless youth. And in a society with too few opportunities to go around, it insured that those in power, put there by adult voters, could arrange that competition from the young would be effectively walled off.

■

Liberal journalists like Mitchell had the insight to see these problems with some clarity. But perhaps only someone with the cross-cultural perspective of the anthropologist could perceive what was really at work here: the creation of a new minority group—youth. In 1941 Ruth Benedict undertook the analysis of this phenomenon for *New Republic* readers.[44] She pointed out the inaccuracy of the adult charge that youth had abandoned the values of their elders. On the contrary, they had learned those values all too well: "We taught them our own standard of success: it lay in the material world and money was the measure of it." But having built these values into the character structure of the young, society then proceeded to let the economy smash up, thereby creating a world in which youth could not hope to realize those values.

Benedict was describing a situation in which ideas and beliefs were out of congruence with a new reality. The economic and employment situation had changed drastically, yet the young continued to hold old ideas of independence and personal autonomy. In a depressed job market the young had difficulty exercising their independence—of "marrying and having children, of choosing which house they'd live in." Many relied on their families for support and felt deeply guilty for doing so. And government youth programs presented some of the same psychological burdens: "The CCC and the NYA are as confusing therefore as being dependent on one's father for ten years after school is over."

In such a situation adults should not blame the young for organizing and protesting. By doing so they were demonstrating politically the initiative it was fruitless to express economically. "Youth has felt humiliated by unemployment and its way of lessening that humiliation is by youth organizations which devote themselves principally to the grinding of teeth." The

young had "special treatment, special disabilities," and then
were made to feel guilty about their plight in a social world they
had not created. But it was still within the power of adults to
rectify the situation—to restore the harmony of inner values
and outer realities:

> The elder generation should say, "There but for the grace
> of God go I," and learn from them how it would have be-
> haved if it had been bred to the extra-materialistic dream
> of the twenties and then cut loose without a sou to earn.
> Such attitudes would go far toward closing the breach be-
> tween youth and its elders and we should not be so apt to
> scold. Our attention would be concentrated instead on
> providing the conditions under which our favorite Ameri-
> can virtues can operate without individual and social trag-
> edy. If we are in earnest about preserving our American
> virtues, we will count no price too high.

Through such reactions to the needs of youth in the Depression and to the federal government's responses to those needs,
we can gain further insight into the liberal journals' general
stance on educational matters. Editors and writers deplored the
economic and social developments and policies that had weakened already inadequate educational opportunities; they supported programs that restored or extended some of these same
opportunities; and they argued in favor of more effective educational activities in programs like the CCC and the NYA.
Throughout their commentary, the two journals fulfilled their
functions as critics, pointing out the quantitative inadequacies
of the new programs as well as their administrative deficiencies.
    More fundamental, however, was the demonstration by the
journals that government youth programs were not merely attempted solutions for temporary ills; they were responses to
underlying social, economic, and educational injustices. In
their writings on the CCC and the NYA the journals put forth
again the positions they had expressed for decades: America,
with all its strengths, was in many ways a social and economic
failure; it offered unsatisfying lives to many adults, and to the
young it provided clumsy and inexpedient means of growing
into even those thin patterns of life. In the 1930s, while federal
programs in relief and education offered small steps toward
the solution of those difficulties, they provided even more

powerfully a way of making the problems of youth visible and understandable on a nationwide scale.

In their responses to the CCC and the NYA, readers could see elements of both continuity and change in the journals' educational commentary. The continuity was evident in the journals' support for these innovative programs, coupled with criticisms of them as too cautious and limited; in enthusiasm for progressive Deweyan integration of work and education; in their insistence that they should be part of a broad reform program; in their opposition to taints of militarism in the programs; and in their demand that they be implemented in ways that provided academic freedom for students and instructors alike.

The elements of change were chiefly ones of tone and emphasis. While continuing much of the substance of their earlier educational positions, the journals were more strident in their denunciations of conservatism in education and society, less sanguine about the separate role of education in reform, and yet—somewhat ironically—more willing to support a significant federal role in education. And through all this commentary occasionally glimmered the journalists' visions of a society in which realistic education would lead to an informed citizenry doing productive, satisfying work in a healthy egalitarian economy.

14

Conclusion: The Weapon of Criticism

In 1925, H. L. Mencken, a longtime contributing editor of *The Nation*, wrote:

The Nation is unique in American journalism for one thing:
it is read by its enemies. . . . That is, the more intelligent of
them—the least hopeless minority of them. It is to such
minorities that *The Nation* addresses itself, on both sides of
the fence. It has penetrated to the capital fact that they
alone count—that the ideas sneaked into them today will
begin to sweat out of the herd day after tomorrow. . . . Editorial writers all over the land steal ideas from it daily; it
supplies, indeed, all the ideas that most of them will ever
have. It lifts them . . . above the sedimentary stratum of
Rotarians and ice-wagon drivers; they are conscious of its
pull when they resist. . . . It is my contention that *The Nation* has led the war in the reform of American journalism—that it will be followed by many papers tomorrow as
it is followed by a few today. . . . Its politics are often outra-
geous. . . . But who will deny that it is honest? And who will
deny that . . . it is generally right—that its enthusiasms, if
they occasionally send it mooning after dreamers, at least
never send it cheering after rogues—that its wrongness,

when it is wrong, is at all events, not the dull, simian wrongness of mere stupidity?[1]

Thus the dean of American iconoclasts attested, in his usual exuberant fashion, to the impact of Villard's *Nation*. A more judicious assessment of the role of its fellow journal, *The New Republic*, appears in Joyce Antler's biography of Lucy Sprague Mitchell. Mitchell was a leading progressive educator, and her husband, Wesley Clair Mitchell, was an influential liberal economist. Antler writes that Lucy Mitchell "was sympathetic to the goals of Marxism, anarchism and syndicalism, but she believed in the power of education, rather than political revolution, to end exploitation. The Mitchell's own beliefs accorded more with what Wesley termed the 'respectable fringe' of intellectual radicalism rather than with its left wing. Their favorite journal was not *The Masses* but the left-of-liberal *New Republic*, whose first issue of November 1, 1914 they excitedly read aloud together."[2]

These two quotations suggest the range of readers of the liberal journals—from the maverick Mencken to the respectably radical Mitchells. The Mitchells provide particularly good examples of the kinds of people reached by the journals. Both studied under John Dewey and shared his views on education and reform. They lived in Greenwich Village, were friends with such *New Republic* insiders as Walter Lippmann and Walter Weyl, and were at the center of progressive causes in New York City and the nation from 1914 until the 1940s.

Looking back over the entire period from 1914 to 1941, how might such disparate readers as Mencken and the Mitchells have seen the educational commentary of the liberal journals? The twenty-seven years from 1914, the high noon of the Progressive Era, to America's entry into World War II included a major war, a decade of Republican dominance, the Depression and New Deal, and the outbreak of a new and more disastrous world conflict. These were obviously momentous years for the world and for the United States; they were no less eventful for the liberals and educators who were writing and acting during this period.

A review of trends, recurrent issues, and comparisons and contrasts in the liberal journals will provide background for an assessment of their role in educational criticism. The 1914–1921 period traversed the "crossroads of liberalism," with two branches of progressivism and their divergent educational expressions. During these seven years the journals focused their educational coverage on the efficiency movement in the schools, issues of academic freedom, and education as an instrument of reform. During the 1921–1930 period their educational interests encompassed the worker education movement, child-centered schooling, and the reputed anti-intellectual overtones of this strand of progressivism. And during the 1930s the journals gave particular attention to the effects of the Depression on schools and colleges, to political struggles in the American Federation of Teachers, to the growth of a militant student movement, and to the problems of youth and the federal responses to their difficulties.

This book's first chapter ended with a statement of four messages derived from this study: that the journals consistently supported education as part of their program for reform; that through their educational commentary the journalists presented their vision of a future society; that reform could be promoted through coalitions among journalists, educators, workers, politicians, and others; and that "connected critics" could play a key role in educational and social change. A brief review of these messages will provide background for some concluding comments on the current educational scene and on the continuing need for sound educational criticism.

■

The first message is that American liberals, as represented by *The New Republic* and the post-1918 *Nation*, were consistent proponents of a reformist role for education. This position was evident in a number of areas over the years and showed itself in support for some movements and opposition to others. Both journals, for example, opposed efficiency measures in schools when they were tied to conservative ends, but endorsed them when they could be used as tools of democracy and social progress. They resisted the separation of liberal and vocational studies, fearing that this would rigidify class lines and retard social mobility. Both advocated workers' education as a means of promoting reform within the labor movement and making unions instruments of broader social change.

The desire to make schools agents of social progress naturally led *The Nation* and *The New Republic* to promote reformist curricula. Editors and writers encouraged schools to make critical studies of social trends so that graduates would be able to participate in needed economic and political transformations. The journals thus recommended that workers' schools go beyond technical subjects of short-term value and study politics, economics, and other social sciences. For the same reason Villard in the early 1930s encouraged colleges to help students analyze the causes of the economic disaster befalling the country. And even the most avid proponents of child-centered schools felt it necessary to claim that their graduates would be active agents of reform.

A key point in all this is that the educational policies of the journals varied less than their political and economic positions. The editors never lost their conviction that humans were at least partially rational, that this rationality could be enhanced, that it could be turned to reformist ends, and that education, broadly construed, was an instrument of that belief. The journals thus provide additional support for Rush Welter's position that the democratic consensus on education was more fundamental than that in almost any other area.[3]

■

The second message is that through their educational commentary the journalists presented their visions of a future and better society. They served the function noted recently by Carol Polsgrove: "Magazines help us proclaim who we are: They are tokens of our aspirations."[4] As the liberal journalists wrote about the education they wanted, they projected pictures of the kinds of individuals and social arrangements such education might lead to. They thus foresaw a world in which young people, through democratic education, would be prepared to participate in an egalitarian economy and polity; in which organized workers, including teachers and professors, would control their conditions of work; in which intellectual freedom would pervade educational, political, and social institutions; in which schools would prepare people for constructive labor and workplaces would also be sites for education; in which social change would be peaceful, rational, evolutionary, and continuous. In short, they hoped and planned for what Dewey called "a spiritually democratic society" in which "every individual would realize distinction." Such a society "would then be for the first time in human history an individual achievement and not a class possession."[5]

■

The third message is that reform would require the creation and development of coalitions of socially concerned groups, including intellectuals, journalists, educators, students, political activists, social workers, and union members. This emphasis on coalition-building was part of the journalists' movement from a social theory based on persuasion to one grounded in power. Fuller's *Nation*, and even Croly for a time, hoped that needed social change might come to pass through the enlightened ethical actions of business and political leaders. On the basis of such a belief, the role of journalists was to persuade such leaders to institute reforms. But Croly moved away from this emphasis soon after *The New Republic* was launched, and when Villard took over *The Nation* he drastically modified that journal's position on this issue. From that point on both weeklies devoted more energy to encouraging exploited groups—including educators—to organize with others and to apply political and economic pressure in their struggles for justice.

■

The final message is that the journals performed an essential function as "connected critics" of society in general and education in particular. For nearly three decades *The Nation* and *The New Republic* commented extensively and thoughtfully on educational developments. They described and analyzed educational reality, identified developments and trends, and proposed fundamental changes in schools and colleges. And some journal personnel took a more active role and participated directly in educational organizations and endeavors.

■

Having seen all this, one may ask: So what? What was the significance of all this writing and activity? Did the journalists have any perceptible effect on American education or any part of it? One can only speculate about the impact of the journals, but a bit of conjecture in this area may help at least to delineate what

the journalists were trying to do in their educational commentary. Clearly one cannot measure in any precise way the out-
comes of the words and actions of these men and women. One
cannot rerun history without them to see if it would come out
differently. As Penn Kimball has written, "One has to be wary
when writing about so-called molders of public opinion."[6] But,
acknowledging the lack of conclusive evidence in this area, one
can at least point out circumstances in which people appeared
to be influenced by educational material in the weeklies. The
journals were blessed with active, articulate, and responsive
readers who reacted strongly, for example, to Bourne's essays,
to George Counts's 1932 articles, to the AFT fellow-traveler
controversy, to Dewey's and Kilpatrick's educational statements, and to academic freedom issues.[7] The journals were
clearly getting through to some readers. They were provoking
thought on the part of teachers and others concerning a wide
range of educational issues. If one cannot trace ideas directly
from the journals into people's minds and then into visible social change, one can at least cite *The New Republic*'s claim: "As a
journal of ideas we may contribute something to the formulation of the tendencies and forces which do end in action." Theodore Peterson has written: "New ideas are essential if society is
not to stagnate. The minority magazine is an especially suitable
vehicle for introducing them, weighing them pro and con, and
if they have merit, feeding them into the mainstream of
thought."[8]

This takes a broad view of the utility of such journals to society in general. But if one looks at *The Nation* and *The New Republic* from the position of the educator, their value lies largely
in the perspective they provide. Educators receive comment
and criticism on their work from a variety of periodical sources,
which may be grouped into three broad categories.

The first group includes professional journals, which are
generally written by and for educators, provide a quantity of
often useful and technical ideas and proposals, and tend to give
an essentially "inside" view of educational developments. But as
will be noted below, these provide more deep-seated criticism
than was formerly the case.

The second group includes mass magazines, which are often
conservative or ostensibly neutral in politics and provide "outside," nonprofessional, nontechnical coverage of education.
Their treatment of educational developments may be placed in

a broader social context than much of the professional literature, but it often reflects a disinclination to modify the status
quo in any significant way. Heavily dependent on advertising,
these magazines often engage in sensationalism and exaggeration in an effort to build circulation.

Mass periodicals are limited in their role as analysts of education because they are only the mildest of social critics. While
willing to castigate educators for their most obvious failures,
their analysis rarely goes deep enough to make fundamental
connections between educational issues and basic social trends.

The third group includes the liberal journals, which are outside both the world of professional educators and the shallow
political consensus represented by popular magazines. This
gives them a perspective unavailable to either the professional
or the popular press.[9]

During the 1914–1941 period, *The Nation* and *The New Republic*, as the foremost liberal journals, played a constructive
role in American education. They conveyed information and
ideas between educators and political liberals, while criticizing
many of the practices and ideas that were being transmitted.
Had the journals served only as a pipeline for facts and theories, they would have been helpful in building political support
for educational innovation and in keeping educators aware of
the social context of their work.[10] But they went well beyond
this disseminating role; they analyzed, evaluated, and sometimes advocated the educational ideas and policies that came
under their scrutiny.

Journal readers who were not directly involved in education
were thus kept informed of developments in the field, and political reformers were constantly reminded that education
should not be ignored in their plans for social reconstruction.
Equally important, educators were constantly helped to see
their work in a broader context; those who proposed a reformist role for education could, with the help of the journals, see
more clearly the possibilities and limitations of the schools as instruments of creative change. The journals provided a continual corrective to the naive assumption that education was *the*
key to progress and reform. And they never took the simplistic
position in which, as Michael Katz says, "educational reform
has substituted for social and economic reform."[11]

The journals had a role as conveyors, promoters, interpreters, and critics of educational ideas and policies. But many

educators welcomed the journals also as allies in the struggle for academic freedom, and progressives appreciated the support *The New Republic* and the post-1918 *Nation* gave to educational innovation. They may, however, have occasionally been stung by the fact that the journals were as willing to criticize as to praise educational developments. In "The Schools from the Outside," published in the thirteenth issue of *The New Republic*, the editors of that journal gave clear expression to their position. They claimed that educators, with their emphasis on "constructive criticism," effectively screened from view any really fundamental critiques of their policies or programs: "Educators, it is true, welcome 'fair criticism,' and they have a fond belief that they get it from one another in the educational press. But in this mass of books and journals . . . the whole setting, language, philosophy are professional. The very bases and premises which the lay critic wishes to criticize are taken for granted."[12]

Educators, like businessmen, union leaders, government officials, or members of any other group, were inevitably limited in their ability to criticize themselves. They had difficulty getting beyond their own experiences and assumptions. And, as Michael Katz has noted, the growth of educational bureaucracy and professionalism reduced educators' receptivity to "the informed, constructive criticism that makes progress possible."[13] What was needed—and this was a role the liberal journals fulfilled—was criticism "from the outside." That these journals were able to provide such criticism with insight and perspective may be partly ascribed to the fact that they were not only outside the schools but were deeply alienated from mass society as well.[14]

Walter Lippmann has written that "in a democracy, the opposition is not only tolerated as constitutional, but must be maintained as indispensable." This is as true of opposition journalism as it is in the strictly political realm. If our major social institutions—schools and colleges among them—are to avoid rigidity and retain the plasticity that will enable them to respond to new challenges, they will continue to need supporters who are also critics. It is to the credit of the liberal journals that they have served both of these functions during much of this century.

■

Thorstein Veblen wrote in 1899:

Institutions are products of the past process, are adapted
to past circumstance, and are therefore never in full accord with the requirements of the present. . . . The read-
justment of institutions and habitual views to an altered
environment is made in response to pressure from without. . . . If any portion or class of society is sheltered from
the action of the environment in any essential respect, that
portion of the community, or that class, will adapt its views
and its scheme of life more tardily to the altered general
situation; it will in so far tend to retard the process of social
transformation.[15]

The editors of the liberal journals shared Veblen's view.
Institutions, including education, could not live a "peculiarly
sheltered life." They could not be depended on to be deeply
self-critical; it was thus the responsibility of outsiders, including
socially concerned journals of opinion, to provide needed criticism. And, as the previous chapters indicate, *The Nation* and *The
New Republic* during the 1914–1941 period, exercised that responsibility by searchingly analyzing educational developments
from their liberal political perspectives.

■

This analysis of liberal commentary on education leads to
some final speculation on the current status of American society, education, and educational criticism. The United States
enters the decade of the 1990s with curiously scrambled economics and politics. The "Reagan Revolution," while it reinforced conservative American beliefs, failed to roll back all the
reforms of the previous decades.[16] Our mixed economy, with its
elements of "welfare capitalism," survives in spite of massive
budgetary and trade deficits. The apocalyptic predictions of the
economic collectivists of the 1930s have not come to pass. The
so-called free enterprise system (which is in fact heavily managed, however ineptly, by various elements of the political process) has shown a resilience that seemed impossible in the midst
of the Depression.

Robert Heilbroner, while still supporting a role for socialism,
has gone so far as to say that "the contest between capitalism

and socialism is over: capitalism has won."[17] Patrick Moynihan has declared the "End of the Marxist Epoch" in a *New Leader* article by that title.[18] And Irving Howe, commenting on the events of 1989 in Eastern Europe and Russia, has written that "we have lived to see the end of Stalinism/communism as a serious political force, everywhere except in a few underdeveloped countries." But he optimistically concludes that "this means that, fairly soon if not immediately, there should be new opportunities for social democratic parties."[19]

Although our mixed economy survives, the Reagan/Bush years brought economic bipolarism: the rich got richer and the poor got poorer. Structural unemployment, particularly for minorities, survives through prosperity and recession. And the growth of crowds of homeless people in our cities brings a reminder of the Hoovervilles of the 1930s. America has demonstrated that the economy as a whole can flourish in spite of the exclusion of large numbers from even its minimal benefits.

The American political system, though it continues to deny participation and justice to many citizens, has shown its ability to last through depression, hot and cold wars, McCarthyism, civil rights and antiwar struggles, imperial adventurism in Southeast Asia and Central America, and other challenges. And amidst all this, perceptible but insufficient gains have been made in extending the franchise (but not in getting people to use it), in racial and gender equity, and in civil liberties. Limited though this progress has been, few minorities or women would choose to return to their status of fifty years ago.

Educational developments paralleled those in politics and the economy. The schools survived in spite of the limited resources occasioned by the Depression, wars, and massive and continuous defense spending; higher education expanded dramatically in response to the G.I. Bill and the baby boom; the Brown decision of 1954, with all-too-deliberate speed, gradually dismantled the structure of *de jure* segregation and was followed by limited integration, white flight and *de facto* resegregation. The schools, battered and bruised, outlasted shrill conservative criticism from such people as Max Rafferty in the 1950s and William Bennett in the 1980s. Educators endured insulting calls for "teacher-proof curricula" and the imposition of "accountability," top-down reform, and massive and inappropriate testing and comparison among schools. Teachers were blamed for a "rising tide of mediocrity" among American students.[20] They were asked to promote both excellence and equality, while being given the resources to do neither. In spite of some scattered successes like the Head Start program, we still have what one observer describes as "the other school system"—one that "is characterized by lower student achievement, lower per capita educational expenditures, and lower social-class status of parents."[21]

So while the worst fears of the liberal journalists have not been realized, neither have their fondest hopes. We find ourselves near the end of this millenium facing new versions of old problems: how to create a more democratic polity, a more just economy, and an educational system that serves justice and excellence rather than privilege and mediocrity.

Where now is the wisdom that may help us confront our challenges as creatively as the liberal journalists did earlier in the century? It can be found in many places, of course, but it is consistent with the spirit of this study to look to those contemporary intellectuals who carry on the tradition of the earlier liberal journalists and who continue to speak through periodicals and books. If, as Russell Jacoby has reported, too many intellectuals have retreated to secure academic posts and ceased to participate in real-world politics, the tradition of the "public intellectual" is not entirely dead.[22] *The Nation* and *The New Republic* have evolved into somewhat different journals, but continue to present educational commentary consistent with their political positions. *The Nation* has maintained a left-liberal position in the tradition of Kirchwey's journal. *The New Republic* has shifted to a hard-headed realism that might merit the appellation Croly once hurled at traditional liberalism: it was, he said, "a species of the higher conservatism."[23] In fact, *Nation* writers occasionally enjoy reminding *The New Republic* of its decline from liberal virtue.[24]

Format indicates something here: *The Nation* maintains its proletarian look, printed mostly in black and white on cheap paper; *The New Republic* is now published on slick paper, with artistic colored covers. And, while the two weeklies do not consistently carry educational commentary of the caliber of the Croly-Bliven or Villard-Kirchwey years, they do continue to critique educational developments from a range of liberal political perspectives.[25]

The Nation and *The New Republic* are far from alone in their role as progressive political/educational critics. *The Progressive*

continues to promote the liberal, peace-oriented faith of its
Wisconsin LaFollette tradition. And new liberal-to-radical periodicals have joined the field. *Dissent*, founded in 1954, presents
the thoughtful democratic socialism of editors Irving Howe
and Michael Walzer. *In These Times*, edited by historian James
Weinstein, provides a more frequent and topical socialist interpretation of news and culture. *Mother Jones* delivers sometimes-
sensational muckraking investigative journalism.[26] *Tikkun: A
Quarterly Jewish Critique of Politics, Culture and Society* speaks for
Jewish liberals. *New Politics: A Journal of Socialist Thought* occasionally carries thoughtful critiques of educational developments.[27]

So the liberal-radical tradition in American journalism continues to flourish and to provide for readers alternatives to the
superficiality and conformism of mainstream periodicals. But
one significant change in *educational* periodicals is that in general they carry more critical and radical commentary than was
the case during the 1914–1941 period. While periodicals aimed
at specific levels and fields continue to emphasize professional
matters, other journals now carry a wider range of educational
criticism—much of it from the left. As educators have acquired
greater security through unions, professional organizations,
and tenure, they have become freer to criticize society and its
schools. And as educators have responded, along with their fellow academics, to the crises of recent decades, they have indicted schools and colleges along with other apparently failed
institutions.[28]

While major educational journals carry a range of opinion,
from Reaganism to neo-Marxism, the weight of the dialogue
has shifted to the left. Neo-conservatives do not lack outlets for
their views, but much of the educational argument is between
those whom *The New Republic* calls "paleo-liberals" and their
more radical colleagues.[29] The recent leftward shift of educational criticism was foreshadowed in the 1930s in *The Social
Frontier*, which—according to Theodore Brameld—was "mod-
eled roughly after *The New Republic* and *The Nation*" and was
"the most sophisticated medium for education writing in the
U.S. at that time."[30] Radical critiques of schooling were also carried in *Progressive Education* and a few other educational journals, but it was not until the New Left movement of the 1960s
that such criticism began appearing frequently in mainstream
education journals. In 1966 *The Harvard Educational Review* car-

ried Noam Chomsky's slashing attack on American foreign policy and on those intellectuals and educators who supported it. That same journal introduced readers to the ideas of Brazilian radical educator and literacy expert Paulo Freire. As Michael Schudson has noted, "The growing political movements of the 1960s opened the pages of the review to radical opinion."[31]

A parallel development can be seen in the University of Chicago's educational journal. Former editor Harold Dunkel recalls that *The School Review* (now *The American Journal of Education*) announced in 1969 that it would go beyond its previous educational coverage and "publish exchanges of opinions, insights and reactions to articles, and reviews from people actively involved in *education and social change*" (Dunkel's emphasis).[32]

Similarly, Lewis Paul Todd, editor of *Social Education*, wrote in 1967 that "the 'revolution' in social studies . . . is not going to come through the development of better methodology or the reorganization of content . . . but rather through a clearer vision of what man can and should be in this new age that has already dawned. In brief, I am convinced that what we desperately need is a complete reorientation of values."[33] And journals such as *Educational Theory, Teachers College Record, Journal of Education, Curriculum Inquiry, Democracy and Education*, and *The Journal of Curriculum Theorizing* carry frequent radical and revisionist critiques of education and society.[34] Even the *Phi Delta Kappan*, widely read among administrators and teacher educators, provides a hearing for fundamental social-educational critiques. A recent book review in that journal closed with these Deweyan words: "As one reads the literature on school reform, one realizes that societal reform and school reform go hand in hand. One .without the other, especially in the inner cities and rural areas, will provide only the same kinds of Band-Aid solutions that have failed to meet our expectations for so long."[35]

How may we explain the fact that educational journals are now more open to radical critiques of education? Many of the activists of the 1960s, once the "revolt of youth" of that decade was over, looked for careers in which they could continue their work. If they were to undertake "the long march through the institutions of society," they had to locate themselves in settings in which they could survive and have some effect.[36] Schools and colleges were obviously more hospitable to such activists than most business, military, or governmental institutions. Andrew Kopkind has written that "many intellectuals of the old New Left had sequestered themselves in universities, think tanks and public advocacy organizations and kept teaching, thinking and advocating while the rest of the country was swinging in the 1970s and investing in the 1980s."[37] Academia, and particularly education, received a disproportionate share of such intellectuals. And over the past two decades many of them have become productive scholars and have used educational journals and other academic periodicals as outlets for their research and ideas.[38]

What has happened then is that many of the people who once might have been true outsiders like Randolph Bourne are now "in but not of" academic and educational institutions. They have become what were called in the 1960s "establishment radicals." While working within the world of education they maintain a judgmental stance toward it. Kenneth Clark once observed that it "may be that only the seemingly alienated can provide a critical basis by which the American nation can mobilize its real positives, its strength and its powers."[39] So the "seemingly alienated" have an important role to play in reminding us that educational institutions fall far short of the ideals we claim for them.

In spite of their continuing difficulties, then, the schools are better off in one important respect than they were in 1914: they are receiving more fundamental criticism, both from inside and outside the world of education. Insiders speak on the basis of their intimate knowledge of educational institutions; outsiders like the liberal journalists continue to analyze and critique educational developments from the perspective of the pragmatic, reformist left. If educators and their allies cannot creatively confront the many challenges that face them, it will not be for lack of informed and deep-seated criticism.

■

There are, then, magazines and journals to provide some of the criticism and proposals our schools and colleges need. But what should be the content of that criticism and those suggestions? What are the ideas and programs that liberals should pursue as we enter the 1990s? And are those ideas consistent with the programs put forth by the liberal journals earlier in this century? Out of the many thinkers from across the political spectrum we may select two who provide a "margin of hope" for educators and their socially concerned allies.[40] Michael Walzer presents a thoughtful argument for fundamental social criticism and Amy Gutmann provides a persuasive public philosophy of society and education.[41]

Walzer, who has been writing for both academic and political audiences for many years, provides the best current rationale for radical criticism. Maurice Isserman has noted that Walzer was one of the links between the new leftists of the 1960s and part of the old left—the democratic socialists associated with *Dissent*.[42] (Or as some used to say in the 1960s, "New Left and Old Leftovers.") Along with Irving Howe, Walzer continues to edit *Dissent*; he also serves as a contributing editor of *The New Republic*. Thus he is one of those "public intellectuals" who reaches beyond the confines of academia with his ideas. His latest book, *The Company of Critics*, is a perceptive analysis of the historical and contemporary role of social criticism, presented through case studies of selected twentieth-century thinkers. Amidst such luminaries as Martin Buber, Antonio Gramsci, George Orwell, and Michel Foucault, the only American included is Randolph Bourne. Walzer discusses Bourne primarily in the context of his fierce opposition to America's entry into World War I and the break that this occasioned with his earlier hero, John Dewey. But he reports that in spite of this rift, Bourne remained a "philosophical pragmatist, committed to the experimental life, sharing the sense of openness, process, participation that pragmatism at its best still stimulates."[43]

Bourne is included because he, like the other thinkers considered in the book, is a good example of what Walzer calls the "connected critic" or the "engaged intellectual."[44] As the labels literally suggest, these are intellectuals who are involved with the larger society and in attempts to influence public opinion. Walzer writes that the problem central to the contemporary period is "the connection of specialists and commoners, elite and mass."[45] He reminds us of three tasks of the critic: he "exposes the false appearances of his own society; he gives expression to his people's deepest sense of how they ought to live; and he insists that there are other forms of falseness and other, equally legitimate hopes and aspirations."[46] The "general intellectual" will be "critical of the power structures that inhibit popular participation in political life (including the power structures of popular parties and movements). . . . Himself a participant, he works at a certain difficult distance, balancing 'solidarity' and 'service.' He is, whenever he can be, the enemy of disconnection. To find one's way in the little battles as well as the big ones, to be faithful to the hopes of popular revolt, to outlast the defeats, to sustain a form of criticism internal to, relevant to, loyal to, democratic politics—that is courage in social criticism."[47]

Writing in *The New Republic*'s Seventy-fifth Anniversary Issue, Walzer sets forth two principles of social democracy: "First, that all citizens ought to be included on equal terms in the political community (this is the democratic principle); and second, that this community is collectively responsible for the well-being . . . of all its members (this is the social principle)."[48] Amy Gutmann's book *Democratic Education* provides the kind of "connected criticism" Walzer calls for and in so doing explores how education promotes "the democratic principle." Gutmann, who also writes for *The New Republic*, probes below the traditional left-right, liberal-conservative dialogue in which many thinkers have been trapped.[49] In a closely reasoned, carefully developed theoretical book she cuts through much of the rhetoric and many of the issues that plague educational thinkers. Updating, critiquing, and extending ideas derived from many thinkers (including John Dewey, John Stuart Mills, John Rawls, Jean-Jacques Rousseau, and Michael Walzer), Gutmann proposes a democratic educational theory that "faces up to the fact of difference in our moral ideals of education by looking toward democratic deliberations not only as a means to reconciling those differences, but also as an important part of democratic education."[50]

Gutmann proposes a primarily political role for the schools: "A society that supports conscious social reproduction must educate all educable children to be capable of participating in collectively shaping their society."[51] For her, the main purpose of elementary and secondary education "is to develop democratic character."[52] She suggests that teachers should be the kinds of "connected critics" that Walzer calls for: "Teachers must be sufficiently connected to their communities to understand the commitments that their students bring to school, and sufficiently detached to cultivate among their students the critical distance necessary to reconsider commitments in the face of conflicting ones."[53]

Applying her democratic criteria of "nonrepression and

nondiscrimination" to a series of major educational issues, Gutmann supports integrated public education (including compensatory education), responsible teacher unions, greater professional autonomy for teachers, more participatory pedagogy, and less bureaucratic school structures. She acknowledges the limitations of schooling as instruments of economic change, noting that a fairer distribution of income is the best way to overcome many "inequities in the ability of citizens to make use of their freedoms."[54] Recognizing that schools cannot solve the economic problems that constrain political participation, she also knows that schools need the help of other institutions in promoting democracy: "The primary educational purpose of the mass media, industry, and government, like that of schools, is to cultivate the knowledge, skills, and virtues necessary for democratic deliberation among citizens."[55]

Gutmann has been unfairly criticized for leaving "unquestioned existing political arrangements" and for not believing "that inequality fundamentally shapes American politics."[56] But, in fact, a major point of her book is that by making basic (and expensive) improvements in schooling and other educative institutions we can reduce the inequality that distorts our politics. While Gutmann's book may be seen as moderate in comparison with (for example) Aronowitz and Giroux's *Education Under Siege*, implementation of her proposals for education would require a massive infusion of public funds and would radically transform the schools. If a radical agenda for education is not likely to be implemented in the near future, a more democratic one is within the realm of possibility, and should be supported by all concerned with the future of our children and our society.

Gutmann's point is reinforced in a broader context by James MacGregor Burns. He has recently written: "When political leaders fail, Americans often turn to the next most available saviors or scapegoats—the educators." And the challenge to educators and their allies is to provide equal opportunity, which is "a most radical doctrine."

> If the nation actually wanted persons to achieve positions for which their basic potentials of intelligence and character fitted them, then government must be more than a referee at the starting line; it must intervene at every point where existing structures of inequality barred people from

realizing those potentials. If the nation wanted to open the way for people to realize their 'life chance,' than government or some other agency must act early in their lives to help them obtain the motivation, self-assurance, literacy, good health, decent clothes, speech habits, education, job opportunity, self-esteem that would enable them really to compete.[57]

The Nation and *The New Republic*—for all their differences— still carry on the tradition of political-educational commentary that characterized them a half-century ago. The 6 March 1989 issues of each journal provide examples that parallel Walzer's call for criticism and Gutmann's appeal for democratic education. Hendrik Hertzberg, a senior editor of *The New Republic*, wrote: "A free and critical press may sometimes be a *tactical* disadvantage for a society. But surely it is a huge advantage strategically, because it enables a society to apprehend and correct its own defects."[58] In *The Nation*, Gerald Graff and William Cain presented a critique of educational traditionalism and a proposal for educational change very consistent with Gutmann's. They wrote: "We do not pretend to be taking a politically neutral position, somehow above the battle. We see ours as a left position; its goal is a democratic culture in which traditions are not simply given or fixed but are open to criticism and negotiation."[59]

In our deeply defective society, we can be grateful that the liberal tradition of criticism and advocacy is still being vigorously maintained. As Harold Rosenberg has written, "The weapon of criticism is undoubtedly inadequate. Who on that account would choose to surrender it?"[60]

Nearly three decades ago, Lawrence Cremin concluded *The Transformation of the School* with these words: "And for all the talk about pedagogical breakthroughs and crash programs, the authentic progressive vision remained strangely pertinent to the problems of mid-century America. Perhaps it only awaited the reformulation and resuscitation that would ultimately derive from a larger resurgence of reform in American life and thought."[61] The decades that followed saw further educational breakthroughs and programs and—during the Kennedy, Johnson, and Carter administrations—brief and limited flurries of reform. To keep alive the vision of the earlier liberal journalists, we may hope that the social and economic disasters of the Nixon, Reagan, and Bush years will, as we go through the 1990s, stimulate progressives and dissenters to struggle for a deeper and longer-lasting "resurgence of reform in American life and thought"—in politics, economics, and education. Our history reminds us that there has been no golden age in American society or American education; the promise of progressivism lies yet ahead.

Notes

In the citations that follow *The Nation* will be identified as *TN* and *The New Republic* (following current practice in that journal) as *TNR*. The authorship of some unsigned material from *The Nation* has been identified through Daniel Haskell, ed., *The Nation: Index of Titles and Contributors, 1865–1917* (New York: New York Public Library, 1951).

Chapter 1. Introduction ■

1. This, and the quotations immediately following, are from Randolph Bourne's "In a Schoolroom," *TNR* 1 (7 November 1914): 23–24. Seymour Lipset has written that Bourne was "perhaps the most impressive young radical intellectual the United States ever produced" (*Rebellion in the University* [Boston: Little, Brown, 1971], 118). The definitive study of Bourne is Bruce Clayton, *Forgotten Prophet: The Life of Randolph Bourne* (Baton Rouge: Louisiana State University Press, 1984). Clayton cites this article, and quotes Bourne's concluding statement, in chapter 7.

2. Bourne had studied under John Dewey at Columbia University and shared Dewey's antipathy to artificial separations between processes like thinking and talking. See Louis Filler, *Randolph Bourne* (Washington: American Council on Public Affairs, 1943), 37.

3. The phrase "cult of efficiency" is from the title of Raymond Callahan's book, *Education and the Cult of Efficiency* (Chicago: University of Chicago Press, 1962).

4. Letter, 28 October 1914, Bourne Papers, Special Collections, Butler Library, Columbia University.

5. Walter Lippmann, "Remarks on the Occasion of this Journal's 50th Year," *TNR* 150 (21 March 1964): 14.

6. David Seideman, *The New Republic: A Voice of Modern Liberalism* (New York: Praeger, 1986), 10.

7. Quoted by editor Michael Straight in "The New Republic: 1914–1954," *TNR* 131 (6 December 1954): 17.

8. Editorial, "Teachers' Manifesto," *TNR* 98 (3 May 1939): 366.

9. Letter, Croly to Bourne, 3 June 1914, Bourne Papers.

10. Letter, Croly to Bourne, 15 September 1914, Bourne Papers.

11. Quoted by Alan P. Grimes in *The Political Liberalism of the New York "Nation"*: *1865–1932* (Chapel Hill: University of North Carolina Press, 1953), 117.

12. C. Wright Mills noted that in 1931 over one-third of the subscribers to *The New Republic* were educators (*Sociology and Pragmatism: The Higher Learning in America*, Irving Horowitz, ed. [New York: Galaxy, 1966], 326).

13. A few examples among many which could be cited: Croly was one of the founders of the American Association of University Professors; Bruce Bliven, his successor, was a participant in the Eight-Year Study of progressive education; Freda Kirchwey, editor of *The Nation*, and Robert Morss Lovett, from *The New Republic*'s editorial board, were advisers to the American Student Union.

14. Seideman, *The New Republic*, 10; Penn Kimball, "American Journalism: From Essay to Assay," *TN*, 100th Anniversary Issue, 201 (20 September 1965): 72.

15. Peter Rutkoff and William Scott, *New School: A History of the New School for Social Research* (New York: Free Press, 1986), passim; Jo Ann Boydston, "John Dewey and the Journals," *History of Education Quarterly* 10 (Spring 1970): 72–77. Dewey also wrote nine articles for *The Nation* (Boydston, "John Dewey," 74).

16. Lawrence Cremin, *The Transformation of the School: Progressivism in American Education, 1876–1957* (New York: Knopf, 1961); also by Cremin, *American Education: The Metropolitan Experience, 1876–1980* (New York: Harper and Row, 1988), 171; Patricia Graham, *Progressive Education: From Arcady to Academe* (New York: Teachers College Press, 1967); Sol Cohen, *Progressives and Urban School Reform* (New York: Teachers College Press, 1964); Chester Bowers, *The Progressive Educator and the Depression: The Radical Years* (New York: Random House, 1969); Walter Feinberg, "On Reading Dewey," *History of Education Quarterly* 15 (Winter 1975): 395–415; in the same issue: Clarence Karier, "John Dewey and the New Liberalism: Some Reflections and Responses": 417–443.

17. Grimes, *New York "Nation"*, viii–ix.

18. Arthur Schlesinger, Jr., writes that Croly's *The Promise of American Life* was the "supreme vindication of the interventionist state" (*The Cycles of American History* [Boston: Houghton Mifflin, 1986], 238).

19. *Revolt on the Campus* was the title of James Wechsler's book on the student rebellion (New York: Covici-Friede, 1935).

20. The role of *The Nation* and *The New Republic* in the popular front is explained in *Liberals and Communism: The "Red Decade" Revisited* by Frank Warren (Bloomington: Indiana University Press, 1966).

21. See, for example, Richard H. Pells, *Radical Visions and American Dreams: Culture and Social Thought in the Depression Years* (New York: Harper and Row, 1973).

22. Peter Filene, "An Obituary for 'The Progressive Movement,'" *American Quarterly* 22 (Spring 1970): 20.

23. William O'Neill, *The Progressive Years: America Comes of Age* (New York: Dodd, Mead, 1975), x; Harold U. Faulkner, *The Quest for Social Justice, 1898–1914* (New York: Macmillan, 1931); Robert Wiebe, *The Search for Order: 1877–1920* (New York: Hill and Wang, 1967).

24. Gabriel Kolko, *The Triumph of Conservatism: A Reinterpretation of American History, 1900–1916* (New York: Free Press, 1963).

25. The best treatment of this question is Otis Graham, Jr., *An Encore for Reform: The Old Progressives and the New Deal* (New York: Oxford University Press, 1967).

26. The crispest summaries of this historiographical struggle can be found in Diane Ravitch, *The Revisionists Revised: A Critique of the Radical Attack on the Schools* (New York: Basic Books, 1978), and in Walter Feinberg, Harvey Cantor, Michael Katz, and Paul Violas, *Revisionists Respond to Ravitch* (Washington, D.C.: National Academy of Education, 1980).

27. David Tyack, Robert Lowe, and Elisabeth Hansot, *Public Schools in Hard Times*:

The Great Depression and Recent Years (Cambridge: Harvard University Press, 1984); William J. Reese, *Power and the Promise of School Reform: Grass-roots Movements During the Progressive Era* (Boston: Routledge and Kegan Paul, 1986); Ira Katznelson and Margaret Weir, *Schooling for All: Class, Race, and the Decline of the Democratic Ideal* (New York: Basic Books, 1985).

28. Katz's and Cremin's observations appear in a "Forum" on *The Metropolitan Experience in Education* in *History of Education Quarterly* 29 (Fall 1989): 419–446. Katz's statement appears on page 431 and Cremin's on pages 438 and 439.

29. Cremin, "Forum," 446.

30. Ibid.

31. I am indebted to David Tyack for suggesting the summary presented in this paragraph (Letter to author, 6 April 1989).

32. Herbert Croly, *The Promise of American Life* (New York: Macmillan, 1909).

33. Cremin, *The Metropolitan Experience*, 154.

34. David Tyack, letter to author, 28 December 1988.

35. Cremin, "Forum," 436.

36. Michael Walzer, *The Company of Critics: Social Criticism and Political Commitment in the Twentieth Century* (New York: Basic Books, 1988), ix.

Chapter 2. Liberalism, Old and New ◼

1. Lawrence Cremin, *The Transformation of the School: Progressivism in American Education, 1876–1957* (New York: Knopf, 1961), viii. Cremin's interpretations of progressivism and progressive education remain quite consistent in *American Education: The Metropolitan Experience* (New York: Harper and Row, 1988). See especially Part II.

2. See, for a recent example, Ira Katznelson and Margaret Weir, *Schooling for All: Class, Race, and the Decline of the Democratic Ideal* (New York: Basic Books, 1985), 14–17 and 224, note 16.

3. Revisionist studies since 1961 have been heavily influenced by Gabriel Kolko, *The Triumph of Conservatism: A Reintrpretation of American History, 1900–1916* (New York: Free Press, 1963), and by Robert Wiebe, *The Search for Order, 1877–1920* (New York: Hill and Wang, 1967).

4. For an exploration of some of these issues in their historiographical context, see Paul E. Peterson, *The Politics of School Reform, 1870–1940* (Chicago: University of Chicago, 1985), particularly chapters 1 and 6.

5. This book is essentially an exercise in the history of ideas, which, as Sol Cohen has noted, "has largely fallen into disfavor with historians of education in recent years" ("The School and Personality Development: Intellectual History," in John H. Best, ed., *Historical Inquiry in Education: A Research Agenda* [Washington, D.C.: American Educational Research Association, 1983], 110).

6. Cremin drew on the liberal journals *The Nation* and *The New Republic* at several points (*Transformation*, 119, 126, 157, 225).

7. Charles Forcey, *The Crossroads of Liberalism: Croly, Weyl, Lippmann, and the Progressive Era, 1900–1925* (New York: Oxford, 1961); see also Christopher Lasch, *The New Radicalism in America, 1889–1963: The Intellectual as a Social Type* (New York: Knopf, 1965), chapters 3, 5, and 6; also David W. Noble, *The Paradox of Progressive Thought* (Minneapolis: University of Minnesota Press, 1958), chapters 1 and 2.

8. See, for example, Wiebe, *The Search for Order*, 314: "Forcey . . . is valuable both as an examination of ideas and as a commentary on the urge to power." William L. O'Neill describes Forcey's book as "a penetrating intellectual history" (*The Progressive Years: America Comes of Age* [New York: Dodd, Mead, 1975], 63). On Croly's elitism and dependence on Roosevelt, see Kolko, *Triumph*, 215–216.

9. See chapter 7 of R. Jeffrey Lustig's *Corporate Liberalism: The Origins of Modern American Political Theory, 1890–1920* (Berkeley: University of California Press, 1982) regarding the ambiguity and elitism of the *New Republic* group. Lustig also acknowledges (page 197) their influence: "These men forged the most complete synthesis of group theory, realist epistemology, and new politics; they presented the country with the first statement of a general theory to replace classical liberalism."

10. David Seideman, *The New Republic: A Voice of Modern Liberalism* (New York: Praeger, 1986), chapter 1; Alan P. Grimes, *The Political Liberalism of the New York "Nation": 1865−1932* (Chapel Hill: University of North Carolina Press, 1953), chapter 4.

11. Edmund Wilson traced some of these changing labels in an article in *The New Republic* in 1931. He described Croly's belief in "the salvation of our society by the gradual and natural approximation to socialism which he himself called progressivism, but which has generally come to be known as liberalism" ("An Appeal to Progressives," *TNR* 65 [14 January 1931]: 235). Robert Crunden says that men like Croly "should be regarded as 'urban liberals' rather than as progressives" (*Ministers of Reform: The Progressives' Achievement in American Civilization, 1889−1920* [New York: Basic Books, 1982], 276).

12. W. A. Swanberg, *Whitney Father, Whitney Heiress* (New York: Scribner's Sons, 1980), 357.

13. Alvin Johnson, *Pioneer's Progress* (Lincoln: University of Nebraska Press, 1960; first published in 1952), 245.

14. Arthur M. Schlesinger, Jr., describes the process of "nationalizing the new freedom" in chapter 5 of *The Crisis of the Old Order, 1919−1933* (Boston: Houghton Mifflin, 1957). Martin Sklar proposes discarding "as a tool of analysis . . . the New Freedom-New Nationalism formula" ("Woodrow Wilson and the Political Economy of Modern United States Liberalism," in *A New History of Leviathan: Essays on the Rise of the American Corporate State*, edited by Ronald Radosh and Murray Rothbard [New York: Dutton, 1972], 65). However these distinctions may have become blurred for historians, during the election of 1912 people thought and acted as though they were significant.

15. Oswald Garrison Villard, *Fighting Years: Memoirs of a Liberal Editor* (New York: Harcourt, Brace, 1939), 349.

16. On the growth of the positive state, see Schlesinger, *The Cycles of American History* (Boston: Houghton Mifflin, 1986), chapter 9: "Affirmative Government and the American Economy." The roles of Lippmann and Croly are considered on pages 237−238.

17. Michael Wreszin, *Oswald Garrison Villard: Pacifist at War* (Bloomington: Indiana University, 1965), chapter 7. See also Richard C. Sterne, "The Nation and Its Century," *TN*, 100th Anniversary Issue, 201 (20 September 1965): 42ff.

18. David Levy, *Herbert Croly of "The New Republic": The Life and Thought of an American Progressive* (Princeton: Princeton University Press, 1985), 234−235.

19. Reviews and articles closely reflected the editorial positions of the two journals. See Villard, *Fighting Years*, 349; Levy, *Croly*, chapter 7; also a 13 June 1914 letter from Harold Fuller to Randolph Bourne (Bourne Papers).

20. "Our Educational Prospect," Unsigned review of John and Evelyn Dewey's *Schools of Tomorrow*, *TNR* 3 (26 June 1915): 211−212. Bourne was at this time a fervent admirer of Dewey, and had just completed his series on the Gary Schools.

21. "The Public Schools," Unsigned review, *TN* 101 (9 September 1915): 326−327.

22. Walter Lippmann, "The Hope of Democracy," Review of John Dewey's *Democracy and Education*, *TNR* 7 (1 July 1916): 231. On Lippmann's career with *The New Republic*, see Ronald Steel, *Walter Lippmann and the American Century* (New York: Random House, 1980), chapters 7−15.

23. Warner Fite, "Dewey's Philosophy of Education," Review of John Dewey's *Democracy and Education*, *TN* 102 (4 May 1916): 480−481. Cremin, *Transformation*, 126. See also Paul Shorey's "The Bigotry of the New Education," *TN* 105 (6 September 1917): Educational Supplement, 253−256. Shorey had mild praise for Dewey, but strong criticism of Bourne's "Education and Living," most of which had been previously published in *TNR*. Villard's *Nation* was more positive about Bourne, probably because Bourne and Villard both firmly opposed America's entrance into World War I. See Bourne's obituary, *TN* 107 (28 December 1918): 79.

24. Walter Lippmann, *Drift and Mastery* (Englewood Cliffs, N.J.: Prentice-Hall, 1961; first published in 1915), chapter 15.

25. D. Joy Humes, *Oswald Garrison Villard: Liberal of the 1920's* (Syracuse, N.Y.: Syracuse University Press, 1960), 4.

26. "En Avant," Letter from W. H. Stone, *TN* 108 (5 April 1919): 503. See also Lewis Gannett, "Villard's 'Nation,'" in Henry M. Christman, ed., *One Hundred Years of "The Nation"* (New York: Macmillan, 1965), 35−41.

27. Cremin, *Transformation*, 221.

28. Boyd H. Bode, "Reconstruction in Philosophy," *TN* 111 (8 December 1920): 658 and 660.

29. H. R. Mussey, "An Independent College of Political Science," Editorial, *TN* 106 (11 May 1918): 559–560. On the founding of the New School, and the involvement of the *New Republic* group, see Peter Rutkoff and William Scott, *New School: A History of the New School for Social Research* (New York: Free Press, 1986), chapters 1 and 2.

30. James Harvey Robinson, "A New Educational Adventure," *TN* 107 (7 September 1918): 264–265.

31. Alexander Meiklejohn, Francis A. Hand, Letters, *TN* 107 (7 September 1918): 266.

Chapter 3. Education and Efficiency ■

1. The most thorough and influential treatment of this topic appears in Callahan's *Education and the Cult of Efficiency*. (Chicago: University of Chicago Press, 1962). Our purpose here is to explore the issue from the standpoint of the liberal journals and to stress more directly than Callahan the fact that progressives, because of their partial alienation from the business ethos, were particularly sensitive to the effects of the efficiency movement.

2. Walter Lippmann, *A Preface to Politics* (New York: Kennerley, 1913). Quoted in Forcey, *The Crossroads of Liberalism: Croly, Weyl, Lippmann, and the Progressive Era, 1900–1925* (New York: Oxford, 1961), 112.

3. On the relationship of the editors to Dorothy and Willard Straight, see David Seideman, *The New Republic: A Voice of Modern Liberalism* (New York: Praeger, 1986), 1–46. Croly later wrote an admiring biography of *The New Republic*'s benefactor: (*Willard Straight* [New York: Macmillan, 1925]). Dorothy Straight's life is recounted in W. A. Swanberg, *Whitney Father, Whitney Heiress* (New York: Scribner's, 1980), Book Two.

4. For the changing views of *The New Republic* group on businessmen and reform, see Forcey, *Crossroads*, 112, 215, 164 ff.

5. Hofstadter draws on Grimes's study in placing Godkin's *Nation* in the "status revolution" framework (*The Age of Reform* [New York: Vintage books, 1960; first published in 1955], 142–143. Aaron Miller reports Godkin's belief that "labor must not be allowed to usurp the prerogatives of the natural aristocracy of a free society" ("The Paradoxical Godkin, Founder of *The Nation*," *Journalism Quarterly* 42 [Spring 1965]: 201).

6. Henry May, *The End of American Innocence: A Study of the First Years of Our Own Time, 1912–1917* (Chicago: Quadrangle, 1964; first published in 1959), 132–136.

7. See ibid., 135; also Samuel P. Hays, *Conservation and the Gospel of Efficiency* (Cambridge: Harvard University Press, 1959), 265, 270–271. The most comprehensive study of this movement is Samuel Haber's *Efficiency and Uplift: Scientific Management in the Progressive Era, 1890–1920* (Chicago: University of Chicago Press, 1964). Chapter 5 deals with Croly, Lippmann, and Louis Brandeis.

8. Editorial, "Democratic Control of Scientific Management," *TNR* 9 (23 December 1916): 204–205; Lippmann, "The Puzzle of Hughes," *TNR* 8 (30 September 1916): 210–213.

9. Randolph Bourne, "Education as Living," *TNR* 8 (5 August 1916): 10–12.

10. Thomas Walters, *Randolph Silliman Bourne: Education Through Radical Eyes* (Kennebunkport, Me.: Mercer House, 1982), 60.

11. Callahan, in *Education and the Cult of Efficiency*, notes (pages 130–134) that as early as 1911 and 1912 educational leaders like J. F. Bobbitt were citing the Gary schools in this way.

12. Bourne, "Schools in Gary," *TNR* 2 (27 March 1915): 198–199.

13. Bourne, "Communities for Children," *TNR* 2 (3 April 1915): 233–234. The other articles in the series appeared on 10 April, 24 April, and 1 May 1915.

14. Bourne, *The Gary Schools* (Boston: Houghton Mifflin, 1916), viii. The most thorough study of the Gary experiment is *The Paradox of Progressive Education: The Gary Plan and Urban Schooling*, by Ronald Cohen and Raymond Mohl (Port Washington,

N.Y.: Kennikat Press, 1979). The authors describe Bourne's study as "a laudatory book" (page 25).

15. Interview by the author with de Lima, 18 November 1965.

16. Letter from Hoyt to Bourne, 22 July 1915, Bourne Papers, Columbia University Library. David Tyack describes Bourne's rather uncritical response to the practices of "administrative progressives" who were heavily influenced by the efficiency movement (*The One Best System: A History of American Urban Education* [Cambridge: Harvard University Press, 1975], 193–194).

17. Letter, Bourne to Sergeant, 23 September 1915, Bourne Papers. Adeline and Murray Levine note that the timing of Bourne's articles and book helped support the campaign (in which the Straights were involved) to import the Gary system into the New York schools (Introduction, reissue of *The Gary Schools* [Cambridge: M.I.T. Press, 1970], xxxvi–xxxvii).

18. John Dewey, "American Education and Culture," *TNR* 7 (1 July 1916): 216.

19. Dewey, Review of Helen Marot's *Creative Industry*, *TNR* 17 (2 November 1918): 20, 23. For an example of Dewey's persistent critique of "scientific management and reform from the top down," see David Tyack and Elisabeth Hansot, *Managers of Virtue: Public School Leadership in America, 1920–1980* (New York: Basic Books, 1982), 201–203.

20. These quotations are all from an editorial, "The National Education Association," *TN* 102 (29 June 1916): 690–691. This issue carried the N.E.A. annual program as a supplement, further evidence that teachers were a significant part of the journal's intended audience. There was a large amount of educational material in this issue, including an indictment of the Gary system by editor Harold Fuller ("The Gary System," Review of Bourne's *The Gary Schools*, 698–699).

21. Editorial, "Universities and Their Money's Worth," *TN* 99 (3 December 1914): 648–649.

22. The phrase "extreme democracy" was used in the editorial on the NEA cited above (*TN* 102: 691).

23. Haber, *Efficiency and Uplift*, 73n.

24. Laski, Review of *The Higher Learning in America*, *TNR* 17 (11 January 1919): 317–318.

25. Joseph Jastrow, "Our Commercialized Universities," Review of Veblen's *The Higher Learning in America*, *TN* 108 (22 February 1919): 286–288. See also "Reviews: Education," *TN* 106 (4 May 1918: 541–543. Several of the reviews suggest that scientific methods and efficiency practices can be reconciled with humane, pragmatic, learner-oriented education.

26. See "The Technicians and Revolution" (1921), in *The Portable Veblen*, edited by Max Lerner (New York: Viking Press, 1948), 438–465.

27. It is likely that Veblen was not as aloof and objective as he tried to appear. See Morton White, *Social Thought in America*, rev. ed. (Boston: Beacon Press, 1957) 89–93.

Chapter 4. Scholars and Their Bosses ■

1. David W. Levy, *Herbert Croly of "The New Republic": The Life and Thought of an American Progressive* (Princeton: Princeton University Press, 1985), 234 and note 40, same page.

2. Willard Elsbree, *The American Teacher: Evolution of a Profession in a Democracy* (New York: American Book Company, 1939), 541–543; Howard K. Beale, *Are American Teachers Free?* (New York: Scribner's, 1936), x–xviii.

3. Lawrence Veysey, *The Emergence of the American University* (Chicago: University of Chicago Press, 1965), 384–418.

4. Ellen Schrecker, *No Ivory Tower: McCarthyism and the Universities*, (New York: Oxford University Press, 1986), chapter 1.

5. Morris Jastrow, "Learning in America: Professors in Council," *TN* 100 (4 February 1915): 146–147. See also the editorial, "Free Speech and the Professors," *TN* 98 (15 January 1914): 51.

6. George Dykhuisen, *The Life and Mind of John Dewey* (Carbondale: Southern Illi-

nois University Press, 1973), 170−171; Walter P. Metzger, *Academic Freedom in the Age of the University* (New York: Columbia University Press, 1961), 200−203.

7. Editorial note, *TNR* 1 (9 January 1915): 4−5.

8. Editorial note, *TN* 100 (24 June 1915): 698.

9. F. I. Davenport, "Reconstructing Boards of Education," *TNR* 2 (3 April 1915): 229−230. John Dewey had made a similar point in the journal in "A Policy of Industrial Education," *TNR* 1 (19 December 1914): 11−12. David Levy notes that during the 1914−1918 period "the editors printed numerous articles advocating progressive education and the academic freedom of teachers" (*Croly*, 234.)

10. Editorial, "Who Owns the Universities?" *TNR* 3 (17 July 1915): 269−270. A similar statement, objecting to exclusive university governance by trustees as "absentee landlordism," appeared in an editorial on 10 March 1917 (*TNR* 10: 149−150).

11. Charles Beard, "A Statement," *TNR* 13 (29 December 1917): 249−251. For a crisp summary of this Columbia University dispute, see Schrecker, *No Ivory Tower*, 22. Thomas Bender describes these events and the founding of the New School in chapter 8 ("Professors as Intellectuals") of *New York Intellect: A History of Intellectual Life in New York City from 1750 to the Beginnings of Our own Time* (New York: Knopf, 1987).

12. Peter Rutkoff and William Scott, *New School: A History of the New School for Social Research* (New York: Free Press, 1986), 20. Chapters 1 and 2 explain the connections between *The New Republic* and the early New School.

13. Ibid., 10−11.

14. Oswald Garrison Villard, "*The Nation*, 1865−1925, *TN* 121 (1 July 1925): 9; Henry Mussey called the 1918−1919 period "The Heroic Age" of *The Nation* in an article with that title in the same issue (pages 9−11).

15. William MacDonald, Editorial note, *TN* 107 (23 November 1918): 613. MacDonald was associate editor at this time (Joseph Swain, "The Crisis in the Schools," *TN* 107 [7 September 1918]: 246−248.

16. Robert K. Murray, *Red Scare: A Study of National Hysteria, 1919−1920* (New York: McGraw-Hill, 1964; first published 1955), 169−170. Murray drew frequently on *The New Republic* and *The Nation* in describing liberal responses to the Red Scare.

17. William MacDonald, Editorial note, *TN* 111 (21 August 1920): 202−203.

18. Editorial, "The Unionizing of Professors," *TN* 109 (23 August 1919): 237.

19. For a brief discussion of the arguments for and against unions of educators during this period, see Metzger, *The Age of the University*, 196n.

20. Croly, Lippmann, More, Fuller, and Villard were Harvard graduates; Weyl was a graduate of the Wharton School of the University of Pennsylvania. See Charles Forcey, *The Crossroads of Liberalism: Croly, Weyl, Lippmann and the Progressive Era, 1900−1925* (New York: Oxford University Press, 1961), 11, 53, 101; D. Joy Humes, *Oswald Garrison Villard: Liberal of the 1920's* (Syracuse, N.Y.: Syracuse University Press, 1960), 8; Alan P. Grimes, *The Political Liberalism of the New York "Nation": 1865−1932* (Chapel Hill: University of North Carolina Press, 1953), viii. For the readership of the journals see Forcey, *Crossroads*, 175; also James P. Wood, *Magazines in the United States* (New York: Ronald Press, 1949), 189. Forcey writes that *The New Republic* was aimed at "teachers, professors, civil servants, social workers, enlightened politicians and businessmen" (*Crossroads*, 175).

21. Editorial note, *TNR* 3 (26 June 1915): 185−186. The call to "discipline the democracy" also suggests the elitism which Croly and the other editors occasionally expressed. See Forcey, *Crossroads*, 19.

22. Murray, *Red Scare*, passim.

23. Editorial, *The Outlook* 116 (29 August 1917): 644−646.

24. Oswald Garrison Villard, *Fighting Years: Memoirs of a Liberal Editor* (New York: Harcourt, Brace, 1939), 354ff. For *The Nation's* relationships with the federal government since 1921, see Penn Kimball, "The History of *The Nation* According to the F.B.I.," *TN* 242 (22 March 1986): 399−426. The current editor's reflections on *The Nation's* history are given by Victor Navasky in his afterword to "*The Nation, 1865−1990: Selections from the Independent Magazine of Politics and Culture*, edited by Katrina Vanden Heuvel (New York: Thunder's Mouth Press, 1990), 513−530.

25. Beale, in *Are American Teachers Free?*, describes (through 1934) various attacks on *The Nation* and *The New Republic* as well as their defenses of academic freedom. See pages 830 and 832 of his index for a number of such references.

Chapter 5. Education and Reform ■

1. Lawrence Cremin, *The Transformation of the School: Progressivism in American Education, 1876–1957* (New York: Knopf, 1961), 179, 288. As early as 1924 Agnes de Lima had identified three comparable groups. See "The New Education: In the Ethical Culture, Horace Mann, and Lincoln Schools," *TN* 119 (2 July 1924): 9–11.

2. Cremin, *Transformation*, 85.

3. Rush Welter, *Popular Education and Democratic Thought in America* (New York: Columbia University Press, 1962), 285.

4. Editorial, *TN* 99 (17 December 1914): 705.

5. Harold Fuller, "The Gary System," *TN* 102 (29 June 1916): 699.

6. Warner Fite, "The State-University Idea," *TN* 101 (9 September 1915): 322–324.

7. Editorial, *TN* 102 (29 June 1916): 691.

8. Concern for blacks was a tradition with *The Nation*'s owners and editors. The first literary editor was abolitionist William Lloyd Garrison's son; the current owner, Oswald Garrison Villard, was his grandson (Oswald Garrison Villard, *Fighting Years: Memoirs of a Liberal Editor* [New York: Harcourt, Brace, 1939], chapter 1).

9. Oswald Garrison Villard, Editorial, *TN* 100 (18 February 1915): 187–188; see also pages 99–100 in the same volume. Villard owned *The Nation* at this time, but did not assume the editorship until 1918.

10. Thorstein Veblen, *The Theory of the Leisure Class* (New York: Heubsch, 1918; first published 1899), 191.

11. Randolph Bourne, *Education and Living* (New York: The Century Company, 1917), vi. This book consisted of papers "reprinted with slight additions from the pages of the "New Republic" (Preface, v).

12. Bourne, "John Dewey's Philosophy," *TNR* 2 (13 March 15): 153.

13. John Dewey, "A Policy of Industrial Education," *TNR* 1 (19 December 1914): 11–12. Groff Conklin wrote in 1936 that "John Dewey, next to the editors themselves, has been the N.R.'s most influential contributor" (*The New Republic Anthology: 1914–1935*, edited by Groff Conklin [New York: Dodge, 1936]). Dewey was a contributing editor of the journal from 1922 to 1937. Jo Ann Boydston has calculated that Dewey published a total of 179 articles in *The New Republic*, "exactly the same number of articles that appeared in the next four most frequently used journals together" ("John Dewey and the Journals, *History of Education Quarterly* 10 [Spring 1970]: 72–77).

14. Dewey, "Splitting Up the School System," *TNR* 2 (17 April 1915): 283–284. Bruce Bliven, a *New Republic* editor during much of Dewey's association with that journal, said that Dewey wrote "in clumsy English" but knew that he needed good editors and never complained about the drastic revisions which his articles often required (Interview with author, August 28, 1965.)

15. Welter, *Popular Education*, 271–276.

16. Walter Lippmann, "Insiders and Outsiders," *TNR* 5 (13 November 1915): 35–36.

17. Cremin, *American Education: The Metropolitan Experience, 1876–1980* (New York: Harper and Row, 1988), 522.

18. In *Drift and Mastery* (page 148), for example, Lippmann recognized the role of the unconscious in politics and life, but advocated "the substitution of conscious intention for unconscious striving" (Englewood Cliffs: N.J.: Prentice-Hall, 1961; originally published 1914). Of Lippmann's many books, *Drift and Mastery*—which appeared in 1914, the same year that *The New Republic* began publishing—was closest in spirit to his *New Republic* articles. Lawrence Cremin presents a broad interpretation of Lippmann's changing educational thought and compares it to Dewey's in *American Education: The Metropolitan Experience*, 180–187.

19. William L. Stoddard, "The Boston Trade Union College," *TN* 109 (30 August 1919): 298–300. See also the reviews of books on education in *TN* 106 (4 May 1918): 541–543.

20. "Books in Brief," *TN* 111 (4 September 1920): 277.

21. Carl Van Doren, Editorial note, *TN* 112 (23 February 1921): 279.

22. Harold Laski, "British Labor and Direct Action, *TN* 106 (21 September 1920): 291–292.

23. Samuel Bowles and Herbert Gintis have written the most influential statement of educational reproduction theory: *Schooling in Capitalist America: Educational Reform and the Contradictions of Economic Life* (New York: Basic Books, 1976). See chapter 7 for their treatment of progressive education.

24. See Cremin, *Transformation*, chapter 6; also Sidney Kaplan, "Social Engineers as Saviors," *Journal of the History of Ideas* 17 (June 1956): 347–369. For some differences between the journals regarding the effects of the war, see the editorial in *TN* 111 (3 November 1920): 489.

25. Editorial, "Americanism in Education," *TNR* 19 (10 May 1919): 38–40.

26. Welter, *Popular Education*, 301.

27. Editorial, "Americanism in Education." The editors were quoting from Dewey's *Democracy and Education: An Introduction to the Philosophy of Education* (New York: Macmillan, 1916), 317.

28. This phrase comes from the title of Gene Smith's *When the Cheering Stopped: The Last Years of Woodrow Wilson* (New York: Morrow, 1964).

29. James Gouinlock stresses Dewey's conviction that a variety of institutions have a part to play in educating and organizing people for democratic social change (*Excellence in Public Discourse: John Stuart Mill, John Dewey, and Social Intelligence* [New York: Teachers College Press, 1986], 70).

30. Nietzsche's phrase "Twilight of Idols" was used by a disillusioned Randolph Bourne as the title of an article in which he indicted Dewey and other liberals for their support of World War I ("Twilight of Idols," *The Seven Arts* 2 [October 1917]: 688–702).

31. James Weinstein, *The Corporate Ideal in the Liberal State* (Boston: Beacon Press, 1968), 216.

Chapter 6. The Eclipse of Progressivism ■

1. Editorial note, *TNR* 26 (2 March 1921): 1.

2. Editorial, "Inaugurated," *TNR* 26 (16 March 1921), 57.

3. Editorial, *TN* 112 (16 March 1921): 389.

4. For an analysis of Theodore Roosevelt as "pseudo-progressive," see chapter 8 of Daniel Aaron, *Men of Good Hope* (New York: Oxford University Press, 1961; first published in 1951). After Wilson's death H. L. Mencken referred to him as "The Archangel Woodrow," and "the late Messiah," and reminded his readers that Wilson's book *The New Freedom* was "once a favorite text of *New Republic* liberals, deserving Democrats, and the tender-minded in general" ("The Archangel Woodrow," *The Smart Set* [January 1921], included in *The Vintage Mencken*, gathered by Alistair Cooke [New York: Vintage, 1955], 116–120. The quotation is from page 117).

5. Henry Fairlie, "War Against Reason," *The New Republic*, 75th Anniversary Issue, 201 (6 November 1989): 58.

6. Wilson may have acquired the phrase "peace without victory," which was first used in *The New Republic*, from that journal (David Seideman, *The New Republic: A Voice of Modern Liberalism* [New York: Praeger, 1986], 48). On Villard's opposition to the Versailles Treaty, see Michael Wreszin, *Oswald Garrison Villard: Pacifist at War* (Bloomington: Indiana University Press, 1965), chapter 9.

7. Editorial, "How Will You Vote?" *TN* 111 (4 September 1920): 260.

8. John B. Judis, "Herbert Croly's Promise," *The New Republic*, 75th Anniversary Issue, 201 (6 November 1989): 84. See also Herbert Croly, "The Eclipse of Progressivism," *TNR* 24 (27 October 1920): 210–216. In this editorial article, Croly gave a capsule history of his political past, describing himself as "an American who called himself a reformer from 1890 to 1908, a Republican insurgent from 1908 to 1912, and since 1912 a progressive, and who shared most of the mistakes and illusions of the reformers, insurgents, and progressives" (page 215).

9. John Hicks, *The Republican Ascendancy* (New York: Harper, 1960), 184.

10. Henry May's 1956 article is still useful: "Shifting Perspectives on the 1920s," *Mississippi Valley Historical Review* 43 (December 1956): 405–427. Richard H. Pells identifies the groups that did not share in 1920s prosperity in *Radical Visions and American*

Dreams: Culture and Social Thought in the Depression Years. (New York: Harper and Row, 1973), 12. Pells's first chapter provides excellent perspective on the decade and on the role of the liberal journals.

11. Quoted in Frederick J. Hoffman, *The Twenties: American Writing in the Postwar Decade* (New York: Collier, 1962; first published 1954), 378n. The most influential study of the expatriates was Malcolm Cowley's *Exiles Return: A Literary Odyssey of the 1920s* (New York: Viking, 1956; first published 1934).

12. Page Smith, *Redeeming the Time: A People's History of the 1920s and the New Deal* (New York: McGraw-Hill, 1987), 182.

13. Arthur S. Link, "What Happened to the Progressive Movement in the 1920's?" *American Historical Review* 64 (July 1959): 833–851.

14. Link in "What Happened to the Progressive Movement?" could have distinguished more clearly between goal and method. Some measures (e.g., prohibition, immigration restriction) that he labeled "progressive" were such only in using collective governmental methods to carry out their illiberal intentions.

15. David W. Levy, *Herbert Croly of "The New Republic": The Life and Thought of an American Progressive* (Princeton: Princeton University Press, 1985, chapter 9, "Years of Despair, 1919–1930"; Oswald Garrison Villard, *The Fighting Years: Memoirs of a Liberal Editor* (New York: Harcourt, Brace, 1939), passim.

16. Judis, "Herbert Croly's Promise," 87.

17. Weyl's article was published posthumously in *Tired Radicals and Other Essays* (New York: Huebsch, 1921). Norman Thomas's use of the phrase is quoted in Hoffman, *The Twenties*, 378n; William Leuchtenberg used it as the title of chapter 7 of *The Perils of Prosperity: 1914–1932* (Chicago: University of Chicago Press, 1958); the quotation about Villard is by William Hard, in Grimes, *Political Liberalism*, ix.

18. Seideman, *The New Republic*, 64.

19. Croly, "Sick of Politics," *TNR* 31 (7 June 1922): 34; Arthur Schlesinger, Jr., "Sources of the New Deal," in *Paths of American Thought*, edited by Schlesinger and Morton White (Boston: Houghton Mifflin, 1963), 379. Schlesinger overstates the case in saying that "successive disenchantments had destroyed [Croly's] interest in politics." Croly was clearly less optimistic than previously about social salvation through political action, but continued to comment vigorously on political developments.

20. Schlesinger, *Paths*, 375–376; Bliven, "The First Forty Years", *TNR* , 40th Anniversary Issue, 131 (November 1954): 10.

21. Preston W. Slosson, *The Great Crusade and After, 1914–1928* (New York: Macmillan, 1930), 442. Circulation figures are from N. W. Ayer and Son, *American Newspaper Annual and Directory* (Philadelphia: Ayer, 1914–1930). For a rather poignant discussion of the financial difficulties of the journals, see the letter from Villard to Jane Addams, 11 October 1919 (Villard Papers, Houghton Library, Harvard University).

22. See Judis, "Herbert Croly's Promise," for an assessment of Croly and his influence. He describes Croly (page 84) as a "political philosopher who made his living as a journalist and biographer."

23. Levy, *Croly*, chapter 9; Hicks, *The Republican Ascendancy*, 85.

24. Villard's activist orientation was evident in the rationale he gave for abandoning his brief teaching career in history at Harvard. He declared that teaching was "like sitting in a club window and watching the world go by on the pavement outside." Quoted in D. Joy Humes, *Oswald Garrison Villard: Liberal of the 1920's* (Syracuse, N.Y.: Syracuse University Press, 1960), 8–9. Humes's statement about Villard's hatred of war is on page 194.

25. Sinclair Lewis, "An American Views the Huns," *TN* 121 (1 July 1925): 20.

26. *Current Biography*, 1940, 831–832.

27. On Croly's stroke and death, see Levy, *Croly*, 299–300.

Chapter 7. A New Means for Liberals ■

1. For further evidence of Croly's disillusion with politics, see his unpublished 1920 manuscript "The Breach in Civilization" (Houghton Library, Harvard University); also David W. Levy, *Herbert Croly* of *"The New Republic": The Life and Thought of an*

American Progressive (Princeton: Princeton University Press, 1985), 290–293. A persuasive analysis of Croly's thought during this period was written by fellow editor George Soule shortly after Croly's death: "Herbert Croly's Liberalism, 1920–1928," *TNR* 63 (16 July 1930), Part II: 253–257. For other recent interpretations, see John Diggins, "*The New Republic* and its Times," *TNR* 191 (10 December 1984): 23–73; also John B. Judis, "Herbert Croly's Promise," *TNR*, 75th Anniversary Issue, 201 (6 November 1989): 84–87.

2. On the history of adult education, see Malcolm Knowles, *The Adult Education Movement in the United States* (Melbourne, Fla.: Krieger, 1977; rev. ed.); worker education through the 1930s is dealt with on pages 44–45, 107–111, and 166–168.

3. David Stewart, *Adult Learning in America: Eduard Lindeman and His Agenda for Lifelong Education* (Melbourne, Fla.: Krieger, 1987), 89–90. On Lindeman's relationship with Croly and *The New Republic*, see particularly chapters 4–6.

4. Marius Hansome, "The Development of Workers' Education," chapter 3 of *Workers' Education in the United States*, Theodore Brameld, ed. (New York: Harper, 1941), 52–53; William Stoddard, "The Boston Trade Union College," TN 109 (30 August 1919): 298–300.

5. C. Hartley Grattan, *In Quest of Knowledge: A Historical Perspective on Adult Education* (New York: Association Press, 1955) 247, 325.

6. Ibid., 250.

7. These include only those editorials, articles, and reviews that gave major attention to adult and workers' education. *The New Republic*'s particular interest in adult and worker education is suggested by the fact that it published three books in its Dollar Series dealing with these topics ("Dollar Reprints," *TNR* 64 [20 August 1930]: 11).

8. Arthur Mann, "British Social Thought and American Reformers of the Progressive Era," provides excellent perspective on this influence (*Mississippi Valley Historical Review* 42 [March 1956] 672–692).

9. Joyce Kornbluh, *A New Deal for Workers' Education: The Workers' Service Program, 1933–1942* (Urbana: University of Illinois Press, 1987), 9, 14–15; Brameld, *Worker's Education*, 10; Horace Kallen, *Education, the Machine and the Worker* (New York: New Republic, 1925), vii–viii.

10. Herbert Horwill, "The Education of the Adult Worker," *TN* 108 (10 May 1919): 738–739. (Horwill was *The Nation*'s London correspondent.) R. H. Tawney, "Adult Education in England," *TNR* 40 (19 November 1924): 292–293; Harold Laski, "On the Prospects of Adult Education," *TNR* 54 (22 February 1928): 47–50.

11. Joyce Kornbluh and Lyn Goldfarb, "Labor Education and Women Workers: An Historical Perspective," in *Labor Education for Women Workers*, edited by Barbara Wertheimer (Philadelphia: Temple University Press, 1981), 15–31; Rose Pesotta, *Bread Upon the Waters* (Ithaca: ILR Press, 1987; first published in 1944), 15–16.

12. Roger Daniels, "Worker's Education and the University of California," *Labor History* 4 (Winter 1963): 34. Irving Bernstein titled his book on American workers from 1920 to 1933 *The Lean Years* (Boston: Houghton Mifflin, 1960).

13. Richard B. Morris, *Encyclopedia of American History* (New York: Harper, 1953), 525.

14. James Maurer, "Labor's Demand for its Own Schools," *TN* 115 (29 September 1922): 276. A. J. Muste expressed a similar viewpoint: "The educational movement is becoming larger and more complex now simply because the unions have larger and more complex tasks to perform." ("Workers' Education in the United States," *TN* 119 [1 October 1924]: 334.)

15. On the effects of workers' education in England, see W.H.G. Armytage, *Four Hundred Years of English Education* (Cambridge: Cambridge University Press, 1964), 192ff.

16. Levy, *Croly*, chapter nine; Alan P. Grimes, *The Political Liberalism of the New York "Nation": 1865–1932* (Chapel Hill: University of North Carolina Press, 1953), chapter 6; David Seideman, *The New Republic: A Voice of Modern Liberalism* (New York: Praeger, 1986), 61–79.

17. As early as 1918, according to Steve Fraser, "the editors of the *New Republic* were swept away" with their hopes for labor. He quotes them as saying: "We have already passed to a new era, the transition to a state in which labor will be the predominating element. The character of the future democracy is largely at the mercy of the

recognized leaders of organized labor" ("The 'Labor Question,'" in *The Rise and Fall of the New Deal Order, 1930–1980,* edited by Steve Fraser and Gary Gerstle, [Princeton: Princeton University Press, 1989], 56).

18. John Dewey, "Labor Politics and Labor Education," *TNR* 57 (9 January 1929), 213. Near the end of the decade Dewey, Villard, Paul Douglas, and others attempted to promote a realignment of American parties on more rational lines, hoping that labor, farmers, intellectuals, and others might become the core of a new liberal political grouping. See R. Alan Lawson, *The Failure of Independent Liberalism* (New York: Putnam's, 1971).

19. A. J. Muste, "Workers' Education," *TN* 119 (10 October 1924): 334. Charles Howlett has shown how broadly these purposes were interpreted at Brookwood, particularly with reference to the peace movement ("Brookwood Labor College and Worker Commitment to Social Reform," *Mid-America* 61 [January 1979]: 47–66).

20. George Soule wrote that during the 1920s Croly "advised progressives to approach closer and support labor. And he defined the support which he favored by a characteristic group of adjectives—'candid, discriminating, and loyal.'" Groups such as labor that "at one movement would feel warmed by his support would soon be cooled by his inveterate necessity to qualify and criticize" (Soule, "Herbert Croly's Liberalism," *TNR* 63 [16 July 1930]: 254, 256).

21. Editorial, "Workers' Education," *TNR* 28 (12 October 1921): 173–174.

22. Grattan, *Adult Education,* 245.

23. On this point, see the quotation from Fannia Cohn in "Workers' Education," *TN* 113 (7 December 1921): 673; also James Maurer, "Labor's Demand for its Own Schools," *TN* 115 (20 September 1922): 276–278.

24. Arthur Gleason, "Workers' Education in the United States," *TNR* 34 (28 March 1923): 143.

25. Jean Flexner, "Brookwood," *TNR* 43 (2 August 1925): 288–289.

26. Gleason, "Worker's Education," 143. Similarly, Muste noted that those who advocated cultural education in labor schools were "in danger of attacking the worker's problem at its circumference rather than its center" ("Workers' Education," 334).

27. Lindeman, a *New Republic* contributing editor, wrote that "adult education, whenever it endures long enough to pass through the 'bread and butter' stage, invariably evolves toward cultural ends" (*The Meaning of Adult Education* [New York: New Republic, 1926], 99).

28. Editorial, "The Object of Workers' Education," *TNR* 34 (25 April 1923): 229.

29. Norman Thomas, Letter, *TNR* 34 (9 May 1923): 296.

30. Editorial note, *TN* 112 (13 April 1921): 527. Kornbluh and Goldfarb give a brief description of the Bryn Mawr Summer School in "Labor Education," 19–20.

31. Maurer, "Labor's Demand," 278.

32. Editorial, "The Object," 230.

33. Editorial, "Is Labor a Lost Hope?" *TN* 118 (20 February 1924): 196.

34. Editorial, "Workers' Education," *TNR* 28 (12 October 1921): 174.

35. Dewey, "Labor Politics," 211–214. See also *The New Republic* editorial in support of Dewey's position ("The Federation and Mr. Woll," 57 [9 January 1929]: 205–206); also an editorial note reaffirming the policy four months later (58 [8 May 1929]: 317).

36. Horwill, "Adult Worker," 739.

37. Flexner, "Brookwood," 288.

38. Editorial, "Adult Education," *TNR* 45 (25 November 1925): 8.

39. Lindeman, "Labor's Outlook to Life," Review of *The Philosophy of Labor,* by C. Delisle Burns, *TNR* 48 (25 August 1925): 22; "Adult Education," *TNR* 54 (22 February 1928): 28. Kornbluh also notes the influence of progressivism on worker's education in the 1920s and 1930s (*A New Deal,* 29, 39).

40. Soule, "Herbert Croly's Liberalism," 255–256.

41. Kenneth Benne holds that Dewey's influence "seems to have been equally great among progressive workers in the education of adults as among workers in the education of children and young people" ("John Dewey and Adult Education", *Adult Education Bulletin* 14 [October 1949]: 7).

42. The curriculum of progressive workers' education tended to emphasize the social sciences. Will Durant, in a letter concerning the Labor Temple School, of which he was director, reported that the institution would "aim to acquaint the student with the

sciences that most directly concern the development and direction of human affairs" ("The Labor Temple School," *TNR* 28 [12 October 1921]: 192).

43. Richard Gentry, *Liberalism and the New Republic, 1914–1960* (Ann Arbor: University Microfilms, 1960), 188–189.

44. Alvin Johnson, *Pioneer's Progress*, (Lincoln: University of Nebraska Press, 1960; originally published 1952), chapters 24–27.

45. Michael Walzer, *The Company of Critics: Social Criticism and Political Commitment in the Twentieth Century* (New York: Basic Books, 1980), x; Croly, Introduction to Lindeman's *Social Discovery* (New York: New Republic, Inc., 1924), xvi.

46. James Morris, *Conflict Within the AFL: A Study of Craft Versus Industrial Unionism, 1901–1938*, (Ithaca: Cornell University Press, 1958), chapter 5.

47. Dewey, "Labor Politics," 213.

48. Brian Simon, comment at a joint meeting of the History of Education Society and the Canadian History of Education Society, Vancouver, B.C., 15 October 1983.

49. Richard Dwyer, *Labor Education in the United States: An Annotated Bibliography* (Metuchen, N.J.: Scarecrow Press, 1977), 8–18, 24. Kornbluh and Goldfarb also note this shift toward "more utilitarian programming to meet the practical needs of the labor movement" ("Labor Education," 27–28).

50. Steve Fraser has commented on the phenomenon in which labor's organizing success in the 1930s was accompanied by decreased attention to some of the broader issues of labor's social role (Fraser, "The 'Labor Question,'" chapter 2 of Steve Fraser and Gary Gerstle, eds., *The Rise and Fall of the New Deal Order, 1930–1980* [Princeton: Princeton University Press, 1989]).

51. David Seideman, "Left Turn," *TNR* 191 (10 December 1984): 46.

52. Quoted in Jo Ann Robinson, *Abraham Went Out: A Biography of A. J. Muste* (Philadelphia: Temple University Press, 1981), 36.

Chapter 8. Agnes de Lima and Progressive Education ■

1. John Dewey, *Democracy and Education: An Introduction to the Philosophy of Education* (New York: Macmillan, 1916); *Experience and Education* (New York: Macmillan, 1938).

2. Randolph Bourne, "In a Schoolroom," *TNR* 1 (November 7, 1914): 23–24. Like Dewey, Bourne wrote more articles for *The New Republic* than for any other periodical. See Clayton's *Forgotten Prophet: The Life of Randolph Bourne* (Baton Rouge: Louisiana State University Press, 1984). Chapters seven through the epilogue include material about Bourne's work for *The New Republic*, his educational writing, and his relationships with Dewey, de Lima, and others.

3. On de Lima's role in the New York Gary Plan struggle, see Ronald Cohen and Raymond Mohl, *The Paradox of Progressive Education: The Gary Plan and Urban Schooling* (Port Washingon, N.Y.: Kennikat Press, 1979), 43, 47. A vivid account of this fight is given in chapter 18 of Diane Ravitch's *The Great School Wars: A History of the New York City Public Schools* (New York: Basic Books, 1988, 2nd ed.).

4. Sigrid de Lima Greene, "Biographical notes for Agnes de Lima." (sent with letter to author, 25 September 1986).

5. Helen L. Horowitz, *Alma Mater: Design and Experience in the Women's Colleges from Their Nineteenth-Century Beginnings to the 1930s* (New York: Knopf, 1984), 222.

6. Transcript for Agnes de Lima, provided by registrar's office, Vassar College. Course titles and instructors were identified through the *Annual Catalogs* (Poughkeepsie, N.Y.: Vassar College, 1904–1908).

7. Barbara Miller Solomon notes the existence of settlement clubs at Vassar and Wellesley during this period: (*In the Company of Educated Women: A History of Women and Higher Education in America* [New Haven: Yale University Press, 1985], 110. De Lima's membership was noted in the *Vassarion* (Poughkeepsie: Vassar College, 1908), 223. She was one of five members of the "Committee for Work Among Maids."

8. *Some Conditions in the Schools of San Francisco*, A Report Made by the School

Survey Class of the California Branch of the Association of Collegiate Alumnae (San Francisco: 1914), 8.

9. Interview with Sigrid de Lima Greene; letter from Sigrid De Lima Greene, 25 September 1986. De Lima's formal and informal educational experiences paralleled in many ways those of the five women in Ellen Condliffe Lagemann, *A Generation of Women: Education in the Lives of Progressive Reformers* (Cambridge: Harvard University Press, 1979).

10. Interview with Agnes de Lima, New York City, 18 November 1965; interview with Sigrid de Lima Greene; John A. Moreau, *Bourne, A Biography* (Ann Arbor: University Microfilms, 1964). For information on de Lima, see pp. 9, 57, 164, 180–181, 302–306.

11. David Seideman, *The New Republic: A Voice of Modern Liberalism* (New York: Praeger, 1986), 61–69. For *The Nation* during this period, see Michael Wreszin, *Oswald Garrison Villard: Pacifist at War* (Bloomington: Indiana University Press, 1965), chapters 10–12.

12. Letter from Croly to Bourne, 16 December 1914, Bourne Papers.

13. Material on de Lima's relationship with the journal is from the author's interview with Agnes de Lima. The sexism of *The New Republic* is noted by Seideman in *The New Republic*, 17.

14. De Lima, "The Dalton Plan," *TNR* 37 (13 February 1924): 308–309.

15. De Lima, "A Public School Experiment," *TNR* 38 (9 April 1924): 174–175. For de Lima's later assessment of this famous progressive experiment, see *The Little Red School House* (New York: Macmillan, 1942), written in collaboration with the school faculty. John Dewey wrote an appreciative introduction for what he called this "lively and vital" book, which rendered an "immense practical service" to educational reform. (page ix.)

16. De Lima, "The New Education: In the Public Schools," *TN* 118 (18 June 1924): 702–703.

17. Lawrence Cremin, *The Transformation of the School: Progressivism in American Education* (New York: Knopf, 1961), chapter 6. Cremin drew on *The New Republic* and *Our Enemy the Child* at several points in this chapter. The quotations that follow are from "The New Education: In the Ethical Culture, Horace Mann, and Lincoln Schools," *TN* 119 (2 July 1924): 9–11.

18. "The New Education: Following the Child's Lead," *TN* 119 (30 July 1924): 116–118.

19. "As Students See It," Editorial, *TN* 119 (13 August 1924): 156–157.

20. De Lima, "Any School Morning," *TNR* 40 (12 November 1924): Supplement, "The Public Elementary School," 19–20. The article is similar in content and tone to "In a Schoolroom," which Bourne had written for the first issue of *The New Republic* almost exactly ten years earlier.

21. "Education Moves Ahead," (Reviews of seven books on education), *TNR* 40 (12 November 1924): 23–24.

22. "De Lima, Education in the Making," *TNR* 40 (19 November 1924): 303–304.

23. De Lima, "The 'Best' of School Mornings," *TNR* 42 (1 April 1924): 150–152.

24. De Lima, "From Infancy On," (Reviews of nine books on education), *TNR* 43 (1 July 1925): 157–159.

25. For the context of these developments during the 1920s, see Ravitch, *The Great School Wars*, 233–236.

26. Circulation figures are from *American Newspaper Annual and Directory* (Philadelphia: N. W. Ayer and Son, 1914–1941). Both journals continued to direct advertising specifically to teachers and professors.

27. De Lima, *Our Enemy the Child* (New York: New Republic, 1925), dedication, 11, 85, 125–126, 256, 252.

28. *The Survey* 14 (15 November 1925): 258; Louise A. Dickey, *The World Tomorrow* 8 (October 1925): 316; *The Booklist* 22 (January 1926): 143. See also *The Literary Review*, 9 January 1926: 8; *New York World*, 6 December 1925: 7.

29. "Dollar Reprints," *The New Republic* 64 (20 August 1930): II. *Our Enemy the Child* was considered of enough historical significance so that it was republished in 1969 with an introduction by Lawrence Cremin. It is still in print in 1990 (Salem, N.H.: Ayer Publishing, 1969).

30. Harold Rugg and Ann Shumaker, *The Child-Centered School: An Appraisal of the New Education* (Yonkers: World Book Company, 1928), 327; Cremin, *Transformation*, chapter 6; Sol Cohen, *Progressives and Urban School Reform: The Public Education Association of New York City* (New York: Teachers College Press, 1964), 126, 128–129; Patricia Aljberg Graham, *Progressive Education: From Arcady to Academe* (New York: Teachers College Press, 1967), 45–46, 175, 180, 182; Robert Elias, *"Entangling Alliances with None": An Essay on the Individual in the American Twenties* (New York: Norton, 1973), 34–37, 42–43; Clarence Karier, *The Individual, Society, and Education* (Urbana: University of Illinois Press, 1986), 237–238; Larry Cuban, *How Teachers Taught: Constancy and Change in American Classrooms, 1890–1980* (New York: Longman, 1984), 41–43.

31. There is at least a difference in emphasis between Patricia Graham's and the author's interpretation of de Lima as a critic. Graham does not see her as "a critical analyst of an emerging movement" (Letter to author, 24 November 1986). The author sees her as selectively critical, particularly of the "technicians" and the "socializers."

32. Cremin, *Transformation*, 279, 202; Cohen, *Progressives and Urban School Reform*, 126; Graham, *Progressive Education*, 45–46, 175; Cuban, *How Teachers Taught*, 43.

33. De Lima, *Our Enemy the Child*, 67. Dewey had spoken out three years earlier against a narrow definition of "Social Purposes in Education." This was the title of a speech he gave in 1922, published in *General Science Quarterly* 7 (1923): 79–91. Republished in *John Dewey: The Middle Works* vol. 15, edited by Jo Ann Boydston (Carbondale: Southern Illinois University Press, 1983), 158–169.

34. De Lima, *Our Enemy the Child*, 68.

35. Ibid., 7, 214.

36. Cuban *How Teachers Taught*, 43; de Lima, *Our Enemy the Child*, 260. Cuban writes: "The long extract I used in *How Teachers Taught* (which I paraphrased from De Lima) of a New York City elementary classroom had as its central message: This is what will happen to progressivism when it gets into the schools." (Letter to author, November 1986.) Two points may be made: (l) In spite of the difficulties, this classroom was more progressive than the one described in "Any School Morning"—thus some degree of public school progressivism was possible; (2) de Lima noted in the next chapter (page 33) that even in the New York Public schools "we nevertheless find significant educational experiments, partly under direct official supervision and guidance and partly with the encouragement and approval of the supervisory staff."

37. De Lima, *Our Enemy the Child*, 260.

38. On *The New Republic*'s greater emphasis on nonpolitical matters during the 1920s, see Seideman, *The New Republic*, 61–79; also David Levy, *Herbert Croly of "The New Republic": The Life and Thought of an American Progressive* (Princeton: Princeton University Press, 1985), chapter 9.

39. Richard Hofstadter, *The Age of Reform* (New York: Vintage, 1960; originally published 1955), 186. For the context within which de Lima worked as a woman journalist, see Madelon Golden Schilpp and Sharon Murphy, *Great Women of the Press* (Carbondale: Southern Illinois University Press, 1983).

40. Interview with Sigrid de Lima Greene, 25 August 1986.

Chapter 9. The Eggheads and the Fatheads ■

1. Stephen Whitfield, "The Eggheads and the Fatheads," *Change* 10 (April 1978): 64.

2. Richard Hofstadter, *Anti-intellectualism in American Life* (New York: Knopf, 1963), 7.

3. Ibid., 6, 359–361.

4. Lawrence Cremin, *The Transformation of the School: Progressivism in American Education, 1876–1957* (New York: Knopf, 1961), 210.

5. Sol Cohen, *Progressives and Urban School Reform: The Public Education Association of New York City, 1895–1954* (New York: Teachers College Press, 1964), 217, 220.

6. Diane Ravitch, *The Troubled Crusade: American Education, 1945–1980,* (New York: Basic Books, 1983), 79, 44.

7. Hofstadter, *Anti-intellectualism*, 377, 380n, 389; see also 22n.

8. Max Rafferty, *What They Are Doing to Your Children* (New York: New American Library, 1964), 16, 18; Hyman Rickover, *Education and Freedom* (New York: Dutton, 1959), 136–140, 145, 153.

9. Christopher Lasch, *New Radicalism in America: The Intellectual as a Social Type* (New York: Knopf, 1965), chapter 9, "The Anti-Intellectualism of the Intellectuals." For a more recent discussion of this issue in relationship to Croly, see David W. Levy, *Herbert Croly of "The New Republic": The Life and Thought of an American Progressive* (Princeton: Princeton University Press, 1985), 170 and chapter 9.

10. Richard H. Pells, *Radical Visions and American Dreams: Culture and Thought in the Depression Years* (New York: Harper and Row, 1973), 18.

11. See Agnes de Lima's *Nation* articles cited in the previous chapter for examples of (but not support for) apparent anti-intellectualism.

12. On Croly's change of emphasis from politics to culture, see Levy, *Croly*, chapter 9.

13. Elisabeth Irwin, "Personal Education," *TNR* 40 (12 November 1924): Part II, 8.

14. Agnes de Lima, "A Public School Experiment," *TNR* 38 (9 April 1924): 175.

15. De Lima, "Education Moves Ahead," (Review of seven books on education), *TNR* 40 (12 November 1924): Part II, 24.

16. Elisabeth Irwin, "The Youngest Intellectuals," *TNR* 48 (10 November 1926): 339–341. Note Miss Irwin's appeal to nature for authority—a common habit of antiformalists from Rousseau to the child-centered educators.

17. Editorial, "Fundamentals in Education," *TNR* 34 (14 March 1923): 58; Editorial, "The High School and Democracy," *TNR* 36 (7 March 1923), 269.

18. Irwin, "Personal Education," 8, 9.

19. De Lima, "Education Moves Ahead," 23. This is consistent with De Lima's retrospective evaluation of child-centered education. In an interview with the author, she vigorously rejected the assessment of child-centered education as anti-intellectual. In most child-centered schools, she noted, children were surrounded by good books and did excellent academic work. A few institutions like the Walden School, she felt, did become too Freudian, and some schools let the children run wild. But she believed that even in these settings the children learned more than in conventional schools (Interview, 18 November 1965).

20. Irwin, "The Youngest Intellectuals," 341; Lawrence Morris, "Intelligence as a Physiological Process," *TNR* 51 (27 July 1927): 261; De Lima, "The New Education: In the Public Schools," 702; Evelyn Dewey, "The New Education: The Modern School," *TN* 112 (11 May 1921): 685.

21. Alvin Johnson, "The Walden School," *TNR* 34 (28 March 1923): 135. Joseph K. Hart declared that the continual assertions that the child-centered schools could have the best of both worlds were "rationalizations, wishful thinking, defenses of inertia" ("Judging Our Progresssive Schools," *TNR* 63 [11 June 1930]: 96).

22. Jean Temple, "The Modern School and Our Present Culture" (Review of Rugg and Shumaker's *The Child-Centered School*), *TNR* 57 (2 January 1929): 199.

23. Boyd Bode, "The New Education Ten Years After: Apprenticeship or Freedom," *TNR* 63 (4 June 1930): 62. Hofstadter's earliest citation of Bode is from his 1938 book *Progressive Education at the Crossroads* (New York: Newson). See Hofstadter, *Antiintellectualism*, 373n, 386–387. See also Dewey's 1924 article in which he stated that "freedom of mind is not something that spontaneously happens. It is not achieved by the mere absence of obvious restraints. It is a product of constant, unremitting nurture of right habits of observation and reflection" ("Science, Belief, and the Public," *TNR* 38 [2 April 1924]: 145).

24. Bode ("Apprenticeship," 63) here pointed to the danger of what David Riesman later labeled "other-directedness" (*The Lonely Crowd* [New Haven: Yale University Press, 1950], 17–24. Bode noted the "defenselessness of children against external stimuli" and cited William James's comment on an environment that "makes the child seem to belong less to himself than to every object which happens to catch his notice." Dewey reinforced this point in protesting against the substitution of "child-dictation" for "adult-dictation" ("How Much Freedom in the New Schools?" *TNR* 63 [9 July 1930]: 205).

25. Bode, "Apprenticeship," 63–64.

26. Hart, "Judging Our Progressive Schools," 95.

27. The Naumberg and Pratt articles are in *TNR* volume 63, 145–146, and 172–176. The quotations that follow are from John Dewey's "How Much Freedom in the New Schools?" *TNR* 63 (9 July 1930): 204–206. Francis Froelicher's contribution to the series, "A Program for Progressive Schools," was also critical of child-centered excesses: "'Freedom' is a word too often profaned by modern educators. . . . Freedom in academic work must first of all be founded upon thorough, authentic scholarship" (*TNR* 63 [18 June 1930]: 123–125.

28. John Dewey, *Democracy and Education: An Introduction to the Philosophy of Education* (New York: Macmillan, 1916), 337–338.

29. John Dewey, "How Much Freedom in the New Schools?," 206. This is one point at which reference to Dewey's journalistic writings might have balanced Hofstadter's treatment of Dewey. On this issue, Hofstadter cites Dewey's early and optimistic *My Pedagogic Creed* (New York: Kellogg, 1897) and misses more tough-minded and critical statements from his articles for the liberal journals (Hofstadter, *Anti-intellectualism*, 387).

30. See Jo Ann Boydston, "John Dewey and the Journals," *History of Education Quarterly* 10 (Spring 1970): 72–77.

31. Editorial, "The High School and Democracy," 68. Ellen Condliffe Lagemann, *Private Power for the Public Good: A History of the Carnegie Foundation for the Advancement of Teaching* (Middletown: Wesleyan University Press, 1983), chapter 2.

32. Pritchett's views were presented in the *17th Annual Report of the Carnegie Foundation for the Advancement of Teaching* (New York: Carnegie Foundation, 1922), 93–117.

33. Editorial, "Fundamentals in Education," 58. Cremin points out that *The New Republic* carried editorials favoring the limitation of college enrollments (*Transformation*, 189). But the motivation here was similarly class-conscious: the editors believed that existing colleges were often "social clubs for the aristocracy" (Editorial, "Who Should Go to College?" *TNR* 32 [4 October 1922]: 137–138).

34. "Fundamentals," 58–59.

35. "The High School," 269–270.

36. George Counts, "The Social Composition of the High School," *TNR* 36 (7 November 1923): Part 2, 5–7. On the context for Counts's article, see Gerald Gutek, *The Educational Theory of George S. Counts* (Columbus: Ohio State University Press, 1970), chapter 2.

37. "The High School," 269–270.

38. Richard Gilman, "The Intellect and its Enemies" (Review of Hofstadter's *Anti-intellectualism*), *TNR* 149 (13 July 1963): 19–22.

39. Alfred Kazin has recently written: "I understood Malcolm Cowley all too well when he lamented the amount of time he had spent in the old days rewriting that clumsy stylist John Dewey" ("The New Republic: A Personal View," *TNR*, 75th Anniversary Edition, 201 (6 November 1989): 80.

40. Gilman, "The Intellect," 21.

41. Merle Borrowman, Review of *Anti-intellectualism in American Life*, *History of Education Quarterly* 3 (December 1963): 223–225.

42. Michael B. Katz, "Not the Whole Story" (Review of *The Troubled Crusade: American Education, 1945–1980*, by Diane Ravitch), *History of Education Quarterly* 25 (Spring-Summer 1985): 175–176.

43. Merle Curti, *American Paradox: The Conflict of Thought and Action* (New Brunswick: Rutgers University Press, 1956), 63.

44. Arthur Zilversmit, "The Failure of Progressive Education, 1920–1940," in Lawrence Stone, ed., *Schooling and Society: Studies in the History of Education* (Baltimore: Johns Hopkins University Press, 1976), 252–263; David Tyack, *The One Best System: A History of American Urban Education* (Cambridge: Harvard University Press, 1975), 193–198; Larry Cuban, *How Teachers Taught: Constancy and Change in American Classrooms, 1890–1980* (New York: Longman, 1984), Part I.

45. Michael B. Katz, *Class, Bureaucracy and Schools: The Illusion of Educational Change in America* (New York: Praeger, 1971), 125.

46. Richard J. Bernstein, "The Varieties of Pluralism," *Current Issues in Education* 5 (Fall 1985): 17.

47. Bernstein, *John Dewey* (New York: Washington Square Press, 1966), 144–145.

Chapter 10. Liberals Move Left ■

1. Robert McElvaine, *The Great Depression: America, 1929–1941* (New York: Times Books, 1984), 71.

2. On Hoover's efforts to deal with the Depression, see Arthur Schlesinger, Jr., *The Crisis of the Old Order, 1919–1933* (Boston: Houghton Mifflin, 1957), chapter 25.

3. Steward Holbrook, *Dreamers of the American Dream* (Garden City, N.Y.: Doubleday, 1957), 338.

4. William Leuchtenberg, *Franklin Roosevelt and the New Deal* (New York: Harper, 1963), 17.

5. An editorial in *The New Republic* was titled "Roosevelt Steps Left and Right." Volume (72 [28 September 1932]: 164–165).

6. Editorial, "How Shall We Vote?" *TNR* 72 (17 August 1932): 5. James Mac-Gregor Burns cites another *New Republic* 1932 critique of Roosevelt in *The Crosswinds of Freedom* (New York: Knopf, 1989), 12.

7. Editorial, *TN* 135 (6 July 1932): 1; "Governor Roosevelt's Campaign," *TN* 135 (2 November 1932): 414. Thomas had once been an associate editor of *The Nation* and was for many years a contributing editor. See Murray Seidler, *Norman Thomas: Respectable Rebel* (Syracuse, N.Y.: Syracuse University Press, 1967), 73.

8. Frank Warren III, *Liberals and Communism: The "Red Decade" Revisited* (Bloomington: Indiana University Press, 1966), 41ff.

9. *TN* 136 (11 January 1933): 34; Sara Alpern, *Freda Kirchwey: A Woman of "The Nation"* (Cambridge: Harvard University Press, 1987), 98.

10. Michael Wreszin, *Oswald Garrison Villar: Pacifist at War* (Bloomington: Indiana University Press, 1965), in chapters 13–15, describes Villard's increasing estrangement from *The Nation*, and Kirchwey's efforts to keep the peace among the melange of pacifists, interventionists, collectivists, New Dealers, pragmatists, and ideologues who staffed the journal.

11. Quoted in Wreszin, *Villard*, 130. Otis Graham, Jr. traces Villard's political transitions (along with those of other progressives) in *Encore for Reform: The Old Progressives and the New Deal* (New York: Oxford University Press, 1967), 183–185.

12. Henry Wallace and Norman Thomas, "Comments on *The Nation*," *TN* 150 (10 February 1940): 190.

13. On Croly's final years, see David W. Levy, *Herbert Croly of "The New Republic": The Life and Thought of an American Progressive* (Princeton: Princeton University Press, 1985), chapter 9, "Years of Despair: 1919–1930". John B. Judis contrasts Croly's proposed program with the New Deal in "Herbert Croly's Promise," *TNR*, 75th Anniversary Edition, 201 (6 November 1989): 87.

14. Bruce Bliven, interview with the author, 28 August 1965. A persuasive analysis of the role of both journals during these years, particularly *The New Republic*, is given by William O'Neill in *A Better World: The Great Schism—Stalinism and the Intellectuals* (New York: Simon and Schuster, 1982), chapter 1.

15. Alfred Kazin, *Starting Out in the Thirties* (Boston: Atlantic Monthly Press, 1962), 16; see also 138 and 141. Kazin's more recent assessments of *The New Republic*, Bliven, and other writers and editors appear in "The New Republic: A Personal View," *TNR*, 75th Anniversary Issue, 201 (6 November 1989): 78–83.

16. Daniel Aaron, *Writers on the Left* (New York: Avon, 1965; first published 1961), 99, 213–215, 437. Cowley's reflections on this period appear in *The Dream of the Golden Mountain: Remembering the 1930s* (New York: Viking, 1980).

17. Wreszin, *Villard*, 240. Bliven later expressed his regret that he opposed collective security so long (Interview with author, 28 August 1965).

18. Benjamin Stolberg, "Muddled Millions," *Saturday Evening Post* 213 (15 February 1941): 82; "Liberals," *Time* 34 (13 November 1939): 21–22.

19. Warren, *Liberals*, 46.

20. Leuchtenberg, *Roosevelt*, chapter 7, "The Second Hundred Days."

21. Heywood Broun, "Shoot the Works: Only a Boy," *TNR* 96 (17 August 1938): 45; quoted in Warren, *Liberals*, 115.

22. Villard vigorously protested the Popular Front; the trend of Croly's thought at

the end of his life makes it likely that he would have been, like Dewey, an anti-Communist liberal.

23. Bruce Bliven, "The First Forty Years," *TNR*, 40th Anniversary Issue, 131 (22 November 1954): 9. These alliances were made easier by the fact that during the mid-1930s the Communists deemphasized their radicalism and promoted their ideas as "twentieth-century Americanism" See Aaron, *Writers*, on "The Appeal of Communism," 166ff.

24. Quoted in Aaron, *Writers*, 347.

25. "Liberals," 21–22.

26. Letters to the editor, *TNR* 101 (1 November 1939): 378; (8 November 1939):III.

27. Letters to the editor, *TN* 150 (27 January 1940): 112; (3 February 1940): 139; (10 February 1940): 190–191.

28. David Seideman, *The New Republic: A Voice of Modern Liberalism* (New York: Praeger, 1986), 97; Wreszin, *Villard*, 12–3.

29. On the influence and the changing positions of *The Nation* and *The New Republic* during the 1920s and 1930s see Richard H. Pells, *Radical Visions and American Dreams: Culture and Social Thought in the Depression Years* (New York: Harper and Row, 1973), 13–14, 46–48, 112–113.

30. United States Bureau of the Census, *Historical Statistics of the United States* (Washington, D.C.: Government Printing Office, 1960), 209. The most thorough study of the Depression and education is David Tyack, Robert Lowe, and Elisabeth Hansot, *Public Schools in Hard Times: The Great Depression and Recent Years* (Cambridge: Harvard University Press, 1984). See page 20 regarding the delayed impact of the Depression on school budgets.

31. Editorial note, *TN* 130 (5 February 1930): 140; "In the Driftway," *TN* 130 (5 March 1930): 270. See also Tyack, Lowe, and Hansot, *Public Schools*, "The Uneven Impact of Retrenchment," 27–41.

32. Wayne Parrish, "The Plight of Our School System," *The Literary Digest* 116 (23 September 1933): 32.

33. Editorial, *TN* 136 (18 January 1933): 60–61. For further information on the Depression and education, see Harry Zeitlin, "Federal Relations in American Education, 1933–1943," Unpublished Ph.D. Dissertation, Columbia University, 1958), chapter 2.

34. Villard, "Issues and Men: The Plight of Higher Education," *TN* 138 (28 March 1934): 349.

35. Bureau of the Census, *Historical Statistics*, 207–209.

36. Editorial, "Our Public Schools," *TN* 138 (18 April 1934): 431–432. See also editorial notes in volume 136 (1 February 1933): 107 and volume 141 (11 September 1935): 283. Denny Hammond's article in *The New Republic*, "Education on the Skids," surveys the whole problem from the perspective of 1939, and includes a consideration of the effects of the 1937–1938 recession (*TNR* 99 [26 July 1939]: 326–327). Tyack, Lowe, and Hansot draw on several other studies in contrasting developments in Chicago and Detroit: (*Public Schools*, pages 85–91 and notes, 238).

37. Harold Ward, "The Poverty Belt," *TNR* 84 (2 October 1935): 212–213. Tyack, Lowe, and Hansot, *Public Schools*, 144–150, provide a detailed analysis of enrollment trends from 1920 to 1950.

38. Martha Gruening, Review of *Schoolhouse in the Foothills*, by Ella Enslow in collaboration with Alvin Harlow, *TNR* 84 (2 October 1935): 223.

39. Eunice Langdon, "The Teacher Faces the Depression," *TN* 137 (16 August 1933): 182. For evidence of the journals' commitment to equal educational opportunity, see "It Seems to Heywood Broun," *TN* 129 (17 July 1929) 59; also editorial notes, *TN* 132 (22 April 1931): 439, and *TN* 149 (9 December 1939): 639. See *The New Republic* 84 (2 October 1935): 200 for that journals' concern over the treatment of blacks in textbooks. See Tyack, Lowe, and Hansot, *Public Schools*, 30–32, 142–143, 176–186, regarding black education, both rural and urban, during the Depression.

40. Villard, "Slumbering Fires in Harlem," *TN* 142 (22 January 1936): 99–100. See also Carleton Beals and Abel Plenn, "Louisiana's Black Utopia," *TN* 141 (30 October 1935): 503–505. Villard, grandson of the great abolitionist William Lloyd Garrison, was

a founder and early chairman of the board of the National Association for the Advancement of Colored People. See Wreszin, *Villard*, 30–31.

41. Editorial, "From Campus to Breadline," *TNR* 75 (17 May 1933): 7. Richard Pells has written perceptively about the dilemmas of intellectuals, especially those associated with *The New Republic*, during this period. See "The Radical as Critic," *Radical Visions*, 187–193.

42. Editorial note, *TN* 136 (1 February 1933): 107.

43. See, for example, Villard, "The Plight of Higher Education," *TN* 138 (23 March 1934): 349.

44. William Thomas, "The Educator and the Depression: The College Instructor," *TN* 137 (23 August 1933): 213–215.

45. Villard, "Plight": 349.

46. Editorial, "From Campus to Breadline," 6–7.

47. Editorial note, *TN* 146 (5 February 1938): 143.

48. "A Call to Unemployed College Graduates" (Letter from Joseph Lash and others), *TNR* 74 (5 April 1933): 218. See also "Scholars on Relief," (letter from O. R. Fuss, secretary of the Associated Office and Professional Emergency Employees), *TNR* 84 (21 August 1935): 49. For Lash's later perspective on these events, see chapter 45 of *Eleanor and Franklin* (New York: Norton, 1971).

49. Editorial, "Graduates of 1936," *TNR* 87 (17 June 1936): 164–165.

50. Editorial, "Baccalaureate," *TNR* 95 (22 June 1938): 171.

51. Ibid., 171.

52. Editorial, "Graduates of 1936," 164–165.

53. "Plight," 349.

54. Jon Cheever, "Expelled," *TNR* 64 (1 October 1930): 171, 174. Cheever, who went on to become a distinguished American writer, later spelled his first name John. *The New Republic* republished this essay on the occasion of Cheever's death. (187 [19 and 26 July 1982]: 32–36).

55. Editorial note, *TN* 141 (11 September 1935): 283.

56. Editorial, "Assault," 173.

Chapter 11. From Campus to Breadline ■

1. David Tyack, Robert Lowe, and Elisabeth Hansot, *Public Schools in Hard Times: The Great Depression and Recent Years* (Cambridge: Harvard University Press, 1984), chapter 1.

2. Robert McElvaine, *The Great Depression: America, 1929–1941* (New York: Times Books, 1984), 223.

3. Charles Alexander, *Nationalism in American Thought, 1930–1945* (Chicago: Rand McNally, 1971), 141–142.

4. Arthur Ekirch, *Ideologies and Utopias: The Impact of the New Deal on American Thought* (Chicago: Quadrangle Books, 1969), 186–187.

5. Anthony Cresswell, Michael Murphy, and Charles Kerchner, *Teachers, Unions, and Collective Bargaining in Public Education* (Berkeley: McCutchan, 1980), 110–111.

6. "From Campus to Breadline," Editorial, *TNR* 75 (17 May 1933): 7; Eunice Langdon, "The Teacher Faces the Depression," *TN* 137 (16 August 1933): 182–183. See also chapter 19, "The 1930's: To Save the Public Schools," of Celia Zitron's *The New York City Teachers Union, 1916–1964* (New York: Humanities Press, 1968).

7. Langdon, "The Teacher Faces the Depression," 182; Edith Smith (pseud.), "Chicago Teachers Are Paid," *TN* 139 (19 September 1934): 322.

8. "Saving on the Schools," (Letter from Unemployed Teachers Association), *TNR* 71 (25 May 1932): 49; "False Economy," (Letter from UTA), *TN* 135 (28 September 1932): 284.

9. Ellsworth Schnebly, "Teaching on Promises," *TN* 137 (26 July 1933): 105.

10. William Thomas, "The Educator and the Depression: The College Instructor," *TN* 137 (23 August 1933): 213–214. See also Villard, "Issues and Men: The Plight of Higher Education," *TN* 138 (28 March 1934): 349.

11. William Thomas, "The Educator and the Depression," 214–215.

12. Robert Conklin, "A Job for Students," *TNR* 85 (29 January 1936): 340.

13. Howard K. Beale, *Are American Teachers Free?* (New York: Scribner's, 1936), 545, 686. See also Sol Cohen, *Progressives and Urban School Reform: The Public Education Assocation of New York City* (New York: Teachers College Press, 1964), 170–173.

14. Editorial note, *TN* 141 (21 August 1936): 198.

15. Editorial note, *TNR* 86 (4 March 1936): 95.

16. Editorial note, *TN* 141 (10 October 1935): 422.

17. Editorial notes, *TN* 139 (12 September 1934): 282–283; (17 October 1934): 422.

18. Norman Thomas, "'Hire Learning' at Ohio State," *TN* 132 (17 June 1931): 654–656.

19. Editorial note, *TN* 140 (9 January 1935): 30–31. Hearst considered Counts to be a dangerous subversive and "ordered that Counts's name was not to be mentioned in any of his publications" (Gerald Gutek, *The Educational Theory of George S. Counts* [Columbus, Ohio: Ohio State University Press, 1970], 76.

20. Editorial note, *TNR* 83 (12 June 1935): 115.

21. Editorial note, *TNR* 87 (20 May 1936): 31. Ellen Schrecker summarizes the Hicks and Schappes cases in *No Ivory Tower: McCarthyism and the Universities* (New York: Oxford University Press, 1986), 65–67.

22. Editorial, "Trouble in Paradise: Academic Freedom in Westchester," *TN* 141 (24 June 1935): 107.

23. Blanche Hofrichter, "The Loyalty Oath," (Letter), *TN* 139 (10 October 1934): 407.

24. Irving Howe and Lewis Coser, like many other scholars, note Stalinist influence in *The Nation* and *The New Republic* during the 1930s (*The American Communist Party: A Critical History* [New York: Praeger, 1962], 314. They also acknowledge that the Communists controlled "major parts of the Teacher Union" during this period (page 374).

25. Paul E. Peterson, *The Politics of School Reform, 1870–1940* (Chicago: University of Chicago Press, 1985), chapter 9; also Tyack, Lowe, and Hansot, *Public Schools*, 85–88.

26. Editorial, "Teachers' Progress," *TN* 136 (10 May 1933): 516.

27. Smith (pseud.), "Chicago Teachers Are Paid," 322–323.

28. Unemployed Teachers Association, Letter, *TN* 135 (28 September 1932): 284.

29. "Teachers in Distress," Letter from Paul Gastwirth of the Classroom Teacher Groups, *TN* 139 (15 August 1934): 185; Langdon, "The Teacher Faces the Depression": 185.

30. Robert Morss Lovett, "The Sovereignty of Teaching," (Reviews of four books on education), *TNR* 73 (23 November 1932): 52.

31. Editorial note, *TN* 142 (11 March 1936): 299–300; Editorial note, *TN* 144 (6 March 1937): 254.

32. Editorial, "Three R's Beleaguered," *TN* 147 (9 July 1938): 33.

33. Editorial, "Education Versus the Legion," *TNR* 95 (6 July 1938): 235.

34. See, for example, James Maurer, "Labor's Demand for Its Own Schools," *TN* 115 (20 September 1922): 276. Regarding the journalists' involvement in other unions, see Bruce Bliven's article, "Union Card Journalist," written when he joined the Newspaper Guild: (*TNR* 88 [9 September 1936] 125–126).

35. Editorial note, *TN* 132 (18 March 1931): 287.

36. Caroline Whitney and Albion Hartwell, "Professional Workers Unionize," *TNR* 86 (19 February 1936): 41–43; Editorial, "Organized Teachers Speak Out," *TNR* 88 (9 September 1936): 118.

37. Whitney and Hartwell, "Professional Teachers Organize": 42.

38. Villard, "The Plight of Higher Education," *TN* 138 (28 March 1934): 349.

39. The figures are from Milton Derber, "Growth and Expansion," in Milton Derber and Edwin Young, eds., *Labor and the New Deal* (Madison: University of Wisconsin Press, 1957), 3; see also Bernstein, *Turbulent Years: A History of the American Worker, 1933–1941* (Boston: Houghton MIfflin, 1970), chapters 8–12.

40. Howe and Coser, *American Communist Party*, 368–386. Richard Flacks acknowledges that "Communist-led unionizing efforts in the thirties achieved substantial gains for workers." (*Making History: The American Left and the American Mind* [New York: Columbia University Press, 1988], 126. See also 158).

41. Charles Miller, *Democracy in Education* (Ann Arbor: University Microfilms, 1967), chapter 6.

42. Robert W. Iversen, *The Communists and the Schools* (New York: Harcourt, Brace, 1959), 108.

43. Quoted in William Eaton, *The American Federation of Teachers, 1916–1961* (Carbondale: Southern Illinois University Press, 1975), 92.

44. Sidney Gould, "A History of the New York City Teachers Union and Why It Died," *The Educational Forum* 29 (January, 1965): 211; also Chester Bowers, *The Progressive Educator and the Depression: The Radical Years* (New York: Random House, 1969), 144, 166.

45. Abraham Lefkowitz, "Crisis in the Teachers' Union: The Case for the Union," *TN* 141 (9 October 1935): 410–411; United Committee to Save the Union, "The Opposition Replies," (Letter), *TN* 141 (9 October 1935): 411–412.

46. The roles of *The Nation* and *The New Republic* in the united front are considered in chapter 6 of Frank Warren III, *Liberals and Communism: The "Red Decade" Revisited* (Bloomington: Indiana University Press, 1966). See also Harvey Klehr, *The Heyday of American Communism: The Depression Years* (New York: Basic Books, 1984), chapter 18; Sara Alpern, *Freda Kirchwey: A Woman of "The Nation"* (Cambridge: Harvard University Press), chapter 5; and David Seideman, *The New Republic: A Voice of Modern Liberalism* (New York: Praeger, 1986), 145–160. Kirchwey's positions on the united front, feminism, and other issues are crisply explained by June Sochen in *Movers and Shakers: American Women Thinkers and Activists, 1900–1970* (New York: Quadrangle, 1973), 134–140.

47. Editorial note, *TN* 143 (29 August 1936): 227; Editorial, "Organized Teachers Speak Out," editorial, *TNR* 88 (9 September 1936): 118; Jerome Davis, "The Teachers' Struggle for Democracy," *TNR* 98 (15 March 1939): 161.

48. Editorial,"Teachers Together," *TNR* 98 (15 March 1939): 151–152; George Hartmann, "Union Teachers and Intellectual Integrity," (Letter), *TNR* 98 (26 April 1939): 337, 340; see also Bowers, *The Progressive Educator and the Depression*, chapter 5.

49. Hartmann, "Union Teachers": 338.

50. See letters from the following: Executive Board, New York College Teachers' Union, *TN* 148 (14 January 1939): 76; in the same issue, John Childs, *TN* 148 (14 January 1939): 76; Howard Langford, "Dr. Langford's Advice," *TN* 148 (28 January 1939): 132; Leo Huberman, "The Teachers' Union," *TNR* 97 (18 January 1939): 317.

51. Eaton, *American Federation of Teachers*, 112; Miller, *Democracy in Education*, 97–102.

52. For the liberal journals' halting response to the Hitler-Stalin Pact and subsequent events, see chapter 1 of William O'Neill, *A Better World: The Great Schism—Stalinism and the Intellectuals* (New York: Simon and Schuster, 1982).

53. Editorial, "Communists and Teachers," *TNR* 104 (24 February 1941): 265. Some members who had resigned during the period of Communist domination now returned. At the 1941 AFT convention, President George Counts announced, "to the delight of those assembled, that John Dewey, now eighty-two years old . . . had just rejoined." Miller, *Democracy in Education*, 159).

54. Editorial, "Communists and Unions," *TN* 152 (1 March 1941): 228–229.

55. Editorial, "The Purge in the A.F.T.," *TNR* 104 (16 June 1941): 809–810; Editorial, *TN* 152 (21 June 1941): 711.

56. Editorial, "Communists and Teachers," 265; Editorial, "Communists and Unions," 228–229; Editorial note, *TN* 152 (8 February 1941): 143.

57. Editorial note. *TN* 152 (8 February 1941): 143; Editorial, "Communist Teachers," *TNR* 104 (17 March 1941): 359–360. Schrecker deals with the Rapp-Coudert Committee in chapter 3 of *No Ivory Tower*. See also chapter 2 regarding academics in the AFT during this period.

58. Mark Starr, Letter, *TNR* 104 (14 April 1941): 503.

59. Max Kline, "Communists and Unions," (Letter), *TN* 152 (12 April 1941): 456.

60. The same pattern of support for the Popular Front, followed by a break with the Communists, was evident during this period in the journals' response to the social reconstructionists at Teachers College. The dialogue between the liberal journalists and the reconstructionists can be traced in the pages of the weeklies and *The Social Frontier*, the reconstructionists' magazine.

61. Editorial, "Mr Frey is Scared," *TNR* 96 (24 August 1938): 59–60.
62. Editorial, "Communists and Unions," 228–229.
63. Editorial, "Mr. Frey is Scared," 60.
64. O'Neill, *A Better World*, 31.
65. Editorial, "Teachers Together," *TNR* 98 (15 March 1939): 152; Editorial, *TN* 146 (12 February 1938): 171.
66. Editorial, "Mr. Frey is Scared," 60.
67. Editorial, "The Purge in the A.F.T.," 809; Editorial note, *TN* 152 (21 June 1941): 711.
68. The struggle in the AFT had an impact on the union's later positions. Wayne Urban notes "the significance of the long fight over communism and communist influence in the labor movement in explaining the AFT's hardline stand" on cold war issues ("Essay Review: Old and New Problems in Teacher Unionism," *Educational Studies* 20 [Winter 1989]: 357.

Chapter 12. Revolt on the Campus ■

1. James Wechsler, *The Age of Suspicion*, (New York: Random House, 1953), 18.
2. Ibid., 18–19.
3. Ibid., 17.
4. Ibid., 18. Ralph Brax incorrectly states that this took place while Wechsler was an editor of the Columbia *Spectator* (*The First Student Movement: Student Activism in the United States*) [Port Washington, N.Y.: Kennikat Press, 1981), 58.
5. Wechsler, *The Age of Suspicion*, 24.
6. Quoted by Hal Draper in "The Student Movement of the Thirties," in Rita Simon, ed., in *As We Saw the Thirties: Essays on Social and Political Movements of A Decade* (Urbana: University of Illinois Press, 1967), 156.
7. Wechsler, *The Age of Suspicion*, 57–66.
8. The student radicals were, however, more visible than numerous. See Draper, "The Student Movement," 182–189, for a persuasive discussion of the numbers and impact of the student activists of the period.
9. On the role of the Communists in the student movement, see Harvey Klehr, *The Heydey of American Communism: The Depression Years* (New York: Basic Books, 1984), especially chapter 16, "The Youth."
10. The context for these developments is explained by David Seideman in *The New Republic: A Voice of Modern Liberalism* (New York: Praeger, 1986), 145–160 and by Michael Wreszin in *Oswald Garrison Villard: Pacifist at War* (Bloomington: Indiana University Press, 1965), chapters 13–15.
11. Richard H. Pells, *Radical Visions and American Dreams: Culture and Social Thought in the Depression Years* (New York: Harper and Row, 1973), chapter 2.
12. Editorial, "Revolt at Yale," *TN* 132 (6 May 1931): 496. Eileen Eagan explores the relationship between progressive education and campus activism in *Class, Culture, and the Classroom: The Student Peace Movement of the 1930s* (Philadelphia: Temple University Press, 1981), chapter 6.
13. Editorial note, *TN* 132 (22 April 1931): 439.
14. Editorial, "Leaders or Followers,", *TN* 132 (17 June 1931): 649.
15. A thorough treatment of these developments is George Rawick, *The New Deal and Youth: The Civilian Conservation Corps, the National Youth Administration, and the American Youth Congress* (Ann Arbor: University Microfilms, 1957), chapters 12–14. See also Philip Altbach, *Student Politics in America: A Historical Analysis* (New York: McGraw-Hill, 1974), especially chapter 3 on the 1930s.
16. Sherwood Anderson and others, "Militant Students" (Letter to editors), *TNR* 74 (15 March 1933): 133. Some of the other signers were Theodore Dreiser, Scott Nearing, Corliss Lamont, and John Dos Passos.
17. Editorial note, *TN* 138 (10 January 1934): 30–31.
18. Seldon Rodman, "Youth Meets in Washington," *TN* 138 (17 January 1934): 70–71. See also the editorial note in *The Nation* 138 (4 April 1934): 373.
19. Wechsler, "Ferment in the Colleges," *TNR* 84 (16 October 1935): 266–268.

20. See, for example, Edgar Johnson, "Campus Activity," Review of Wechsler's *Revolt on the Campus, TNR* 85 (4 December 1935): 110; Eagan, *Class, Culture, and the Classroom,* 298; also Brax, *The First Student Movement,* 116. *Revolt on the Campus* was considered of sufficient historical significance that it was republished in 1973 with a new introduction by the author (Seattle: University of Washington Press).

21. Robert Morss Lovett, Introduction to *Revolt on the Campus,* xiii–xvii.

22. Johnson, "Campus Activity," 110.

23. "A Letter to You," (from the ASU), *TNR* 86 (12 February 1936): back cover. Draper, "Student Movements," 172–173, explains the founding of the ASU.

24. Joseph Lash and James Wechsler, *War Our Heritage* (New York: International Publishers, 1936). Robert W. Iversen identifies this as the first publication of the student united front. See his *The Communists and the Schools* (New York: Harcourt, Brace, 1959), 385.

25. Draper, "Student Movement," 188.

26. Ibid., 176.

27. *The New York Times* estimated that 500,000 students took place in the 1937 demonstrations. (Rawick, *The New Deal and Youth,* 318.) The most complete study of these events is Eagan, *Class, Culture, and the Classroom.* See especially chapter 5, "Students Strike Against War."

28. Wechsler, *The Age of Suspicion,* 118.

29. Ibid., 128–129.

30. Wechsler, "Politics on the Campus," *TN* 149 (30 December 1939): 732–733. This parallels explanations cited in the previous chapter concerning the effectiveness of Communists in the union movement.

31. Editorial, "Have the Young Gone Sour?" *TNR* 104 (13 January 1941): 39.

32. Robert G. Spivack, "Youth Reorganizes," *TN* 152 (18 January 1941): 71–73.

33. On the liberal journals' slow break with the popular front, see chapter 1 of O'Neill, *A Better World: The Great Schism—Stalinism and the Intellectuals* (New York: Simon and Schuster, 1985).

34. Spivack, "Youth Reorganizes," 73.

35. See for example, Bruce Bliven, Jr., "Citizens of Tomorrow," *TNR* 97 (11 January 1939): 283.

36. Alan Wald, *The New York Intellectuals: The Rise and Decline of the Anti-Stalinist Left from the 1930s to the 1980s* (Chapel Hill: University of North Carolina Press, 1987), 246.

37. "Youth in College," *Fortune* 13 (June 1936): 99–102, 155–162. Quoted in Seymour Lipset, *Rebellion in the University* (Boston: Little, Brown, 1972), 185.

38. Joseph Lash, "Action Notes," *Student Advocate* 1 (October-November, 1936): 28. Quoted in Lewis Feuer, *The Conflict of Generations: The Character and Significance of Student Movements* (New York: Basic Books, 1969), 371.

39. Altbach, *Student Politics,* 92; Wechsler, *The Age of Suspicion,* 85–86.

40. Brax, *The First Student Movement,* 48.

41. "The Nation's Honor Roll for 1934," *TN* 140 (2 January 1935): 3. For some additional references to college publications see: Editorial note, *TN* 138 (10 January 1934): 30–31; Editorial note, *TN* 138 (18 April 1934): 428; Wechsler, "Politics on the Campus," 733.

42. Bliven, *Five Million Words Later* (New York: John Day, 1970), chapter 2; Sara Alpern, *Freda Kirchwey: A Woman of "The Nation"* (Cambridge: Harvard University Press, 1987), 4–16; Robert Morss Lovett, *All Our Years* (New York: Viking, 1948), 34–47.

43. Wechsler, "Politics on the Campus," 732–733. For Lash's later interpretation of these events and of the Roosevelts' support for the American Youth Congress, see his *Eleanor and Franklin* (New York: Norton, 1971), chapter 45.

44. Editorial note, *TN* 150 (18 May 1940): 611.

45. Wechsler, *The Age of Suspicion,* 157.

46. Ibid., 10. Two recent books show that for some 1930s radicals at least, anti-Stalinism did not necessarily lead to conservatism: Alexander Bloom, *Prodigal Sons: The New York Intellectuals and Their World* (New York: Oxford University Press, 1986), chapters 11 and 14; Wald, *The New York Intellectuals,* part III.

47. Wechsler, Introduction to 1973 edition of *Revolt on the Campus,* x.

Chapter 13. A New Deal for Youth   ■

1. Michael Katz has noted that during the Depression, "a mass of respectable, hard-working family men" were unemployed (*In The Shadow of the Poorhouse: A Social History of Welfare in America* [New York: Basic Books, 1986], 211).

2. Kazarian's articles, titled "The Starvation Army," appeared in *The Nation* 136 (12 April 1933): 396–398; (19 April 1933): 443–445; (26 April 1933): 472–473. The material that follows is from these articles.

3. See David A. Shannon, ed,. *The Great Depression* (Englewood Cliffs, N.J.: Prentice-Hall, 1960), Part 4, "Nomads of the Depression"; also Edward Ellis, *A Nation in Torment: The Great American Depression, 1929–1939* (New York: Coward-McCann, 1970), chapter 18, "Migrants and the Civilian Conservation Corps."

4. James MacGregor Burns, *The Crosswinds of Freedom: The American Experiment,* vol. 2 (New York: Knopf, 1989), 25.

5. Page Smith, *Redeeming the Time: A People's History of the 1920s and the New Deal* (New York: McGraw-Hill, 1987), 439–441; Kenneth S. Davis, *FDR: The New Deal Years, 1933–1937* (New York: Random House, 1986), 77–79; Arthur M. Schlesinger, Jr., *The Coming of the New Deal* (Boston: Houghton Mifflin, 1959), 336–340.

6. Lindley and Lindley, *A New Deal,* 13.

7. Schlesinger, "Sources of the New Deal," in Arthur M. Schlesinger, Jr., and Morton White, eds., *Paths of American Thought* (Boston: Houghton Mifflin, 1963), 377–381. The other two were Charles Beard and Thorstein Veblen, close associates of Croly and Dewey.

8. Jonathan Mitchell, "Roosevelt's Tree Army, I" *TNR* 83 (29 May 1935): 64.

9. Bob Crandall, quoted by Alan Gibbs in *Institutional History as an Element of Community History: Civilian Conservation Corps in the Okanagan Country* (Okanagan, Wash.: U.S. Forest Service, 1986), 5.

10. Ellis, *A Nation in Torment,* 307.

11. Schlesinger, *Coming of the New Deal,* 340.

12. Editorial, "The Peacetime Army," *TNR* 74 (5 April 1933): 202. This issue had gone to press before the actual passage of the bill. Regarding opposition to the program see George Rawick, *The New Deal and Youth: The Civilian Conservation Corps, the National Youth Administration, and the American Youth Congress* (Ann Arbor: University Microfilms, 1957), chapter 3. The quotation from William Green is from page 47.

13. Editorial note, *TN* 137 (22 November 1933): 581; Raymond Gram Swing, "Take the Army out of the CCC," *TN* 141 (23 October 1935): 459; Editorial note, *TN* 144 (15 May 1937): 551.

14. Quoted in John A. Salmond in *The Civilian Conservation Corps, 1933–1942: A New Deal Case Study* (Durham, N.C.: Duke University Press, 1967), 48.

15. This information, and that immediately following, is from Harry Zeitlin, "Federal Relations in American Education, 1933–44: A Study of New Deal Efforts and Innovations" (Dissertation, Columbia University, 1958), chapter 3. The political issues surrounding the education program are traced in detail by Salmond in *The Civilian Conservation Corps,* 47–54 and passim.

16. David Tyack, Robert Lowe, and Elisabeth Hansot, *Public Schools: in Hard Times: The Great Depression and Recent Years* (Cambridge: Harvard University Press, 1984), 116.

17. Frances Perkins, *The Roosevelt I Knew* (New York: Viking Press, 1946), 181.

18. Ibid., 180.

19. Rawick, *The New Deal and Youth,* 119.

20. The quotation is from Walter Krah, a CCC veteran interviewed by Judy Caughlin, 6 November 1981 (Vancouver, Wash.: Gifford Pinchot National Forest, Oral History Tapes). The figures on the numbers of enrollees who became literate are from Fred Leake and Ray Carter, *Roosevelt's Tree Army: A Brief History of the Civilian Conservation Corps* (Arlington, Va.: National Association of Civilian Conservation Corps Alumni, 1982), 3.

21. Editorial note, *TN* 137 (22 November 1933): 581.

22. Swing, "Take the Army," 460. On Roosevelt's interest in the CCC for promoting conservation, see Ellis, *A Nation in Torment,* 296–307.

23. This and the material following is from Mitchell, "Roosevelt's Tree Army: II," 83 (12 June 1935) 127–129.

24. Dorothy Bromley, "They're in the Army Now," *TNR* 104 (6 January 1941): 14.

25. Robert McElvaine, *The Great Depression: America, 1929–1941* (New York: Times Books, 1984), 155. However, McElvaine adds that "in terms of 'regimentation' the camps were probably little worse than the practice sessions of high school football teams."

26. Editorial, "Sedition in the C.C.C.," *TNR* 86 (12 February 1936): 6–7.

27. Bernard Harkness, Letter, *TN* 146 (5 February 1938): 168; Wayne McMillen, "Make the CCC Civilian," Letter, *TNR* 74 (15 March 1933): 168.

28. Editorial note, *TN* 144 (15 May 1937): 551.

29. Lindley and Lindley give personal accounts of many NYA students and workers (*A New Deal for Youth*, chapter 7).

30. Dixon Wecter, *The Age of the Great Depression* (New York: Macmillan, 1948), 188.

31. Smith, *Redeeming the Time*, 823; Wecter, *Age of the Great Depression*, 187–188.

32. McElvaine, *The Great Depression*, 191.

33. Zeitlin, "Federal Relations," 201–214. In 1939 *The New Republic* reported that some businessmen "wanted to destroy the National Youth Administration and the Civilian Conservation Corps, by turning them over to the far-from-tender mercies of the individual states" (Editorial, "Democracy or Chautauquacy?" *TNR* 100 [30 August 1939]: 90).

34. Editorial note, *TN* 141 (10 June 1935): 30; Editorial note, *TNR* 83 (10 July 1935): 234. See also the *Nation* editorial, "Our Noble Educators," which applauded the government's decision to spend NYA funds through the Federal Emergency Relief Administration instead of the National Education Association: 141 (17 June 1935): 61–62.

35. Jonathan Mitchell, "Without Work Experience," *TNR* 85 (22 January 1936): 307.

36. Jonathan Mitchell, writing as "TRB," *TNR* 86 (6 May 1936): 366–367.

37. John Chamberlain, "Self-Help and Government Aid," *TNR* 95 (27 June 1938): 338.

38. Editorial, "Training for Defense," *TNR* 104 (21 April 1941): 520.

39. Wecter, *Age of the Great Depression*, 188.

40. Editorial note, *TN* 142 (1 April 1936): 399.

41. William Mangold, "On the Labor Front," *TNR* 83 (17 June 1935): 279. Ivar Berg later made a similar point in *Education and Jobs: The Great Training Robbery* (New York: Praeger, 1970), 191; also Eli Ginzberg's foreword, xiv.

42. For the larger dimensions of this feud see Robert Sherwood, *Roosevelt and Hopkins* (New York: Harper, 1955), 78–79.

43. Mitchell "Without Work Experience,": 306–308.

44. The quotations that follow are from Ruth Benedict's article, "Our Last Minority: Youth," *TNR* 104 (24 February 1941): 271–272.

Chapter 14. Conclusion: The Weapon of Criticism ▪

1. Quoted by Carey McWilliams in *A View of "The Nation"—An Anthology, 1955–1959*, Henry M. Christman, ed. (New York: Grove Press, 1960), 12.

2. Joyce Antler, *Lucy Sprague Mitchell: The Making of a Modern Woman* (New Haven: Yale University Press, 1987), 203–204. Antler says that "the Mitchells were avid readers of *The New Republic* . . . and knew its editors well" (Letter to author, 23 March 1989).

3. See Rush Welter, *Popular Education and Democratic Thought in America* (New York: Columbia University Press, 1962), 1–6, regarding the larger American consensus on education. In chapter 16 Welter explores Croly's, Lippmann's, and Dewey's commitment to an educative politics.

4. Carol Polsgrove, "Missing Ms.," *The Progressive* 54 (January 1990): 34.

5. John Dewey, "American Education and Culture," *TNR* 7 (1 July 1916): 216.

6. Penn Kimball, "Modesty Was Not a Family Affliction" (Reviews of two books on journalism), *New York Times Book Review* (27 February 1966): 7.

7. See the correspondence columns of the journals for reader responses to articles and editorials on education.

8. Editorial, "How Shall We Vote?" *TNR* 72 (17 August 1932): 4; Theodore Peterson, "The Role of the Minority Magazine," *Antioch Review* 23 (Spring 1963): 58.

9. The liberal journals, of course, have their counterparts on the right, such as *National Review* and *Human Events*. I leave to some other scholar the disheartening chore of analyzing their commentary on education.

10. Lawrence Cremin writes: "Given the politics of American education, lay opinion is always a crucial factor, a truism occasionally ignored by historians." He lists eight journals, including *The New Republic*, as "the most fruitful periodical sources for the progressive education movement." *The Transformation of the School: Progressivism in American Education, 1876–1957* (New York: Knopf, 1961), 357.

11. Michael B. Katz, *Reconstructing American Education* (Cambridge: Harvard University Press, 1987), 157.

12. Editorial, "The Schools from the Outside," *TNR* 1 (30 January 1915): 10–11.

13. Katz, *Reconstructing Education*, 109.

14. On the need for educational criticism, and some of the problems in obtaining it, see E. Patrick McQuaid, "A Story at Risk: The Rising Tide of Mediocre Education Coverage," *Phi Delta Kappan* 70 (January 1989): K1–K8.

15. Thorstein Veblen, *The Theory of the Leisure Class* (New York: Heubsch, 1918; first published in 1899), 191–193.

16. John Judis puts the "Reagan Revolution" in perspective in "We Are All Progressives Now," a review of Martin Sklar's *The Corporate Reconstruction of American Capitalism* (*TNR* 200 [13 March 1989]: 37–39).

17. Robert Heilbroner, "Reflections: The Triumph of Capitalism," *The New Yorker* 64 (23 January 1989): 98–109.

18. Patrick Moynihan, "End of the Marxist Epoch," *The New Leader* 72 (23 January 1989): 9–11.

19. Irving Howe, "Glasnost Watch: A New Political Situation," *Dissent* 37 (Winter 1990): 88.

20. National Commission on Excellence in Education, *A Nation at Risk* (Washington, D.C.: Government Printing Office, 1983).

21. Milton Schwebel, "The Other School System," in Beatrice Gross and Ronald Gross, eds., *The Great School Debate: Which Way for American Education?* (New York: Touchstone, 1985), 237–242.

22. Russell Jacoby, *The Last Intellectuals: American Culture in the Age of Academe* (New York: Basic Books, 1987), chapters 5 and 6.

23. Herbert Croly, *The Promise of American Life* (New York: Macmillan, 1909), 153–154.

24. Alexander Cockburn takes particular pleasure in castigating *The New Republic*. See, for example, "Beat the Devil," *TN* 248 (20 February 1988): 223; also "Ashes and Diamonds," *In These Times* 13 (March 1–14, 1989): 16. Martin Peretz, editor-in-chief of *The New Republic*, returns the criticism. Referring to Cockburn, he observed "how little one can trust him on anything" ("Cambridge Diarist: Old Scores and New," *TNR* 200 [8 May 1989]: 43).

Jude Winniski wrote in 1988 that "TNR continues to be the nation's most important political journal." He says that *The Nation* "along with *Mother Jones*, takes its place as the leading publication of the leftist political community" (*The 1988 Media Guide: A Critical Review of the Print Media* [Morristown, N.J.: Polyconomics, 1988], 103, 97). David Bromwich has recently written: "What there is of a live debate on issues of current importance goes on in journals like the *New Republic* and the *Nation*" ("The Future of Tradition," *Dissent* 36 [Fall, 1989]: 543).

25. For two recent examples, see Frank Oski, "How to Raise Money for the Class of 2000," *TN* 248 (20 February 1989) 217, 221; Amy Gutmann, "Principals, Principles," *TNR* 199 (12 December 1988): 32–38.

26. A recent cover shows Joe Clark holding a baseball bat; the cover article is titled "Bad Ass Principal: Who's Challenging Joe Clark, America's Most Famous Educator?"

The article itself, however, has the more restrained title "Education: The Movie," by David L. Kirp, *Mother Jones* 14 (January 1989): 34–45.

27. See, for example, Lois Weiner, "Democratizing the Schools," in *New Politics* 1, new series (Summer 1987): 81–94.

28. An early compilation of radical critiques in the humanities in academia was an "anti-text" titled *The Dissenting Academy*, edited by Theodore Roszak (New York: Vintage, 1969). For a somewhat similar treatment of education, see *Radical Ideas and the Schools*, eds. Jack Nelson, Kenneth Carlson, and Thomas E. Linton (New York: Holt, Rinehart and Winston, 1972).

29. Editorial, "See How They Run," *TNR* 196 (4 May 1987): 9.

30. Theodore Brameld, "Social Frontiers: Retrospective and Prospective," *Phi Delta Kappan* 59 (October 1977): 118–120.

31. Michael Schudson, "A History of *The Harvard Educational Review*, in *Conflict and Continuity: A History of Ideas on Social Equality and Human Development, The Harvard Educational Review*, reprint series no. 15 (Cambridge, 1981), 14–15.

32. Harold Dunkel, "Reviewing *School Review*," *School Review* 83 (May 1975): 391–396.

33. Quoted by Billie Day in "A Brief History of *Social Education*," *Social Education* 51 (January 1987): 10–15.

34. See, for example, the journal articles cited by Stanley Aronowitz and Henry A. Giroux in *Education Under Siege: The Conservative, Liberal, and Radical Debate Over Schooling* (South Hadley, Mass: Bergin and Garvey, 1985), 221–225. Ira Shor cites some of the same journals as well as *The Radical Teacher, The American Educator, The New Republic, The Progressive* and others in *Culture Wars: School and Society in the Conservative Restoration, 1969–1984* (Boston: Routledge and Kegan Paul, 1986).

35. Ann Marie Haase, "High School Reform: More Than Band-Aids," *Phi Delta Kappan* 70 (February 1989): 490.

31. Rudi Dutschke used this phrase in proposing a strategy for the left. Quoted in Samuel Bowles and Herbert Gintis, *Schooling in Capitalist America: Educational Reform and the Contradictions of Economic Life* (New York: Basic Books, 1976), 287.

37. Andrew Kopkind, "Seed and Compost" (Review of *The Year Left 2*, edited by Mike Davis and others), *TN* 244 (30 May 1987): 739.

38. Aronowitz and Giroux, in *Education Under Siege*, (221–225), provide an excellent bibliography of books and journal articles that reflect a radical perspective.

39. Kenneth Clark, quoted in *Newsweek* 66 (9 August 1965): 76.

40. *A Margin of Hope* is the title of Irving Howe's intellectual autobiography (New York: Harcourt Brace Jovanovich, 1982).

41. Walzer and Gutmann are also paired in a recent issue of *Dissent*. Walzer wrote the introduction to, and edited, a symposium on "The State of Political Theory," and Gutmann contributed the lead article, "The Central Role of Rawls's Theory" (*Dissent 36* [Summer 1989]). Walzer's introduction is on page 337 and Gutmann's article is on pages 338–342.

42. Maurice Isserman, *If I Had a Hammer: The Death of the Old Left and the Birth of the New* (New York: Basic Books, 1987), 120–122.

43. Michael Walzer, *The Company of Critics: Social Criticism and Political Commitment in the Twentieth Century* (New York: Basic Books, 1988), 58.

44. Ibid., x, 225.

45. Ibid., 4.

46. Ibid., 232.

47. Ibid., 239–240.

48. Walzer, "Socialism Then and Now," *TNR* 102 (6 November 1989): 75.

49. Amy Gutmann, "Principals, Principles," *TNR* 199 (12 December 1988): 32–38.

50. Gutmann, *Democratic Education* (Princeton: Princeton University Press, 1987), 11.

51. Ibid., 39.

52. Ibid., 127.

53. Ibid., 77.

54. Ibid., 70.

55. Ibid., 288.

56. Daniel Perlstein, "The Parameters of Participation: Schooling and Democratic

Theory" (Review of Amy Gutmann's *Democratic Education*), *Educational Researcher* 18 (January-February 1989): 49–50.

57. James MacGregor Burns, *The Crosswinds of Freedom: The American Experiment*, vol. 3 (New York: Knopf, 1989), 663, 668.

58. Hendrik Hertzberg, "TRB From Washington: Casualties of War," *TNR* 200 (6 March 1989): 42.

59. Gerald Graff and William Cain, "Peace Plan for the Canon Wars," *TN* 248 (6 March 1989): 312.

60. Quoted by Isserman in *If I Had a Hammer*, 95.

61. Cremin, *Transformation*, 353.

Selected Bibliography

Books ▪

Aaron, Daniel. *Men of Good Hope.* New York: Oxford University Press, 1951; Galaxy Books, 1961.
———. *Writers on the Left.* New York: Harcourt, Brace, 1961; Avon, 1965.
Alexander, Charles. *Nationalism in American Thought, 1930–1945.* Chicago: Rand McNally, 1971.
Alpern, Sara. *Freda Kirchwey: A Woman of "The Nation."* Cambridge: Harvard University Press, 1987.
Altbach, Philip. *Student Politics in America: A Historical Analysis.* New York: McGraw-Hill, 1974.
Antler, Joyce. *Lucy Sprague Mitchell: The Making of a Modern Woman.* New Haven: Yale University Press, 1987.
Armytage, W.H.G. *Four Hundred Years of English Education.* Cambridge: Cambridge University Press, 1964.
Aronowitz, Stanley, and Henry A. Giroux. *Education Under Siege: The Conservative, Liberal, and Radical Debate Over Schooling.* South Hadley, Mass.: Bergin and Garvey, 1985.
Ayer, N. W. and Son. *American Newspaper Annual and Directory.* Philadelphia: Ayer, 1914–1941.
Beale, Howard K. *Are American Teachers Free?* New York: Scribner's, 1936.
Bender, Thomas. *New York Intellect: A History of Intellectual Life in New York City from 1750 to the Beginnings of Our Own Time.* New York: Knopf, 1987.
Berg, Ivar. *Education and Jobs: The Great Training Robbery.* New York: Praeger, 1970.
Bernstein, Irving. *The Lean Years: The American Worker, 1920–1933.* Boston: Houghton Mifflin, 1960.
———. *Turbulent Years: A History of the American Worker, 1933–1941.* Boston: Houghton Mifflin, 1970.
Bernstein, Richard J. *John Dewey.* New York: Washington Square Press, 1966.
Bird, Caroline. *The Invisible Scar.* New York: Longman, 1966.
Bliven, Bruce. *Five Million Words Later.* New York: John Day, 1970.

Bloom, Alexander. *Prodigal Sons: The New York Intellectuals and Their World.* New York: Oxford University Press, 1986.

Blum, John. *The Progressive Presidents: Roosevelt, Wilson, Roosevelt, Johnson.* New York: Norton, 1980.

Bode, Boyd. *Progressive Education at the Crossroads.* New York: Newson, 1938.

Bourne, Randolph. *Education and Living.* New York: The Century Company, 1917.

———. *The Gary Schools.* 1916. Reprint with introductions and annotations by Adeline Levine and Murray Levine. Cambridge: M.I.T. Press, 1970.

———. *The World of Randolph Bourne.* Edited by Lillian Schlissel. New York: Dutton, 1965.

Bowers, Chester. *The Progressive Educator and the Depression: The Radical Years.* New York: Random House, 1969.

Bowles, Samuel, and Herbert Gintis. *Schooling in Capitalist America: Educational Reform and the Contradictions of Economic Life.* New York: Basic Books, 1976.

Brameld, Theodore, ed. *Workers' Education in the United States.* New York: Harper, 1941.

Brax, Ralph. *The First Student Movement: Student Activism in the United States.* Port Washington, N.Y.: Kennikat Press, 1981.

Burns, James MacGregor. *The Crosswinds of Freedom: The American Experiment* Vol. 3. New York: Knopf, 1989.

Callahan, Raymond. *Education and the Cult of Efficiency.* Chicago: University of Chicago Press, 1962.

Charles, Searle. *Minister of Relief: Harry Hopkins and the Depression.* Syracuse: Syracuse University Press, 1963.

Christman, Henry M., ed. *A View of "The Nation"—An Anthology, 1955–1959.* New York: Grove Press, 1960.

———. ed. *One Hundred Years of "The Nation": A Centennial Anthology, 1865–1965.* New York: Macmillan, 1965.

Clayton, Bruce. *Forgotten Prophet: The Life of Randolph Bourne.* Baton Rouge: Louisiana State University Press, 1984.

Cohen, Ronald, and Raymond Mohl. *The Paradox of Progressive Education: The Gary Plan and Urban Schooling.* Port Washington, N.Y.: Kennikat Press, 1979.

Cohen, Sol. *Progressives and Urban School Reform: The Public Education Association of New York City, 1895–1954.* New York: Teachers College Press, 1964.

———. "The School and Personality Development: Intellectual History." In *Historical Inquiry in Education: A Research Agenda,* edited by John H. Best. Washington: American Educational Research Association, 1983.

Cohen, Stan. *The Tree Army: A Pictorial History of the Civilian Conservation Corps, 1933–1942.* Missoula, Mont.: Pictorial Histories, 1980.

Conklin, Groff, ed. *The New Republic Anthology: 1914–1935.* New York: Dodge Publishing, 1936.

Conlin, Joseph, ed. *The American Radical Press, 1880–1960.* Westport, Conn.: Greenwood Press, 1974.

Cowley, Malcolm. *The Dream of the Golden Mountains: Remembering the 1930s.* New York: Viking, 1980.

———. *Exile's Return: A Literary Odyssey of the 1920s.* New York: Viking, 1934.

———. *Think Back on Us: A Contemporary Chronicle of the 1930s, The Social Record.* Edited by Dan Piper. Carbondale: Southern Illinois University Press, 1967. Arcturus edition, 1972.

Cremin, Lawrence. *American Education: The Metropolitan Experience, 1876–1980.* New York: Harper and Row, 1988.

———. *The Transformation of the School: Progressivism in American Education, 1876–1957.* New York: Knopf, 1961.

Cresswell, Anthony, Michael Murphy, and Charles Kerchner. *Teachers, Unions, and Collective Bargaining in Public Education.* Berkeley: McCutchan, 1980.

Croly, Herbert. *The Promise of American Life.* New York: Macmillan, 1909.

———. *Willard Straight.* New York: Macmillan, 1925.

Crunden, Robert M. *Ministers of Reform: The Progressives' Achievement in American Civilization, 1889–1920.* New York: Basic Books, 1982.

Cuban, Larry. *How Teachers Taught: Constancy and Change in American Classrooms, 1890–1980.* New York: Longman, 1984.

Cummins, E. E. *The Labor Problem in the United States.* New York: Van Nostrand, 1932.

Curti, Merle. *American Paradox: The Conflict of Thought and Action.* New Brunswick, N.J.: Rutgers University Press, 1956.

Davis, Kenneth S. *FDR: The New Deal Years, 1933–1937.* New York: Random House, 1986.

Derber, Milton, and Edwin Young, eds. *Labor and the New Deal.* Madison: University of Wisconsin Press, 1957.

De Lima, Agnes. *The Little Red School House.* New York: Macmillan, 1942.

———. *Our Enemy the Child.* New York: New Republic, 1925. Reprinted with a foreword by Lawrence Cremin. Salem, N.H.: Ayer Publishing, 1969.

Dewey, John. *Democracy and Education: An Introduction to the Philosophy of Education.* New York: Macmillan, 1916.

———. *Experience and Education.* New York: Macmillan, 1938.

———. *My Pedagogic Creed.* New York: Kellogg, 1897.

Dwyer, Richard. *Labor Education in the U.S.: An Annotated Bibliography.* Metuchen, N.J.: Scarecrow Press, 1977.

Dykhuisen, George. *The Life and Mind of John Dewey.* Carbondale: Southern Illinois University Press, 1973.

Eagan, Eileen. *Class, Culture, and the Classroom: The Student Peace Movement of the 1930s.* Philadelphia: Temple University Press, 1981.

Eaton, William. *The American Federation of Teachers: 1916–1961.* Carbondale: Southern Illinois University Press, 1975.

Ekirch, Arthur. *Ideologies and Utopias: The Impact of the New Deal on American Thought.* Chicago: Quadrangle Books, 1969.

Elias, John, and Sharan Merriam. *Philosophical Foundations of Adult Education.* Malabar, Fla.: Krieger, 1984.

Elias, Robert. *"Entangling Alliances with None": An Essay on the Individual in the American Twenties.* New York: Norton, 1973.

Ellis, Edward. *A Nation in Torment: The Great American Depression, 1929–1939.* New York: Coward-McCann, 1970.

Elsbree, Willard. *The American Teacher: Evolution of a Profession in a Democracy.* New York: American Book Company, 1939.

Faulkner, Harold U. *The Quest for Social Justice, 1898–1914.* New York: Macmillan, 1931.

Feinberg, Walter, Harvey Cantor, Michael Katz, and Paul Violas. *Revisionists Respond to Ravitch.* Washington, D.C.: National Academy of Education, 1980.

Feuer, Lewis. *The Conflict of Generations: The Character and Significance of Student Movements.* New York: Basic Books, 1969.

Filler, Louis. *Appointment at Armageddon: Muckraking and Progressivism in the American Tradition.* Westport, Conn.: Greenwood Press, 1976.

——. *Randolph Bourne.* Washington, D.C.: American Council on Public Affairs, 1943.

Flacks, Richard. *Making History: The American Left and the American Mind.* New York: Columbia University Press, 1988.

Forcey, Charles. *The Crossroads of Liberalism: Croly, Weyl, Lippmann, and the Progressive Era, 1900–1925.* New York: Oxford University Press, 1961.

Fraser, Steve, and Gary Gerstle, eds. *The Rise and Fall of the New Deal Order, 1930–1980.* Princeton: Princeton University Press, 1989.

Gentry, Richard. *Liberalism and the New Republic, 1914–1960.* Ann Arbor: University Microfilms, 1960.

Gibbs, Alan. *Institutional History as an Element of Community History. Civilian Conservation Corps in the Okanagan Country.* Okanagan, Wash.: U.S. Forest Service, 1986.

Gouinlock, James. *Excellence in Public Discourse: John Stuart Mill, John Dewey, and Social Intelligence.* New York: Teachers College Press, 1986.

Graham, Otis, Jr. *An Encore for Reform: The Old Progressives and the New Deal.* New York: Oxford University Press, 1967.

——. *From Roosevelt to Roosevelt: American Politics and Diplomacy, 1901–1941.* New York: Appleton-Century-Crofts, 1971.

Graham, Patricia. *Progressive Education: From Arcady to Academe.* New York: Teachers College Press, 1967.

Grattan, C. Hartley. *In Quest of Knowledge: A Historical Perspective on Adult Education.* New York: Association Press, 1955.

Grimes, Alan P. *The Political Liberalism of the New York "Nation": 1865–1932.* Chapel Hill: University of North Carolina Press, 1953.

Gross, Beatrice, and Ronald Gross, eds. *The Great School Debate: Which Way for American Education?* New York: Touchstone, 1985.

Gutek, Gerald. *The Educational Theory of George S. Counts.* Columbus: Ohio State University Press, 1970.

Gutmann, Amy. *Democratic Education.* Princeton: Princeton University Press, 1987.

Haber, Samuel. *Efficiency and Uplift: Scientific Management in the Progressive Era, 1890–1920.* Chicago: University of Chicago Press, 1964.

Haskell, Daniel, ed. *The Nation: Index of Titles and Contributors, 1865–1917.* New York: New York Public Library, 1951.

Hays, Samuel P. *Conservation and the Gospel of Efficiency.* Cambridge: Harvard University Press, 1959.

Heuvel, Katrina Vanden, ed. *"The Nation," 1865–1990: Selections from the Independent Magazine of Politics and Culture.* New York: Thunder's Mouth Press, 1990.

Hicks, John. *The Republican Ascendancy.* New York: Harper, 1960.

Hoffman, Frederick J. *The Twenties: American Writing in the Postwar Decade.* New York: Viking Press, 1955; Collier, 1962.

Hofstadter, Richard. *The Age of Reform.* 1955. New York: Vintage, 1960.

——. *The American Political Tradition and the Men Who Made It.* New York: Knopf, 1948.

——. *Anti-intellectualism in American Life.* New York: Knopf, 1963.

Holbrook, Stewart. *Dreamers of the American Dream.* Garden City: Doubleday, 1957.

Howe, Irving. *A Margin of Hope: An Intellectual Autobiography.* New York: Harcourt Brace Jovanovich, 1982.

Howe, Irving, and Lewis Coser. *The American Communist Party: A Critical History*. New York: Praeger, 1962.

Humes, D. Joy. *Oswald Garrison Villard: Liberal of the 1920's*. Syracuse, N.Y.: Syracuse University Press, 1960.

Isserman, Maurice. *If I Had a Hammer: The Death of the Old Left and the Birth of the New*. New York: Basic Books, 1987.

Iversen, Robert W. *The Communists and the Schools*. New York: Harcourt, Brace, 1959.

Jacoby, Russell. *The Last Intellectuals: American Culture in the Age of Academe*. New York: Basic Books, 1987.

Johnson, Alvin. *Pioneer's Progress*. 1952. Reprint. Lincoln: University of Nebraska Press, 1960.

Kallen, Horace. *Education, the Machine and the Worker*. New York: New Republic, 1925.

Kantor, Harvey, and David Tyack, eds. *Work, Youth, and Schooling: Historical Perspectives on Vocationalism in American Education*. Stanford: Stanford University Press, 1982.

Karier, Clarence. *The Individual, Society, and Education*. Urbana: University of Illinois Press, 1986.

———. *Shaping the American Educational State: 1900 to the Present*. New York: Free Press, 1975.

Katz, Michael B. *Class, Bureaucracy and Schools: The Illusion of Educational Change in America*. New York: Praeger, 1971.

———. *In the Shadow of the Poorhouse: A Social History of Welfare in America*. New York: Basic Books, 1986.

———. *Reconstructing American Education*. Cambridge: Harvard University Press, 1987.

Katznelson, Ira, and Margaret Weir. *Schooling for All: Class, Race, and the Decline of the Democratic Ideal*. New York: Basic Books, 1985.

Kelly, Frank. *The Fight for the White House: The Story of 1912*. New York: Crowell, 1961.

Kerchner, Charles, and Douglas Mitchell. *The Changing Idea of a Teachers' Union*. New York: Falmer Press, 1988.

Klehr, Harvey. *The Heyday of American Communism: The Depression Years*. New York: Basic Books, 1984.

Kliebard, Herbert. *The Struggle for the American Curriculum, 1893–1958*. New York: Routledge and Kegan Paul, 1987.

Knowles, Malcolm. *A History of the Adult Education Movement in the United States*. Rev. ed. Melbourne, Fla.: Krieger, 1977.

Gabriel Kolko. *The Triumph of Conservatism: A Reinterpretation of American History, 1900–1916*. New York: Free Press, 1963.

Kornbluh, Joyce. *A New Deal for Workers' Education: The Workers' Service Program, 1933–1942*. Urbana: University of Illinois Press, 1987.

Krug, Edward. *The Shaping of the American High School: 1920–1941*. Madison: University of Wisconsin Press, 1972.

Lagemann, Ellen Condliffe. *A Generation of Women: Education in the Lives of Progressive Reformers*. Cambridge: Harvard University Press, 1979.

———. *Private Power for the Public Good: A History of the Carnegie Foundation for the Advancement of Teaching*. Middletown, Conn.: Wesleyan University Press, 1983.

Lasch, Christopher. *The New Radicalism in America, 1899–1963: The Intellectual as a Social Type*. New York: Knopf, 1965.

Lash, Joseph. *Eleanor and Franklin*. New York: Norton, 1971.

Lash, Joseph, and James Wechsler. *War Our Heritage*. New York: International Publishers, 1936.

Lawson, R. Alan. *The Failure of Independent Liberalism*. New York: G. P. Putnam's Sons, 1971.

Leake, Fred and Ray Carter. *Roosevelt's Tree Army: A Brief History of the Civilian Conservation Corps*. Arlington, Va.: National Association of C.C.C. Alumni, 1982.

Lerner, Max ed. *The Portable Veblen*. New York: Viking Press, 1948.

Leuchtenberg, William. *Franklin Roosevelt and the New Deal*. New York: Harper, 1963.

———. *The Perils of Prosperity: 1914–1932*. Chicago: University of Chicago Press, 1958.

Levy, David W. *Herbert Croly of "The New Republic": The Life and Thought of an American Progressive*. Princeton: Princeton University Press, 1985.

Lindeman, Eduard C. *The Meaning of Adult Education*. New York: New Republic, Inc., 1926.

———. *Social Discovery*. New York: New Republic, Inc., 1924.

Lindley, Betty and Ernest Lindley. *A New Deal for Youth*. New York: Viking, 1938.

Lippmann, Walter. *Drift and Mastery*. 1914. Reprint. Englewood Cliffs, N.J.: Prentice-Hall, 1961.

———. *A Preface to Politics*. New York: Kennerley, 1913.

Lipset, Seymour. *Rebellion in the University*. Boston: Little, Brown, 1972.

Lovett, Robert Morss. *All Our Years*. New York: Viking, 1948.

Lustig, R. Jeffrey. *Corporate Liberalism: The Origins of Modern American Political Theory, 1890–1920*. Berkeley: University of California Press, 1982.

Martin, James. *American Liberalism and World Politics, 1931–1941*. New York: Devin-Adair, 1964.

Matthews, T. S. *Name and Address*. New York: Simon and Schuster, 1960.

May, Henry. *The End of American Innocence: A Study of the First Years of Our Own Time, 1912–1917*. 1959. Chicago: Quadrangle, 1964.

Mazolf, Marion. *Up from the Footnote: A History of Women Journalists*. New York: Hastings House, 1977.

McElvaine, Robert. *The Great Depression: America, 1929–1941*. New York: Times Books, 1984.

Mencken, H. L. *A Gang of Pecksniffs*. Edited by Theo Lippmann, Jr. New Rochelle, N.Y.: Arlington House, 1975.

———. *The Vintage Mencken*. Gathered by Alistair Cooke. New York: Vintage, 1955.

Metzger, Walter P. *Academic Freedom in the Age of the University*. 1955. Reprint. New York: Columbia University Press, 1961.

Miller, Charles. *Democracy in Education*. Ann Arbor: University Microfilms, 1967.

Mills, C. Wright. *Sociology and Pragmatism: The Higher Learning in America*. Edited by Irving Horowitz. New York: Galaxy, 1966.

Mitchell, Wesley Clair. *Wesley Clair Mitchell: The Economic Scientist*. Edited by Arthur Burns. New York: National Bureau of Economic Research, 1952.

Moreau, John A. *Bourne, A Biography*. Ann Arbor: University Microfilms, 1964.

Morris, James. *Conflict Within the AFL: A Study of Craft Versus Industrial Unionism, 1901–1938*. Ithaca: Cornell University Press, 1958.

Morris, Richard B. *Encyclopedia of American History*. New York: Harper, 1953.

Murray, Robert K. *Red Scare: A Study of National Hysteria, 1919–1920.* 1955. Reprint. New York: McGraw-Hill, 1964.

Muste, A. J. *The Essays of A. J. Muste.* Edited by Nat Hentoff. Indianapolis: Bobbs-Merrill, 1967.

Myers, Norman. *Letters to Home: Life in the C.C.C. Camps of Douglas County, Oregon, 1933–1934.* Edited by Gerald Williams. Roseburg, Oreg.: U.S. Forest Service, 1983.

Nash, Roderick. *The Nervous Generation: American Thought, 1917–1930.* Chicago: Rand McNally, 1970.

National Commission on Excellence in Education. *A Nation at Risk.* Washington, D.C.: Government Printing Office, 1983.

Nelson, Jack, Kenneth Carlson, and Thomas E. Linton. *Radical Ideas and the Schools.* New York: Holt, Rinehart and Winston, 1972.

Noble, David W. *The Paradox of Progressive Thought.* Minneapolis: University of Minnesota Press, 1958.

Nutter, Glen L. *Education and Politics in the "New Republic" Magazine.* Ann Arbor: University Microfilms, 1968.

O'Neill, William. *A Better World: The Great Schism—Stalinism and the American Intellectuals.* New York: Simon and Schuster, 1982.

———. *The Progressive Years: America Comes of Age.* New York: Dodd, Mead, 1975.

Pells, Richard H. *Radical Visions and American Dreams: Culture and Social Thought in the Depression Years.* New York: Harper and Row, 1973.

Perkins, Frances. *The Roosevelt I Knew.* New York: Viking Press, 1946.

Perrett, Geoffrey. *America in the Twenties: A History.* New York: Touchstone, 1983.

Pesotta, Rose. *Bread Upon the Waters.* 1944. Reprint. Ithaca: ILR Press, 1987.

Peterson, Paul E. *The Politics of School Reform, 1870–1940.* Chicago: University of Chicago, 1985.

Pritchett, Henry L. *17th Annual Report of the Carnegie Foundation for the Advancement of Teaching.* New York: Carnegie Foundation, 1922.

Radosh, Ronald, and Murray Rothbard, eds. *A New History of Leviathan: Essays on the Rise of the American Corporate State.* New York: Dutton, 1972.

Rafferty, Max. *What They Are Doing to Your Children.* New York: New American Library, 1964.

Ravitch, Diane. *The Great School Wars: A History of the New York City Public Schools.* 2nd ed. New York: Basic Books, 1988.

———. *The Revisionists Revised: A Critique of the Radical Attack on the Schools.* New York: Basic Books, 1978.

———. *The Troubled Crusade: American Education, 1945–1980.* New York: Basic Books, 1983.

Ravitch, Diane, and Ronald Goodenow, eds. *Educating an Urban People: The New York City Experience.* New York: Teachers College Press, 1981.

Rawick, George. *The New Deal and Youth: The Civilian Conservation Corps, the National Youth Administration, and the American Youth Congress.* Ann Arbor: University Microfilms, 1957.

Reese, William J. *Power and the Promise of School Reform: Grass-roots Movements During the Progressive Era.* Boston: Routledge and Kegan Paul, 1986.

Rickover, Hyman. *Education and Freedom.* New York: Dutton, 1959.

Riesman, David. *The Lonely Crowd.* New Haven: Yale University Press, 1950.

Roosevelt, Eleanor. *This I Remember.* New York: Harper, 1949.

Roszak, Theodore, ed. *The Dissenting Academy.* New York: Vintage, 1969.

Robinson, Jo Ann. *Abraham Went Out: A Biography of A. J. Muste.* Philadelphia: Temple University Press, 1981.

Radosh, Ronald, and Murray Rothbard, eds. *A New History of Leviathan: Essays on the Rise of the American Corporate State.* New York: Dutton, 1972.

Rugg, Harold, and Ann Shumaker. *The Child-Centered School: An Appraisal of the New Education.* Yonkers: World Book Company, 1928.

Rutkoff, Peter, and William Scott. *New School: A History of the New School for Social Research.* New York: Free Press, 1986.

Salmond, John A. *The Civilian Conservation Corps, 1933–1942: A New Deal Case Study.* Durham: Duke University Press, 1967.

Schilpp, Madelon Golden, and Sharon Murphy. *Great Women of the Press.* Carbondale: Southern Illinois University Press, 1983.

Schlesinger, Arthur M., Jr. *The Coming of the New Deal.* Boston: Houghton Mifflin, 1959.

———. *The Crisis of the Old Order, 1919–1933.* Boston: Houghton Mifflin, 1957.

———. *The Cycles of American History.* Boston: Houghton Mifflin, 1986.

Schlesinger, Arthur M., Jr., and Morton White, eds. *Paths of American Thought.* Boston: Houghton Mifflin, 1963.

Schrecker, Ellen. *No Ivory Tower: McCarthyism and the Universities.* New York: Oxford University Press, 1986.

School Survey Class of the California Branch of the Association of Collegiate Alumnae. *Some Conditions in the Schools of San Francisco.* San Francisco: 1914.

Schudson, Michael. "A History of *The Harvard Educational Review.*" In *Conflict and Continuity: A History of Ideas on Social Equality and Human Development, The Harvard Educational Review.* Reprint Series Number 15. Edited by John R. Snaren and others. Cambridge, 1981.

Seideman, David. *The New Republic: A Voice of Modern Liberalism.* New York: Praeger, 1986.

Seidler, Murray. *Norman Thomas: Respectable Rebel.* Syracuse: Syracuse University Press, 1967.

Shannon, David A., ed. *The Great Depression.* Englewood Cliffs, N.J.: Prentice Hall, 1960.

Sheats, Paul, Clarence Jayne, and Ralph Spence. *Adult Education—the Community Approach.* New York: Dryden Press, 1953.

Sherwood, Robert. *Roosevelt and Hopkins.* New York: Harper, 1955.

Shor, Ira. *Culture Wars: School and Society in the Conservative Restoration, 1969–1984.* Boston: Routledge and Kegan Paul, 1986.

Simon, Rita, ed. *As We Saw the Thirties: Essays on Social and Political Movements of a Decade.* Urbana: University of Illinois Press, 1967.

Sklar, Martin. *The Corporate Reconstruction of American Capitalism, 1890–1916: The Market, the Law, and Politics.* New York: Cambridge University Press, 1988.

Slosson, Preston W. *The Great Crusade and After, 1914–1928.* New York: Macmillan, 1930.

Smith, Gene. *When the Cheering Stopped: The Last Years of Woodrow Wilson.* New York: Morrow, 1964.

Smith, Page. *Redeeming the Time: A People's History of the 1920s and the New Deal.* New York: McGraw-Hill, 1987.

Sochen, June. *Movers and Shakers: American Women Thinkers and Activists, 1900–1970.* New York: Quadrangle, 1973.

Solomon, Barbara Miller. *In the Company of Educated Women: A History of*

Women and Higher Education in America. New Haven: Yale University Press, 1985.

Steel, Ronald. *Walter Lippmann and the American Century.* New York: Random House, 1980.

Stewart, David. *Adult Learning in America: Eduard Lindeman and His Agenda for Lifelong Education.* Melbourne, Fla.: Krieger, 1987.

Swanberg, W. A. *Whitney Father, Whitney Heiress.* New York: Scribner's, 1980.

Turner, Steven. *The New Education in the "New Republic" Magazine: 1914–1930.* Ann Arbor: University Microfilms, 1983.

Tyack, David. *The One Best System: A History of American Urban Education.* Cambridge: Harvard University Press, 1975.

Tyack, David, and Elisabeth Hansot. *Managers of Virtue: Public School Leadership in America, 1820–1980.* New York: Basic Books, 1982.

Tyack, David, Robert Lowe, and Elisabeth Hansot. *Public Schools in Hard Times: The Great Depression and Recent Years.* Cambridge: Harvard University Press, 1984.

United States Bureau of the Census. *Historical Statistics of the United States.* Washington, D.C.: Government Printing Office, 1960.

Vassar College. *Annual Catalogs.* Poughkeepsie, N.Y.: Vassar College, 1904–1908.

Vassarion. Poughkeepsie: Vassar College, 1908.

Veblen, Thorstein. *The Portable Veblen.* Edited by Max Lerner. New York: Viking Press, 1948.

———. *The Theory of the Leisure Class.* 1899. Reprint. New York: Heubsch, 1918.

Veysey, Lawrence. *The Emergence of the American University.* Chicago: University of Chicago Press, 1965.

Villard, Oswald Garrison. *Fighting Years: Memoirs of a Liberal Editor.* New York: Harcourt, Brace, 1939.

Wald, Alan. *The New York Intellectuals: The Rise and Decline of the Anti-Stalinist Left from the 1930s to the 1980s.* Chapel Hill: University of North Carolina Press, 1987.

Walters, Thomas. *Randolph Silliman Bourne: Education Through Radical Eyes.* Kennebunkport, Maine: Mercer House, 1982.

Walzer, Michael. *The Company of Critics: Social Criticism and Political Commitment in the Twentieth Century.* New York: Basic Books, 1988.

Warren, Frank III. *Liberals and Communism: The "Red Decade" Revisited.* Bloomington: Indiana University Press, 1966.

Wechsler, James. *The Age of Suspicion.* New York: Random House, 1953.

———. *Revolt on the Campus.* New York: Covici-Friede, 1935. Introduction by Robert Morss Lovett. Republished in 1973 with a new introduction by the author. Seattle: University of Washington Press.

Wecter, Dixon. *The Age of the Great Depression.* New York: Macmillan, 1948.

Weinstein, James *The Corporate Ideal in the Liberal State.* Boston: Beacon Press, 1968.

Welter, Rush. *Popular Education and Democratic Thought in America.* New York: Columbia University Press, 1962.

Wertheimer, Barbara, ed. *Labor Education for Women Workers.* Philadelphia: Temple University Press, 1981.

Weyl, Walter. *Tired Radicals and Other Essays.* New York: Huebsch, 1921.

White, Morton. *Social Thought in America.* Rev. ed. Boston: Beacon Press, 1957.

Wiebe, Robert. *The Search for Order, 1877–1920*. New York: Hill and Wang, 1967.

Willey, Malcolm. *Depression, Recovery and Higher Education: A Report by Committee Y of the American Association of University Professors*. New York: McGraw-Hill, 1937.

Winniski, Jude. *The 1988 Media Guide: A Critical Review of the Print Media*. Morristown, N.J.: Polyconomics, 1988.

Wood, James P. *Magazines in the United States*. New York: Ronald Press, 1949.

Wreszin, Michael. *Oswald Garrison Villard: Pacifist at War*. Bloomington: Indiana University Press, 1965.

Young, Michael. *The Elmhirsts of Dartington: The Creation of An Utopian Community*. London: Routledge and Kegan Paul, 1982.

Zilversmit, Arthur. "The Failure of Progressive Education, 1920–1940." In *Schooling and Society: Studies in the History of Education*, edited by Lawrence Stone. Baltimore: Johns Hopkins University Press, 1976.

Articles, Editorials, Reviews ■

Articles, editorials, reviews, letters, and advertisements from *The Nation* (*TN*) and *The New Republic* (*TNR*) from 1914 to 1941 are cited in the notes and most are not repeated here. A few from that period which deal with journal history and personnel are included, however. Articles from the journals since 1941 are included below along with material from other magazines and journals.

Altenbaugh, Richard. "'The Children and the Instruments of a Militant Labor Progressivism': Brookwood Labor College and the American Labor College Movement of the 1920s and 1930s." *History of Education Quarterly* 23 (Winter 1983): 395–411.

Beck, Robert. "Progressive Education and American Progressivism: Margaret Naumberg." *Teachers College Record* 60 (December 1959): 198–208.

Benne, Kenneth. "John Dewey and Adult Education." *Adult Education Bulletin* 14 (October 1949): 7–12.

Berman, Barbara. "Business Efficiency, American Schooling and the Public School Superintendency: A Reconsideration of the Callahan Thesis." *History of Education Quarterly* 23 (Fall 1983): 297–321.

Bernstein, Richard J. "The Varieties of Pluralism." *Current Issues in Education* 5 (Fall 1985): 1–21.

Bliven, Bruce. "The First Forty Years." *TNR*, 40th Anniversary Issue, 131 (22 November 1954): 6–10.

Borrowman, Merle. Review of *Anti-intellectualism in American Life*, by Richard Hofstadter. *History of Education Quarterly* 3 (December 1963): 223–225.

Jo Ann Boydston. "John Dewey and the Journals." *History of Education Quarterly* 10 (Spring 1970): 72–77.

Brameld, Theodore. "Social Frontiers: Retrospective and Prospective." *Phi Delta Kappan* 59 (October 1977): 118–120.

Bromwich, David. "The Future of Tradition." *Dissent* 36 (Fall 1989): 541–557.

Church, Robert L., Michael B. Katz, Harold Silver, and Lawrence Cremin. "Forum on *The Metropolitan Experience in Education*." *History of Education Quarterly* 29 (Fall 1989): 419–446.

Cockburn, Alexander. "Ashes and Diamonds." *In These Times* 13 (March 1–14, 1989): 16.

———. "Beat the Devil." *TN* 248 (20 February 1988): 223.

Coe, George A. "What Sort of School is a CCC Camp?" *Social Frontier* 1 (May 1935): 24–26.

Cohen, Sol. "The Mental Hygiene Movement, the Development of Personality and the School: The Medicalization of American Education." *History of Education Quarterly* 23 (Summer 1983): 123–149.

———. "The School and Personality Development: Intellectual History." In *Historical Inquiry in Education: A Research Agenda*, 109–137, edited by J. Hardin Best. Washington, D.C.: American Educational Research Association, 1983.

Croly, Herbert. "The Breach in Civilization." Unpublished manuscript. Cambridge: Houghton Library, Harvard University.

Daniels, Roger. "Worker's Education and the University of California." *Labor History* 4 (Winter 1963): 32–50.

Day, Billie. "A Brief History of *Social Education*." *Social Education* 51 (January 1987): 10–15.

Dewey, John. "Social Purposes in Education." *General Science Quarterly* 7 (January 1923): 79–91. Republished in *John Dewey: The Middle Works*, vol. 15, edited by Jo Ann Boydston, 158–169. Carbondale: Southern Illinois University Press, 1983.

Diggins, John. "*The New Republic* and its Times." *TNR* 191 (10 December 1984): 23–73.

Draper, Theodore. "The Class Struggle: The Myth of the Communist Professors." Review of Ellen Schrecker's *No Ivory Tower*. *TNR* 196 (26 January 1987): 29–36.

Dunkel, Harold. "Re-viewing *School Review*." *School Review* 83 (May 1975): 391–396.

Editorial. *The Outlook* 116 (29 August 1917): 644–646.

Feinberg, Walter. "On Reading Dewey." *History of Education Quarterly* 15 (Winter 1975): 395–415.

Filene, Peter. "An Obituary for 'The Progressive Movement.'" *American Quarterly* 22 (Spring 1970): 20–34.

Fairlie, Henry. "War Against Reason." *The New Republic*, 75th Anniversary Issue, 201 (6 November 1989): 58–62.

Forcey, Charles B. "Croly and Nationalism." *TNR* 131 (22 November 1954): 17–22.

Gilman, Richard. "The Intellect and its Enemies." Review of Hofstadter's *Anti-intellectualism*. *TNR* 149 (13 July 1963): 19–22.

Gould, Sidney. "A History of the New York City Teachers Union and Why It Died." *The Educational Forum* 29 (January 1965): 207–215.

Gower, Calvin W. "The Civilian Conservation Corps and American Education: Threat to Local Control?" *History of Education Quarterly* 7 (Spring 1967): 58–70.

Graff, Gerald, and William Cain. "Peace Plan for the Canon Wars." *TN* 248 (6 March 1989): 310–313.

Graham, Patricia Albjerg. "Schools: Cacophony About Practice, Silence About Purpose." *Daedalus* 113 (Fall 1984): 29–57.

Gutmann, Amy. "The Central Role of Rawls's Theory." *Dissent* 36 (Summer 1989): 338–342.

———. "Principals, Principles." *TNR* 199 (12 December 1988): 32–38.

Haase, Ann Marie. "High School Reform: More Than Band-Aids." *Phi Delta Kappan* 70 (February 1989): 490.

Hechinger, Grace, and Fred Hechinger. "In Criticism of Anti-Criticism." *New York Times Magazine* (11 March 1962): 28, 86.

Heilbroner, Robert. "Reflections: The Triumph of Capitalism." *The New Yorker* 64 (23 January 1989): 98–109.

Hertzberg, Hendrik. "TRB From Washington: Casualties of War." *TNR* 200 (6 March 1989): 4, 42.

Hood, Elmer. "A Study of the Attitude of *The New Republic* on Foreign and Domestic Policies of the United States Between November, 1914 and March 3, 1933." Master's thesis, Rutgers University, 1949.

Howe, Irving. "Glasnost Watch: A New Political Situation." *Dissent* 37 (Winter 1990): 87–91.

Howlett, Charles. "Brookwood Labor College and Worker Commitment to Social Reform." *Mid-America* 61 (January 1979): 47–66.

Isserman, Maurice. "Three Generations: Historians View American Communism." *Labor History* 26 (Fall 1985): 517–545.

Judis, John B. "Herbert Croly's Promise." *TNR*, 75th Anniversary Issue, 201 (6 November 1989): 84–87.

——. "We Are All Progressives Now." Review of Martin Sklar's *The Corporate Reconstruction of American Capitalism. TNR* 200 (13 March 1989): 37–39.

Kaplan, Sidney. "Social Engineers as Saviors." *Journal of the History of Ideas* 17 (June 1956): 347–369.

Karier, Clarence. "John Dewey and the New Liberalism: Some Reflections and Responses." *History of Education Quarterly* 15 (Winter 1975): 417–443.

Katz, Michael B. "Not the Whole Story," Review of *The Troubled Crusade: American Education, 1945–1980,* by Diane Ravitch. *History of Education Quarterly* 25 (Spring-Summer 1985): 175–180.

Kazin, Alfred. "The New Republic: A Personal View." *TNR*, 75th Anniversary Edition, 201 (6 November 1989): 78–83.

Kimball, Penn. "American Journalism: From Essay to Assay." *TN*, 100th Anniversary Issue, 201 (20 September 1965): 72–76.

——. "The History of *The Nation* According to the F.B.I." *TN* 242 (22 March 1986): 399–426.

——. "Modesty Was Not a Family Affliction." Reviews of two books on journalism. *New York Times Book Review* (27 February 1966): 7, 38.

Kirp, David L. "Education: The Movie." *Mother Jones* 14 (January 1989): 34–45.

Kopkind, Andrew. "Seed and Compost." Review of *The Year Left 2*, edited by Mike Davis and others. *TN* 244 (30 May 1987): 739.

Kuttner, Robert. "Don't Trade Lenin for Milton Friedman." *The Oregonian* (10 October 1989): B10.

"Lash, Joseph P." *Current Biography* (New York: H. W. Wilson, 1972), 272–274.

"Liberals." *Time* 34 (13 November 1939): 21–22.

Link, Arthur S. "What Happened to the Progressive Movement in the 1920s?" *American Historical Review* 64 (July 1959): 833–851.

Lippmann, Walter. "Remarks on the Occasion of this Journal's 50th Year." *TNR* 150 (21 March 1964): 13–14.

Mann, Arthur. "British Social Thought and American Reformers of the Progressive Era." *Mississippi Valley Historical Review* 42 (March 1956): 672–692.

May, Henry. "Shifting Perspectives on the 1920s." *Mississippi Valley Historical Review* 43 (December 1956): 405–427.

McQuaid, E. Patrick. "A Story at Risk: The Rising Tide of Mediocre Education Coverage." *Phi Delta Kappan* 70 (January 1989): K1–K8.

McWilliams, Carey. "One Hundred Years of *The Nation*." *Journalism Quarterly* 42 (Spring 1965): 189–197.

Miller, Aaron. "The Paradoxical Godkin, Founder of *The Nation*." *Journalism Quarterly* 42 (Spring 1965): 198–202.

Moynihan, Patrick. "End of the Marxist Epoch." *The New Leader* 72 (23 January 1989): 9–11.

Oski, Frank. "How to Raise Money for the Class of 2000." *TN* 248 (20 February 1989): 217, 248.

Parrish, Wayne. "The Plight of Our School System." *The Literary Digest* 116 (23 September 1933): 32.

Peretz, Martin. "Cambridge Diarist: Old Scores and New." *TNR* 200 (8 May 1989): 43.

Perlstein, Daniel. "The Parameters of Participation: Schooling and Democratic Theory." Review of Amy Gutmann's *Democratic Education*. *Educational Researcher* 18 (January-February 1989): 49–50.

Peterson, Theodore. "The Role of the Minority Magazine." *Antioch Review* 23 (Spring 1963): 57–52.

Polsgrove, Carol. "Missing Ms." *The Progressive* 54 (January 1990): 34–35.

Prescott, Peter S. "Report on the Republic." Review of Arthur Schlesinger Jr.'s *Cycles of American History*. *Newsweek* (27 October 1986): 98–99.

Reviews of Agnes de Lima's *Our Enemy the Child: The Survey* 14 (15 November 1925): 258; Louise A. Dickey, *The World Tomorrow* 8 (October 1925): 316; *The Booklist* 22 (January 1926): 143; *The Literary Review* (9 January 1926): 8; *New York World* (6 December 1925): 7.

Roosevelt, Jinx. "Randolph Bourne: The Education of Critic—An Interpretation," *History of Education Quarterly* 17 (Fall 1977): 257–274.

Rose, Amy D. "The Anti-Profession Profession: Adult Education in the 1920s." *Journal of the Midwest History of Education Society* 16 (1988): 194–206.

Schlesinger, Arthur, Jr. "The Point of it All." Review of James Martin's *American Liberalism and World Politics, 1931–1941*. *New York Times Book Review* (23 April 1965): 10–14.

Seideman, David. "Left Turn." *TNR* 191 (10 December 1984): 46.

Smith, Mortimer. "Educators Must Listen Closely." *Phi Delta Kappan* 47 (February 1966): 295–297.

Soule, George. "Herbert Croly's Liberalism, 1920–1928." *TNR* 63 (16 July 1930), Part 2: 253–257.

Sterne, Richard C. "The Nation and Its Century." *TN*, 100th Anniversary Issue, 201 (20 September 1965): 42–53, 241–334.

Stolberg, Benjamin. "Muddled Millions." *Saturday Evening Post* 213 (15 February 1941): 9–10, 82.

Straight, Michael. "The New Republic: 1914–1954." *TNR* 131 (6 December 1954): 17–18.

Straight, Michael. "Something for the Arts." *TNR* 152 (13 March 1965): 11–15.

"The Talk of the Town: Notes and Comment." *The New Yorker* (2 October 1989): 37–38.

Urban, Wayne J. "Essay Review: Old and New Problems in Teacher Unionism." *Educational Studies* 20 (Winter 1989): 355–364.

Villard, Oswald. "*The Nation*, 1865–1925." *TN* 121 (1 July 1925): 7–9.

Walzer, Michael. Introduction to a symposium on "The State of Political Theory." *Dissent* 36 (Summer 1989): 337.

———. "Socialism Then and Now." *TNR*, 75th Anniversary Edition, 102 (6 November 1989): 75–78.

Weiner, Lois. "Democratizing the Schools." *New Politics* 1, new series (Summer 1987): 81–94.

Stephen Whitfield. "The Eggheads and the Fatheads." *Change* 10 (April 1978): 64–66.

Woodring, Paul. "The Role of Responsible Criticism in Educational Reform." *The Education Digest* 31 (December 1965): 1–4.

Wright, Robert. "One World, Max." *TNR*, 75th Anniversary Edition, 201 (6 November 1989): 68–75.

"Youth in College." *Fortune* 13 (June 1936): 99–102, 155–162.

Zeitlin, Harry "Federal Relations in American Education, 1933–1943." Ph.D. dissertation, Columbia University, 1958.

Index